OPIUM CULTURE

THE ART AND RITUAL OF THE CHINESE TRADITION

Peter Lee

Park Street Press

Rochester, Vermont

Park Street Press
One Park Street
Rochester, Vermont 05767
www.InnerTraditions.com

Park Street Press is a division of Inner Traditions International

Library of Congress Cataloging-in-Publication Data

Lee, Peter, 1936–
 Opium culture : the art and ritual of the Chinese tradition / written by Peter
  Lee.
   p. cm.
 ISBN 1-59477-075-1
 1. Opium. 2. Opium abuse. 3. Opium abuse--China--History. I. Title.
 HV5816.L44 2005
 394.1'4—dc22

                                                                 2005018781

Printed and bound in Canada by Transcontinental Printing

10 9 8 7 6 5 4 3 2 1

Text design and layout by Jon Desautels
This book was typeset in Sabon with Beffle as the display font

To send correspondence to the author of this book, mail a first-class letter to the author c/o Inner Traditions • Bear & Company, One Park Street, Rochester, VT 05767, and we will forward the communication.

CONTENTS

PART II – THE ART AND CRAFT OF SMOKING OPIUM

*   *   *

ACKNOWLEDGMENTS

The author would like to acknowledge the encouragement, assistance, and congenial companionship of the many friends and fellow travelers who helped nurture this idea to fruition. Special thanks to D. Davies and J. Goodman for providing photos to illustrate the text, and to Wolf K. for sharing his beautiful collection with us. Thanks also to the New York Botanical Garden and the Vaults of Erowid. A bow of gratitude to the late Martin Matz for contributing the extraordinary poems that give voice to the opium experience in such exquisitely eloquent literary images.

And a tip of the hat from all of us to "Mr. K," the wily old "Chinese master" of Vientiane, for the warm hospitality and fine service he always provided our circle of scribes and scholars whenever we visited his place.

NOTE TO THE READER

The foundation for this book is a historical monograph by the Chinese scholar Peter Lee, whose grandfather and great-grandfather were both opium smokers who lived well into their nineties. The monograph was originally written in Chinese under the title *Da Yen: Jung Guo Ya Pien Yi Shu yu Chiao Miao* (Opium: The Big Smoke, the Chinese Art & Craft of Opium) in 1996, after Peter Lee retired to Thailand. In this edition, the original monograph has been expanded upon to include the pharmacology of opium, its medical uses, and other current issues, such as naturopathic methods of withdrawal, as well as the "Pipe Dreams" series and "Alchemist's Song" poems of Martin Matz.

Introduction
"THE BIG SMOKE"

The Chinese call it *da yen,* "the Big Smoke." For three hundred years, the distinctive bittersweet smell of opium fumes hung redolent in the air of elegant salons and musty alleyways throughout China as millions of smokers reclined on their hips "swallowing clouds and spewing fog." Regarded by many as the ultimate luxury and by some as indispensable to daily life, opium was as common a commodity in China as alcohol and tobacco are in Europe and America today. The idle rich lavished extravagant expense and meticulous attention to every detail of their opium habits, collecting exquisitely crafted utensils of ivory and jade, gold and silver, fashioned by the most renowned artisans of their time; they spent at least as much time each day preparing and smoking opium as the English spend on tea and the French on wine. For the poor, the ultimate reward for their daily toil was to smoke a few pipes of the lowest-grade opium while lying on a coarse mat in a roadside den, much as factory workers during the early days of the industrial revolution in England found cheap respite from their labors in the gin mills and beer houses of urban slums.

The Chinese did not discover opium, but they refined its recreational use into an art and craft of unparalleled sophistication. The Chinese opium pipe, which distills rather than incinerates opium to produce an

1

extremely pure and soothing vapor, may be the most ingenious drug-delivery system ever created throughout the long history of recreational drug use in human civilization. Known as the "Smoking Gun" *(yen chiang)*, the Chinese opium pipe and other requisite paraphernalia became the focus of an elaborate ritual and colorful lore, the tools and the toys of a smoking cult that reached its zenith during the late nineteenth and early twentieth centuries. It is these cultural aspects of opium smoking, including the technical, aesthetic, and pharmacological facets, that are discussed in this book, not the political and moral issues that led to its strict suppression by the mid-twentieth century.

Prior to the prohibition of opium as a legal and socially condoned relaxant, the Chinese art of opium smoking spread far beyond the borders of China and became deeply ingrained in the culture and social fabric of Southeast Asia and India, while also attracting a devoted cult of followers in Europe, particularly France, as well as in America. Writing in 1896, the American author Stephen Crane reports:

> Opium smoking in this country is believed to be more particularly a pastime of the Chinese, but in truth the greater number of smokers are white men and white women. Chinatown furnishes the pipe, lamp, and needle, but let a man once possess a layout and the common American drugstore furnishes him with the opium and afterward China is discernible only in the traditions and rituals that cling to the habit.

During the 1920s and 1930s, the Big Smoke penetrated America's avant-garde art and music underworld, where opium-smoking jazz musicians and blues singers coined the slang term *hip*, from which the words *hipster* and *hippie* were later derived, based on the position one adopts when smoking opium the Chinese way—lying down on one's hip. Hence, the quip, "Are you hip?"

Today, the reasons for opium's prohibition remain obscure and unexplained in the public mind. In a world where alcohol—which causes more damage to the user and more danger to society than any other drug—and such highly addictive substances as tobacco and barbiturates are legally available to one and all, the medical and moral debates regarding the use of opium ring rather hollow. Remarking on the paternalistic and hypocritical attitudes that modern medical authorities express on the subject of opium, Thomas De Quincey notes in *The Confessions of an English Opium-Eater:*

> Indeed, the fascinating powers of opium are admitted, even by medical writers, who are its greatest enemies . . . Perhaps they think the subject of too delicate a nature to be made common; and as many people might then indiscriminately use it, it would take from the necessary fear and caution, which should prevent their experiencing the extensive power of this drug; for there are many properties in it, if universally known, that would habituate the use, and make it more in request with us than the Turks themselves . . .

The underlying assumption behind this parochial attitude is that people in Western societies, where personal liberty and freedom of choice are supposedly sacrosanct rights enshrined by law, are not mature enough to handle information about opium that the Turks and Chinese have known for centuries, and that they are not qualified to make their own informed decisions regarding its use based simply on the facts. But there is also a more cynical reason for the deliberate suppression of information on opium in the Western world. Opium was ostensibly banned as a dangerous drug because of its addictive properties. Yet today, anyone can easily get a prescription from the family doctor for far more dangerous and addictive drugs, such as barbiturates and amphetamines, sleeping pills, and antidepressants. So why are doctors not permitted to prescribe opium to those who prefer an herbal to a chemical remedy?

It's a well-known fact of medical science that opium readily relieves such common conditions as insomnia, hypertension, depression, and chronic pain, for relief of which so many millions of people today have become addicted to expensive tranquilizers, antidepressants, painkillers, and other patented pharmaceutical drugs. The more one investigates the truth about opium, the more one realizes that the real reason it has been prohibited is to protect the profits of the politically powerful pharmaceutical cartels, which have established a lucrative international monopoly in the vast markets for medical drugs throughout the world.

These brief observations are made to preempt the inevitable attacks this book will arouse from self-appointed guardians of conventional morality and medical cant who will surely shake an accusing finger at the author and denounce him for promoting the use of drugs. Promoting drug use is not the purpose of this book. In fact, legally condoned drug use has already become far more rampant in all segments of society throughout the world today than it ever was during the times prior to opium's prohibition. As Berridge and Edwards point out in *Opium and the People:*

> The market stalls or the chandler may no longer be selling opium, but tranquilizers are multinational business . . . All the reasons which formerly made opium so popular for symptomatic medication are still society's common pains and tribulations, but with a variety of drugs now taking a role in different areas—analgesics in particular in place of opium for pain relief or ill-defined malaise, varieties of cough medicine where opium was previously the sovereign remedy, and tranquilizers and antidepressants as present day substitutes on a huge scale for opium's role as a psychoactive drug for the relief of nervous tribulations and the stress of life.

The sole purpose of this book is to provide an accurate account of the art and craft, the nature and the spirit, of the colorful custom of smoking opium for pleasure as it evolved in China and Southeast Asia from the eighteenth to the twentieth century, a custom that is still discreetly practiced by connoisseurs in small private salons in quiet corners of the world.

Not so long ago, frankly informed material on sex was also regarded as a public taboo. But this is the age of information. The author presents this discussion of opium so that readers may judge the legacy of the Big Smoke on its own merits and weigh its pros and cons in their own minds.

Part I

OPIUM AND ITS ALLURE THROUGH TIME

THE HERB OF JOY

HISTORICAL BACKGROUND

The opium poppy *(Papaver somniferum)* is mentioned in the very earliest records of human civilization. Native to the Mediterranean region, opium spread rapidly throughout the Middle East and Greece and was known for both its medicinal and its recreational properties. An Egyptian medical text written during the sixteenth century BCE recommended it as a sedative to quiet crying babies. References to opium as "the herb of joy" appear inscribed on ancient Sumerian tablets excavated in what is now Iraq, dating from about 5000 BCE. In addition to its primary uses as a pain reliever and a reliable inducer of peaceful sleep, opium was also taken for its euphoric and, according to some sources, aphrodisiac properties.

The English word *opium* seems to be derived from the Greek word *opos,* which means "juice," an apparent reference to the fact that opium is obtained by making incisions in the seedpod of the poppy and collecting the gummy latex that oozes from the cuts. Poppies were cultivated in great quantity in Crete during the late Minoan era, and images of the pod appear frequently in ancient Greek iconography. Homer mentions a narcotic drug called "nepenthes" in *The Odyssey,* claiming that it was brought to Greece from Egypt, and both Theophrastes and Dioscordes describe opium as a highly effective painkiller in their historical writings. Opium thus became associated in ancient Greek mythology with Nyx, goddess of the night; with Morpheus, god of dreams; and with Thanatos, god of death, thereby neatly summarizing its primary properties.

The great physician Hippocrates, known as the Father of Medicine in Western history, enthusiastically prescribed opium as a general panacea. Later, the physician Galen recommended it for myriad ailments in ancient Rome, where, during the latter days of the Roman Empire, it was used with the same abandon as heroin is today. While the writers Heraclides of Tarentum and Diagoras of Melos did make mention of opium's habit-forming properties and thus recommended caution in its use, Western physicians seem to have been generally unaware of the drug's addictive nature until the early seventeenth century. In 1613, Samuel Purchas made the observation that opium "being once used, must daily be continued on pain of death, though some escape by taking to wine instead."

The great Swiss alchemist and medical reformer Paracelsus prescribed opium on a grand scale and lavished it with praise as a universal panacea. "I possess a secret remedy," he wrote, "which I call laudanum and which is superior to all other heroic remedies." Laudanum, a tincture of opium extracted in alcohol, was widely used in England during the nineteenth century, especially by writers and poets such as Shelley, Keats, Byron, and Coleridge.

The Arabs, however, believed most strongly in the virtues of opium, and they spread knowledge of the drug far and wide throughout the ancient world, across North Africa and up into Western Europe, as well as eastward into Persia, India, and the southwestern regions of China. During the T'ang dynasty (618–906 CE), Arab traders introduced opium to China as a formal item of trade, and soon thereafter the plant was cultivated in modest quantities as a medicinal herb in southern China. The first mention of the term *poppy milk* appears in a medical treatise of the southern Sung dynasty (1127–1280 CE), indicating that the technique of tapping the sap from the poppy by incising the ripe capsule was by then well known in China. Beside its use for medicinal purposes, the poppy, which puts out a beautiful blossom, was also cultivated in China as an ornamental garden plant. While by this time opium was commonly eaten as a recreational drug by the ruling classes throughout the Middle East and India, in China it remained strictly medicinal, used primarily to relieve dysentery and bronchial congestion and to combat tropical fevers and infections. The momentous discovery that opium could be smoked for pleasure reached China close on the heels of tobacco during the sixteenth century.

The Chinese Learn to Smoke Opium

Sometime during the sixteenth century, tobacco and the tobacco pipe were introduced to China by European traders, and the Chinese took to the habit of smoking tobacco like a duck takes to water. The custom spread swiftly among the upper classes throughout the Ming empire, and soon Chinese craftsmen began to produce their own original designs in tobacco pipes, including handheld water pipes cast from pewter.

The Chinese first learned to smoke opium on the island of Taiwan, however, not on the mainland. At the time, Taiwan was a lonely outpost inhabited mostly by wild headhunting aboriginal tribes and administered on behalf of the imperial government by Chinese magistrates. During the sixteenth century, the Dutch established a trading post at Tainan—a port on the southern coast of Taiwan—seeking a source of precious camphor, which grew abundantly in Taiwan. Preferring to barter another product for camphor rather than paying for it in silver bullion, as the Chinese usually demanded, the Dutch brought opium from Java and taught the Chinese in Taiwan how to mix it with tobacco and smoke it for pleasure in tobacco pipes. Already enamored of tobacco, the Chinese magistrates and merchants living in Taiwan enthusiastically adopted this new habit, and they soon set their artisans to work developing even more efficient utensils for smoking opium.

Back on the mainland, the famous Ming emperor Wan Li, who ruled China from 1573 to 1620, passed the last eighteen years of his long reign without once granting an audience to anyone. Chinese historical annals explain his unprecedented imperial reclusiveness by noting that "[h]e had become a prisoner to the poison of the black perfume." While *poppy milk* was the term used in China to describe drafts of opium taken orally for medicinal purposes, "black perfume" referred to the intoxicating vapors released when opium was dripped onto hot coals in small braziers, to be inhaled for pleasure. Apparently the emperor Wan Li became so enamored of this habit that he grew loath to fulfill even his most basic imperial duties.

By this time, tobacco smoking had become so widespread throughout China that imperial authorities became deeply concerned about its addictive properties and began to worry that the entire nation would soon become dependent upon what was still regarded as a foreign drug. Therefore, in the year 1641, the last emperor of the Ming dynasty, Chung Cheng, issued an edict strictly prohibiting tobacco smoking, on pain of death.

At first, desperate tobacco addicts resorted to the recently acquired Taiwanese habit of mixing opium with tobacco to conserve their dwindling supplies of the now illegal tobacco plant; but due to the severe punishment meted out for possession of tobacco, they soon began to experiment with new methods of smoking pure opium, which, due to its sticky latex quality, could not be smoked alone in an ordinary tobacco pipe. There is no record of who actually invented the Chinese opium pipe, or of exactly when or where it was first developed, but it must certainly have been created sometime between the mid-1600s, shortly after tobacco was banned, and 1729, when the emperor of the Manchu Ching dynasty issued China's first edict banning the import and sale of opium and decreed punishment by strangulation for the proprietors of any establishment where opium smoking was conducted. A hundred strokes of the cane and permanent exile from China was the sentence for anyone else found working in such an establishment.

Unlike the prohibition against tobacco, however, the ban on opium had absolutely no effect on the trade, nor did it prevent the swift spread of the opium-smoking habit throughout China. Demoralized by their defeat and occupation by the foreign Manchu dynasty, the Chinese turned to opium as a convenient and comfortable escape from the realities of the times. Recognizing the enormous potential of the Chinese market for opium created by the discovery and popularization of its recreational use, the Portuguese brought large quantities of opium to China from their colony in Goa, on the west coast of India.

In 1757, the British army marched into India and colonized Bengal, where opium was cultivated in abundance, and soon the British East India Company (known in those days simply as the Company) became China's major opium supplier. The trade grew by leaps and bounds. By 1760, annual imports of opium to China reached one thousand chests, each chest containing 133 pounds of raw opium.

By 1820, British India shipped 4,244 chests of opium to China, and by 1838, the trade saw a tenfold increase to 42,400 chests—or 5,639,200 pounds—of opium per annum. At the time, China contained an estimated two million opium addicts, which guaranteed British traders a constant demand for opium there.

Opium production became big business for the British in India. By 1883, they had 876,454 acres of fertile farmland under poppy cultivation in the Ganges plains around Benares and Bihar. In 1878, the annual income from wholesale opium sales in India came to £9.1 million, and total revenues between 1840 and 1879 added up to a staggering £375 million. Hundreds of Indian workers toiled daily in British opium-processing factories the size of modern airplane hangars in the cities of Patna and Ghazipur, which produced the high-grade opium most favored by Chinese smokers. The raw opium was drained, dried, and pressed into balls weighing about four pounds each, which were then wrapped in the dried leaves

Shipping invoice for five chests of high-grade opium from India, bound for China. (Courtesy of Wolf K.)

and petals of the poppy plant and sealed with *lewa*, the liquid drained from the fresh raw opium paste immediately after harvest. After another period of drying on open racks stacked from floor to ceiling, they were packed into wooden chests of forty balls each and transported to Calcutta for sale and export to China.

Opium Etiquette

In traditional Chinese society from the eighteenth through the mid-twentieth century, opium smoking became an integral part of daily life, governed by the same social etiquette that prevailed in other aspects of Chinese culture. When guests visited a household where opium was smoked, the host would offer tea and snacks, and if the guest was a smoker, the host invited him into the smoking room for a few pipes, just as people in the West today offer their guests a drink in the parlor. Under such circumstances, etiquette dictated that the host would serve as chef, cooking the pellets and preparing the pipes for his guests. In the wealthier households of China and other Asian countries where opium smoking became part of traditional social life, such as Vietnam and Laos, a maid or houseboy was often trained especially to prepare pipes for the smokers in the family; in these households, they would be assigned to serve guests who smoked.

Whenever someone prepared pipes for friends or guests, smoking etiquette called for the chef to hold the bowl end of the pipe over the lamp, guiding the pellet through the heat for optimum vaporization and distillation, while the smoker held the end with the mouthpiece. The same practice prevailed in opium dens when the proprietor or a pipe boy prepared pipes for customers. If the smoker was a novice, good form required the chef to provide some guidance regarding the number of pipes to be smoked, to discourage the tendency toward excessive indulgence so commonly displayed by eager newcomers, and to pace the smoker's rate of consumption with sufficient intervals between pipes.

Interrupting a smoker during a smoking session was regarded as extremely poor manners. Once a smoker lay down to smoke his or her pipes, other members of the household refrained from bothering that person with mundane business or family matters until the smoker had finished the session and blown out the lamp, indicating that he or she was again ready to deal with daily affairs. The time between the lighting and the snuffing of the lamp was considered a sacrosanct part of the smoker's day, and woe be to the child, spouse, or servant who spoiled a smoker's time at the lamp with unnecessary or unwelcome intrusions.

While a man was free to go out with friends and smoke at opium dens, teahouses, and bordellos, the household was the female's only domain for indulging. If the women in a wealthy family liked opium, a room was usually set aside exclusively for smoking, equipped with beautifully crafted opium beds, tea tables, and other fine furnishings, and decorated with landscape paintings, calligraphy, carvings of jade and wood, and other exquisite works of art. These rooms were often appointed with a special table and chairs for mah-jongg. This game was the favorite pastime of China's leisure class, and a group of ladies might retire to the smoking room to play mah-jongg nonstop for two or three days, with pipes of opium, hot tea, and occasional snacks from the kitchen to refresh them.

Chinese friends smoking opium in the smoking salon
of the host's home. (Courtesy of Wolf K.)

Chinese and other Asian families discouraged their younger members from cultivating the opium-smoking habit until they themselves were married and had established their own households. Opium smoking was generally seen as a pleasure for the middle aged and elderly, not for the young. Since opium smoking required special attention to diet, tonics, exercise, and other preventive regimens to preserve health and vitality, a good husband or wife and a stable family life were regarded as important foundations for indulging, at least for the well-established members of society. What went on at opium dens, where actors and gamblers, derelicts and touts, criminals and prostitutes, and other denizens of China's underworld congregated to smoke, was another matter altogether and of no concern to polite society.

The Tao of Opium

Not only did opium smoking become an integral part of daily life in all segments of Chinese society—taking its proper place beside food and sex, tea and medicine, opera and mah-jongg, and other aspects of traditional Chinese culture—but in erudite smoking circles, it also came to be viewed through the lens of classical Chinese philosophy, or the Tao.

Taoist philosophy, with its polar principles of yin and yang and the transformational alchemy of the Five Elemental Energies of Wood, Fire, Water, Metal, and Earth, lies at the heart of traditional Chinese arts and sciences, and it was therefore inevitable that Chinese scholars would eventually develop a theoretical framework based upon these principles to fit opium smoking into the greater Chinese view of life and nature. And so they did.

The fundamental principle in Chinese philosophy, art, and science is the Great Principle of Yin and Yang, whereby all phenomena and activities in the manifest universe are understood in terms of the primordial polarity that governs all forms and functions from the atomic to the galactic, the microscopic to the macrocosmic. Yang is hot, bright, expansive, stimulating, and masculine. Yin is cold, dark, contractive, pacifying, and feminine. All foods and medicines, for example, are categorized as either yin or yang, depending upon the sort of energy and effect they impart to the consumer. The system permits one to achieve optimum metabolic balance in diet, select medicinal herbs for therapeutic properties that specifically suit one's condition, and prevent the systemic imbalances that give rise to disease and degeneration. Yang substances are warming and stimulating to the human system, while yin products are cooling and calming. Thus, in winter, when the weather is cold and the body requires extra warmth, the Chinese favor yang foods; in the heat of summer, yin products are preferred. When one has a fever, which is a yang condition, cooling yin herbs are prescribed; yin conditions of fatigue and flagging vitality, for example, are treated with stimulating yang medicines.

Of all the items listed in the Chinese herbal pharmacopeia, opium is one of the most extremely yin in terms of its effects on human energy. The calming, pacifying properties of opium are well known in Chinese as well as Western medicine. It slows respiration, lowers blood pressure, decreases digestive functions, reduces body temperature, and inhibits perspiration. Consequently, to prevent opium smoking from causing a chronic state of yin imbalance in the body, the Tao of Opium calls for the extreme yin properties of this substance to be counterbalanced with a variety of strongly yang foods, beverages, and herbal tonics.

Thus, Chinese opium smokers who understand these principles and can afford to follow them make certain that their diets include plenty of warming, metabolically stimulating yang foods when they smoke—foods such as fatty meats, shrimp, mushrooms, pumpkin, sesame oil, garlic, and ginger. They always drink a bit of alcohol, not for its intoxicating effects, but for its warming, blood-stimulating medicinal properties. They use herbal tonics prepared with stimulating yang herbs such as cinnamon, wolfberry, and schisandra to balance the medicinally yin effects of the opium, and of course they drink plenty of the best-grade oolong tea they can afford in order to keep their bloodstreams clean, purge their lungs of opium resins, and improve digestive function.

An even more esoteric application of classical Chinese philosophy to the art of opium smoking is based on the theory of the Five Elemental Energies as expounded in the trigrams and hexagrams of the mysterious I Ching, or Book of Change, the ancient book of divination written around the twelfth century BCE that constitutes one of the original fountainheads of Chinese civilization. A detailed exposition on the subtle mysteries and esoteric symbolism of the I Ching is beyond the scope of this book, but the basic idea formulated by Chinese philosophers with a taste for opium runs something like this:

In the art of smoking opium, the pellet of opium clinging to the pipe as it is held over the lamp in preparation for smoking stands for the Water element, the quintessential symbol of yin, represented in the I Ching by the trigram *Kan*. The lamp, with its flame and heat, represents the Fire element, the ultimate embodiment of yang, symbolized by the trigram *Lee*. Thus, Water over Fire is illustrated in the I Ching by the trigram Kan over the trigram Lee, producing the hexagram known as *Chi*, or "Completion," one of the most perfectly balanced and auspicious of all the sixty-four hexagrams in the I Ching. This is the hexagram often cited in Taoist sexual alchemy to represent the perfect balance of male and female energies achieved when the sexual act is properly performed according to the Great Principle of Yin and Yang.

By virtue of the action of the Wind element, or Sun, embodied in the smoker's breath when he draws on the pipe, the Water element of opium is transformed by the Fire energy of the lamp to produce Earth, or *kun*—represented by the crusty dross that remains inside the bowl of the pipe after a pellet is smoked. Water energy liberated from the opium during smoking is transformed into vapor and enters the smoker's body, where it is absorbed into his internal energy system. This leaves the trigram Kun, or Earth, over the trigram Lee, or Fire (i.e., the dross over the lamp), thereby forming a new hexagram called *Ming I*, or "Darkening of the Light." This hexagram symbolizes light hidden within the earth, which is usually interpreted to mean that a man of superior intelligence takes measures to hide the light of his mind within the earth of his body—that is, he conceals his talents from others—to avoid attracting unwanted attention or arousing jealousy, so that he may perform his duties in the world without causing conflict.

On another level, the external perfect balance between the Water element of the opium and the Fire element of the lamp, represented by the hexagram Completion, is transformed by the alchemical act of smoking into an external imbalance and obfuscation between the remaining dross (Earth) and the lamp (Fire), symbolized by the hexagram Darkening of the Light. But internally, a condition of renewed balance is created when the smoker assimilates the Water energy of the opium within his own system. The Water energy absorbed by the smoker from the opium through the action of Wind (breath) and Fire (lamp) cools and calms his overworked body, pacifies his agitated mind, fertilizes his dormant imagination, and balances the hardness and aggression of yang with the softness and receptivity of yin. The smoker thus achieves a state of internal equilibrium by infusing the essential yin energy of opium into his own system through an alchemical transformation involving the elements Fire and Water, catalyzed by Wind and leaving Earth as a by-product. No wonder opium smoking acquired an esoteric cult status in China!

Before the age of biochemistry and high-tech laboratory analysis, this may have been the way the philosophical Chinese mind understood how the herbal essences of opium—for example, the alkaloids—affect human physiology, influence mood, and alter consciousness. As with most aspects of traditional Chinese culture, aesthetic and philosophical considerations were always of paramount interest to the connoisseur, and opium was no exception.

In any case, the traditional Chinese approach to smoking opium was certainly a far cry from the reckless attitude and self-destructive behavior adopted by users of narcotic drugs today. *Dope,* the slang term applied to such drugs in the Western world today, reflects more on the way people in the modern world use these drugs than on the nature of the drugs themselves. In traditional Chinese and other Asian societies, the use of opium was a lifestyle choice, and those who made that decision usually refined it to an art with the same care and attention to detail that went into tea and cooking, gardening, and herbal medicine. The habit was governed by the same universal principles of balance and harmony that informed all aspects of civilized life in traditional Eastern societies. As with any luxury and recreational pastime, those who studied the basic precepts and practiced the proper methods in the art of smoking opium learned how to savor its pleasures and counteract its hazards, always maintaining a healthy balance between its two polar aspects. As Melville noted, "All things in moderation are good; whence, wine in moderation is good." The same wisdom applies to opium.

The Opium Wars

Historians often accuse England of "forcing" opium on China for sheer profit and spite, but in reality the driving force behind the British opium trade with China was England's own addiction to Chinese tea. As early as 1780, the English had developed such an enormous appetite for Chinese tea that the Company was buying about fifteen million pounds of it from China each year and shipping it at great expense to England. At the time, China enjoyed a worldwide monopoly on the production and supply of tea, which was jealously guarded as a state secret. Furthermore, China had no use for any of the manufactured products that England offered in exchange, so the Chinese demanded payment for all tea purchases in silver coin.

As a result of the soaring demand for tea in England, the British treasury was rapidly drained of silver, a situation that threatened England with bankruptcy and economic collapse. The British Crown tried several times to ban, or at least curtail, imports of tea from China, resulting in violent riots in the streets of London. So addicted had the English people become to their daily "cuppa" that they refused to work without it, a situation very similar to opium addiction in China. Thus a solution had to be found whereby British traders could obtain Chinese tea without having to pay for it with silver bullion. The solution the British came up with was to *trade* Indian opium, produced at negligible expense in colonial India, for precious Chinese tea.

Within a few decades, the British East India Company had established a Triangular Trade based on Indian opium in Asia that paralleled the Triangular Trade based on African slaves in America. In the latter case, rum from the West Indies was brought to Africa and traded there for slaves, who were then shipped back and sold in America. The profits were used to purchase cotton and other raw materials required to supply the booming industrial revolution in England. In Asia, the Company brought opium from the British colony in Bengal to China, sold it to Chinese black marketeers for silver, then used the same Chinese silver to purchase tea from official Chinese sources in Canton. In effect, the British got their tea for free, and due to the enormous Chinese demand for opium, they managed to turn a huge profit to boot.

Now it was the Chinese treasury that was drained of silver by the tea trade with England, and it did not take the Chinese long to figure out how British traders had managed to turn the tables on them. Alarmed by the rapid depletion of their hard currency reserves, in 1799 the imperial government of China issued its second edict banning the import of opium, but by that time there were such enormous profits in the trade, and such a huge demand for tea in England and opium in China, that neither British traders nor Chinese black marketeers paid any heed to this prohibition.

Finally, in 1836, the emperor Tao Kuang decided to take firm action to halt economic disaster caused by the opium trade, centered at the time in the southern Chinese port of Canton. He appointed a new viceroy to Canton and invested him with full powers to enforce imperial edicts against opium and to deal decisively with the arrogant foreign merchants residing there. Commissioner Lin Tse-hsu was an upright, honest official who could not be bribed, and he came to his post in Canton determined to eradicate the opium trade. Unlike so many other Chinese officials at the time, not only was Commissioner Lin incorruptible, he also did not smoke opium, and he viewed the habit as a social disgrace as well as an economic threat to China.

In 1838, Lin blockaded the entire European trading community in Canton and forced the traders there, mostly British, to surrender more than twenty thousand chests of opium, the destruction of which he personally supervised. He then ordered the torching of all Chinese warehouses where opium was stored and set fire to the fleet of British ships anchored offshore waiting to unload their cargoes of opium. The fire raged for many days, and witnesses reported that the pungent aroma of opium could be smelled miles away from the scene.

This incident bears some interesting parallels to the Boston Tea Party in pre-Revolutionary America. Like British tea in America, most of the twenty thousand chests of British opium confiscated in Canton were destroyed by throwing them into the sea. In both incidents, angry local authorities seized a product provided by British traders, tea in America and opium in China, because it was draining the domestic economy in order to enrich the British. In America, an exorbitant tax had been arbitrarily imposed on all imports of tea to the colonies ("taxation without representation"), while in China opium from India was peddled to black marketeers in exchange for silver used to buy Chinese tea for England without having to pay for it with British sterling. Even more ironic is that the tea tossed into the sea at Boston Harbor by rebellious colonists was no doubt paid for with profits from the opium trade with China.

From Chinese eyes, this action was viewed as a fully justified and long overdue enforcement of Chinese law on Chinese territory, but to the British East India Company it was seen as an act of piracy. Angry British traders promptly summoned the British navy to avenge this incident, and the resulting conflict became known as the First Opium War (1839–1842). Chinese defenses were no match for the superior British firepower, as evidenced in one battle during which two British frigates sank an armada of twenty-two Chinese war junks. In order to preclude an outright occupation of China by foreign forces, the emperor finally capitulated and the war was concluded in 1842 by the Treaty of Nanking, the first of the so-called unequal treaties forced upon China by victorious European powers. The terms of this treaty required China to pay an indemnity of twenty-one million dollars as reparation to British traders for their loss of opium. It also ceded the island of Hong Kong to Britain in perpetuity and opened the ports of Canton, Amoy, Foochou, Ningbo, and Shanghai to British trade.

Fourteen years later, another Anglo-Chinese conflict erupted over the still illegal opium trade and other simmering disputes, resulting in what has become known as the Second Opium War (1856–1858). Once again, China suffered abject defeat at the hands of modern British weaponry and was forced to surrender. This time, the Treaty of Tientsin added Kowloon to the British colonial territory in Hong Kong, opened another dozen ports to British trade, and, most significant, legalized the import of opium into China. This gave new impetus to the opium trade, which reached a peak of eighty-seven thousand chests (11.6 million pounds) per year by 1879, at which time British traders were shipping more than one hundred million pounds of tea per year out of China to England, almost all of it paid for with cash received from China for opium.

China Grows Her Own

In the wake of opium's legalization in China after the Second Opium War, a rapid growth in domestic cultivation of the poppy occurred. This came about not only to stem the outflow of hard currency, but also to meet the demand of China's ever-growing market of opium smokers, numbering as many as fifteen to twenty million addicts by the turn of the twentieth century. Vast tracts of arable land in the southern and western provinces of Yunnan and Sichuan were given over to opium production, which by 1900 reached more than twenty-two thousand tons per year, far more than the record high of sixty-five hundred tons imported by British traders in 1880. China had now become the world's largest producer of opium, as well as the largest consumer.

Another major factor in the decline of the British opium trade in China toward the end of the nineteenth century was the advent of British tea production in the mountainous regions of its Indian colonies in Darjeeling and Assam. The British had discovered wild tea plants growing in these areas, indicating the suitability of this region for tea cultivation. But it takes many decades to crossbreed hybrid plants suitable for domestic production from wild tea, and the British were eager to start their own production without unnecessary delay. Therefore, sometime during the 1890s, a British missionary in southern China managed to steal a few tea shoots from one of the heavily guarded Chinese tea plantations, and these were swiftly shipped to India and planted in the fertile soil around Darjeeling. Now that England had its own direct source of tea in India, the entire rationale for opium trade with China, which by then had become a political liability for England, collapsed. British imports of opium into China fell rapidly by the turn of the century.

On November 21, 1906, the imperial government of China once again attempted to eliminate the opium trade and curtail the consumption of opium in China by issuing a decree calling for the gradual prohibition of opium over a ten-year period. The British government, which no longer depended on the opium trade to finance its import of tea to England, agreed to cooperate with this policy by reducing importation of opium from India to China from 61,900 chests per year to zero within a ten-year period, commencing in 1908. At this time, the primary foreign suppliers of opium to China were the merchant houses of David Sassoon & Co., E. D. Sassoon, S. J. David, and Edward Ezra. They were none too happy at this turn of events, and subsequently took measures to continue supplying opium to China "under the table."

In 1911, the Manchu dynasty was overthrown and the Republic of China founded; that same year, the British Parliament decreed a ban on the shipment of opium to China in British ships. This finally closed an unpleasant chapter in Anglo-Chinese relations, and henceforth the cultivation, sale, and consumption of opium in China became an entirely Chinese affair, although significant supplies continued to arrive from various foreign merchants, mainly Indians based in Calcutta and Jewish merchants from Baghdad. In 1913, these foreign merchants formed the Shanghai Opium Merchants Combine to protect their monopoly of opium exports to China, and they signed an exclusive marketing agreement with the vicious Swatow gangsters who controlled domestic distribution of opium in China.

Despite repeated attempts by both the imperial and the republican governments of China to suppress opium trade and consumption during the early twentieth century, the business continued to flourish unabated, and ever-greater tracts of land were turned to domestic cultivation of the poppy. Sichuan province alone produced twenty-six million pounds of opium per year, and the provincial capital of Chengdu had one opium den for every sixty-seven of the city's three hundred thousand inhabitants. In Yunnan, where most of the arable land was by now devoted to opium cultivation, nine out of ten males were confirmed opium smokers. From Yunnan province, various minority hill tribes such as the Hmong, Lahu, Lisu, and Akha began to filter down into the highlands of Southeast Asia during the late nineteenth and early decades of the twentieth century, bringing with them seeds and techniques for opium cultivation, thereby establishing what would become the world's major opium-producing region, the so-called Golden Triangle, encompassing the mountainous northern areas of Burma, Thailand, and Laos.

The hill tribes of the Golden Triangle have since become some of the world's most skilled and enthusiastic cultivators of opium, particularly the Hmong in Laos. Opium smoking, which these tribal people originally learned from the Chinese prior to migrating south, still plays an important role in the culture and social life of many of the hill tribes in the Golden Triangle. The Akha, for example, have evolved their own romantic legend about the origin of the opium poppy. They say that once upon a time there was an Akha girl so amazingly beautiful that men came from all over the world to woo her. Of these many suitors, only seven gained her affection, and one day they each appeared at her house at the same time to ask for her hand in marriage. Unwilling to offend any one of them by her refusal, which she knew would arouse jealousy and conflict among them, she decided to make love with each and every one of them, even though she realized that this would cause her death. Before her selfless sacrifice, the girl requested that her people take special care of her grave and promised them that she would cause an exquisitely beautiful flower to grow for them from her heart. She told them that whoever tasted the nectar from this flower would wish to taste it over and over again, and she warned them that they must therefore treat this flower with the utmost care and respect, for its nectar could be the source of good as well as evil. That flower was the opium poppy.

By 1920, the focal point of China's domestic opium trade as well as the area of greatest consumption had shifted decisively to Shanghai, a city that was built entirely on opium revenues. Fabulously wealthy, notoriously decadent—and prior to 1927 virtually free from control by any central government authority—Shanghai was renowned throughout the world as the City of Sin, a place where "money talks, nobody walks" and where, as the writer James Lee observed in his book *The Underworld of the East,* "the very air seemed to be flavored with the faint smell of burning opium."

In 1927, Chiang Kai-shek led the Nationalist Army on the "Northern Expedition" from Canton to Shanghai to secure central government command over regions that, since the collapse of the Manchu dynasty, had been controlled by various warlords. At first, the new Nationalist administration based in Nanking attempted to ban the opium trade and eradicate opium addiction with such lofty social reform programs as the New Life Movement. Before long, the government realized that only opium could provide the enormous revenues required to finance the Nationalists' ambitious economic and social reconstruction programs, and to bankroll the Bandit Suppression Campaign against their bitter Chinese Communist rivals, who were contesting Chiang Kai-shek for control of China. As Frederic Wakeman Jr. writes in his fascinating book on this colorful period of Chinese history, *Policing Shanghai: 1927–1937*:

> Chiang Kai-shek himself seems to have been ambivalent about the ultimate goal of licensing [opium]. On the one hand, it was a very effective way for the Nanjing government to raise revenue: during the period of legalization, from August 1927 to July 1928, the government is said to have made over $40 million. On the other hand, unless the government carried the program through to detoxification and rehabilitation, with a lot of administrative self-policing along the way, legalization was tantamount to condoning the opium habit.

In the end, the Nationalist government decided on the practical policy of creating an opium monopoly to generate revenue by selling opium to licensed addicts, while at the same time establishing Opium Suppression Bureaus to eliminate illicit sources of opium that competed with the government. By 1937, the government's opium monopoly—operated and enforced in conjunction with the notorious boss of the Green Gang in Shanghai, Tu Yue-sheng—was selling opium to at least four million licensed addicts, and during the three-year period from 1934 to 1937, the Chinese government realized net profits on this trade of well over five hundred million U.S. dollars.

Besides selling opium to licensed addicts, the government levied a Pipe Tax on all opium dens, based on the number of pipes in use in each den. This aspect of opium revenue was controlled almost entirely by Tu Yue-sheng's Green Gang thugs, in conjunction with the police bureaus in the various districts of Shanghai, all of whom kept a fat cut of the income for themselves.

When Japan declared war on China in 1937, driving the Nationalist government deep into the hinterlands of Chungching, in western Sichuan, all controls on Chinese opium consumption in the area under Japanese jurisdiction were lifted; Japanese policy encouraged drug addiction in China in order to undermine resistance to Japanese occupation. In his memoirs of Peking, *The City of Lingering Splendor,* John Blofeld gives a lively description of a visit to one of the city's biggest opium houses:

> The Te I Lou was a hotel outside the Ch'ien Men, which owed to Japanese protection its immunity from visits by the police. Equipped with baths, telephones, mahjongg tables and several sorts of cuisine, it had become a nest of small opium dens (one to each room) where some people were said to pass the whole of each day between rising at noon and returning home at dawn to sleep. Pao and others had told me that the Japanese were using every sort of criminal means to soften up North China before swallowing it whole . . . The smoking habit was already so widespread in China that all the Japanese had to do was to give protection to the bigger dens and to ensure that adequate supplies were brought in from Manchuria by Korean roughs with whom the Chinese police interfered at their peril . . . Knowing something of these matters, I expected the Te I Lou to be a sort of chamber of horrors, but I cannot honestly say that the atmosphere we found there that night was vicious. While searching for the Singing-Master, we entered a number of rooms each furnished with padded divans and the six to eight lamps necessary to accommodate about thirty smokers per room per day . . . Some of the customers we saw were busy cooking little pellets of opium over their lamps or inhaling clouds of smoke from their heavy pipes. Others sat or lay upon the divans talking to one another with the noticeable animation which opium smoking produces in almost everyone. Those not ready yet for a smoke were seated at square tables

playing mahjongg or bending over delicious snacks brought in by hawkers or ordered from neighboring restaurants. We saw very few people asleep or sleepy looking; and only two or three elderly and undernourished men resembled my previous conception of "dope fiends." In fact I was disappointed to discover that, if the sour smell of beer could have been substituted for the sweet and all pervading odor of opium, the atmosphere would have been very much indeed like that of a London pub on a Saturday night. This was nothing like the sort of hell I had pictured.

This was the type of opium house where Chinese with plenty of money to spend whiled away much of their leisure time, and every city in China had numerous establishments of this sort. The situation for coolies and vagabonds was not so cozy, for all they could afford to sustain their habits were a few ten-cent pipes of what was known as *tye,* a mixture of the lowest-grade opium blended with the highly toxic dross of opium residues scraped from the inside of pipe bowls smoked by others in better houses. James Lee describes such a place he visited in Shanghai in his book *The Underworld of the East:*

> When my eyes became accustomed to the dim light of the place, I saw that we were in a large room entirely bare of furniture. On the boards of the floor were stretched, alongside of each other, about a dozen grass mats, and on most of them there was a Chinese coolie. Some of them were already lying insensible like dead bodies, while others were still smoking opium. Some were filthy and in rags, and I noticed that some were quite young boys, although there were old men too.

The reason that the smokers Blofeld saw at the Te I Lou in Peking were animated and healthy while the coolies described by Lee in Shanghai were virtually comatose is that the former could afford to smoke purely refined, high-grade opium and feed themselves with the large quantities of nourishing food required to sustain good health when addicted to opium. The latter had to spend what little money they had on highly toxic opium dross and virtually nothing on food. It's a myth that opium per se destroys one's health: What destroys an opium smoker's health is a poorly managed habit, wretched excess, and the sort of poverty that funnels every cent into opium at the expense of nourishment. The same principle applies to the use of alcohol and distinguishes the connoisseur of fine wines from the skid-row wino.

In China as well as throughout the rest of Asia, opium dens were an exclusively male domain. While there was no written rule excluding women from entering an opium den, it was deemed socially unacceptable for a woman to be seen in one, unless she was a prostitute or masseuse summoned to service a male client there. In Asia, women who liked to smoke opium did so at home; men smoked both at home and at the dens.

During the nineteenth and early twentieth centuries, opium dens played a role in Asian societies similar to that of pubs in England, cafés in France, and hashish houses in Egypt. Men would gather there after work to relax and sometimes also before work to fortify themselves for a day of business or labor with a few pipes. Merchants and traders, clerks and magistrates would retire to their favorite den to discuss important affairs in the comfortable ambience and complete privacy that these places provided. Artists and actors, writers and musicians sometimes spent entire days and nights lounging leisurely in their favorite opium den, spending all of their spare time and money on the sensual distractions offered by the better houses. It was also customary among those who smoked habitually to stop off at an opium den to smoke a few pipes prior to going out for lunch or dinner or attending an opera or concert, just as one might go to a bar for a few drinks before going out to dinner or the movies in the West.

The best opium dens were usually located in small, inconspicuous lanes in quiet residential districts, rather than in busy commercial centers of town, occupying large private houses set well off the street and discreetly screened from public view by elaborate gardens. However, in large metropolises like Shanghai and Peking, entire multistory buildings or hotels located in the center of town were also converted into huge opium emporiums with up to several hundred private smoking rooms and a wide range of supplementary services. The Te I Lou described by John Blofeld in his memoirs of Peking was such a place, and in Shanghai the notorious Great World and other entertainment emporiums offered similar services. Here one could spend weeks at a time without ever seeing the light of day, indulging not only in opium but also in virtually every conceivable vice.

For the poor, cheap dens were generally located in cramped quarters above shop houses in the narrow alleyways of public markets, where coolies and rickshaw drivers, sweatshop workers and fishmongers had quick and easy access to them. Such a place is described in the passage previously quoted from James Lee's *The Underworld of the East*. The estimate mentioned previously of one opium den for every sixty-seven inhabitants of Chengdu meant the city supported a total of about five thousand dens at the turn of the century; this was fairly typical of the situation throughout China at that time. Chinese-style opium dens proliferated throughout southeastern Asia as well, catering mostly to the large overseas Chinese communities in those nations. In some of these countries, such as Indonesia, the law required that anyone entering a licensed opium den show a valid identity card proving that he was ethnic Chinese in order to prevent the local populace from taking up the opium habit. The last country to permit legally licensed opium dens to operate was Thailand, which finally banned them in 1959. That year, the journalist and "old Asia hand" Richard Hughes was invited by a friend in Bangkok to pay a visit to the Heng Lak Hung—the largest Chinese opium den in the world.

In his book *Foreign Devil: Thirty Years of Reporting from the Far East,* Hughes describes his evening at this gargantuan opium emporium with the same air of curiosity and pleasant surprise as John Blofeld did twenty-five years earlier in Peking. Hughes's account reveals the Chinese opium den as a self-contained world that marches (or reclines) to the beat of a very different drummer:

> The old and honorable Heng Lak Hung in Bangkok was one of the strangest inns in the world. It bore no name sign. It boasted five thousand permanent boarders, averaged another thousand transients a day, and at a pinch could accommodate eight thousand. Its

main entrance was at the rear of a single front restaurant, open to the rough pavement next to the ancient Buddhist temple on the hot, noisy bustling New Road in Bangkok's Chinatown . . . It was the biggest opium den in the world.

In that rambling, galleried, muted, poppy scented labyrinth, the five thousand permanent boarders enjoyed an average of ten pipes a night, plus accommodation and a frugal meal, at a cost of about ten to fifteen baht (thirty to fifty new pence), less than half their normal day's pay . . . They left in the morning for work, returned in the evening . . . and then, lulled by a couple of hours' unhurried smoking, fell asleep on the plain wooden floors of their cubicles. Virtually the whole of their non-working life was spent in the opium smoke of the Heng Lak Hung . . .

There was a heavy, haunting, sweetish, incense-like smell in the long hot passageways. Some of the inmates were already asleep (it was about 9 p.m.) under the unshaded electric light globes. Others, reclining on their sides, were puffing white clouds of poppy smoke from the long, gleaming pipes, held over the yellow flame of oil lamps . . .

Some smokers were being massaged by kneeling women . . . No one hurried. No one raised his voice. Over all there hung a languorous, hushed, meditative spell that became almost hypnotic.

The brown sticky opium is . . . cooked tenderly on the tip of a needle in the flame from the glass-chimneyed lamp, then inserted in the doorknob shaped (and sized) bowl on the side of the bamboo pipe stem. You rest your head on a blue porcelain "pillow," place your lips against the mouthpiece (not around it), tilt the bowl over the lamp flame, and cultivate a deep, easy, rhythmical inhalation which produces a loud hissing noise and dense smoke . . .

You can "feel" the smoke in your lungs—not as strong as a Havana cigar but curiously, fleetingly and delicately stimulating. One pipe can be smoked in less than two minutes. The opium makes you thirsty; wraith-like attendants pass continually, carrying pots of hot tea—never alcohol—to the smokers. Your sight seems keener and sharper; there is almost an illusion of second sight. Your brain remains clear but there are flashes of lightheaded fantasy in which you find yourself obsessed—as though in the discovery of a great and hidden truth—with trivia like the smoothness of the boards on which you are lying, the texture of the skin of your hand which holds the pipe, or the warmth of the oil lamp beside your head . . .

Outside, I felt a sudden heady exhilaration and a pleasing detached sense of superiority as I halted for a moment in the eruption of noise and traffic along New Road. The neon lights surely looked brighter, sharper, more elegant. The hot wind from the river seemed cooler and even refreshing . . . I realized that I had no idea what time it was, and was surprised to find myself chuckling over this ignorance.

Around the turn of the century, Chinese-style opium dens operated also in New York and in other major cities of the United States. In a monograph entitled *Opium Pipes, Tools, and Paraphernalia,* Martin and Barbara Matz give a colorful description of the opium den scene in New York City during the 1890s:

By the 1890s opium dens were to be found concentrated mostly in Chinatown but also in the Tenderloin there were whole strips of dens where one could go without being introduced. Opium was popular among a certain class that dwelt along the common fringe between the underworld and show business.

As Crane wrote, "Cheap actors, race track touts, gamblers, and the different kinds of confidence men took to it generally. It was equally in vogue among prostitutes and showgirls . . . There was no shortage of wealthy users either. Some of them came in with their own equipment, pieces made of gold, silver, and ivory. At one point there was a house on Forty Sixth Street near 7th Avenue that catered exclusively to the hophead gentry . . . The house had heavy curtains, a piano at which sat a rotating staff of entertainers, and elaborately embroidered cushions and bunks. The newspapers generated a steady stream of blind items that alluded to various celebrities seen entering the house, the women disguised by heavy veils.

Opium, or hop use, was simultaneously condemned and glamorized by the press, and its popularity grew steadily." When Crane published his report in 1896, he estimated that there were at least 25,000 regular users in the city; another writer of the same period guessed a far less plausible 500,000.

The last opium den known to be operating in New York City was located in a tenement at 295 Broome Street, between Forsyth and Eldridge Streets, on the northern flank of Chinatown. The proprietor was a mild-mannered, middle-aged Chinese immigrant surnamed Lau, whose place the police raided on June 28, 1957, after which they hauled him off to jail. While that may well have been the last Chinese opium den to provide traditional smoking services to customers on a commercial basis, there's no telling how many private smoking salons might still exist secretly in various quarters of the city where small circles of intimate friends might gather from time to time to share a few pipes of good opium in congenial company. Suffice it to say that the Big Smoke still wings down the barrel of smoking guns in quiet, curtained corners of cosmopolitan cities like Paris, London, and Amsterdam, and the Big Apple has never been known to lag behind its sisters.

There were also numerous Chinese opium dens operating in London's East End during the late nineteenth century. A reporter for *The Morning Advertiser* visited one of these places expecting to find the proverbial den of iniquity, but discovered instead that "it was not repulsive. It was calm, it was peaceful. There was a placid disregard of trivialities, politics, war, betting, trade and all the cares, occupations and incidents of daily life, which only opium can give." Nor did this reporter find the smokers to be a degenerate, dazed lot of loafers, as users were so frequently depicted by those who know nothing whatsoever of the subject. As noted in *Opium and the People* (Berridge and Edwards), "Opium smoking was an aid to hard work, not a distraction from it, and smokers managed to combine their habit with a normal working existence."

Chinese opium dens were usually divided into semiprivate alcoves with elevated wooden platforms to accommodate the reclining smokers. Some of the bigger houses had special rooms furnished with elabo-

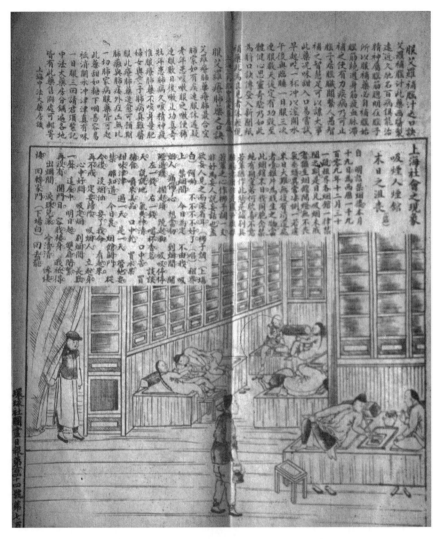

Scene from a traditional Chinese opium den.

rately carved opium beds, carpets, tables and chairs, and other furnishings, in which private parties could entertain themselves without being disturbed—or recognized—by other customers. The lower-class dens were either bare rooms with a few straw mats strewn about the floor or equipped with tiered bunks along the walls to economize on available space.

Upon entering an opium den, one indicated to the proprietor whether one wanted to prepare one's own pipes or have them prepared by a pipe boy. Those who preferred to serve themselves were provided with a pipe and a tray complete with the requisite paraphernalia, while those who wanted to be served, or who did not know how to perform the complex ritual of preparing opium for smoking, were assigned a pipe boy along with the pipe and tray. The opium itself was sold either in thimble-sized "cups" of liquid opium, each cup sufficient for about six pipes, or in small precooked wafers of about three pipes each. Bills were reckoned according to the number of cups or wafers ordered, rather than by the pipe, because some customers enjoyed their pipes prepared with large pellets and others preferred smaller ones.

Almost all opium dens prepared their own *chandoo*—a purified opium paste prepared expressly for smoking—on their premises, refining it from raw opium purchased from established sources in their districts. The better the house, the purer the chandoo it offered its clients. In China, the best dens seasoned the chandoo for three or more years in sealed ceramic jars to improve its flavor and enhance its natural potency. In the cheaper houses frequented by the poor, the chandoo was not as well refined and was heavily dosed with dross in order to increase its strength at the expense of purity. These lower-class houses also sold individual doses of powdered dross in small paper packets for oral consumption by those who could not afford the cost of smoking opium. Virtually all opium dens sold chandoo "to go," so that people who preferred to smoke opium at home could come in and purchase a personal supply. If a private household wanted to buy a large stock of chandoo from an opium den, the order would have to be placed well in advance so that the proprietor could purchase the required amount of raw opium to make it.

Large Chinese opium dens and opium emporiums offered a range of supplemental services to their customers. Some kept their own kitchens on the premises to prepare a variety of foods and snacks; others sent out runners to the better restaurants and food stalls in the neighborhood to fetch various dishes ordered by their clients. One amenity that even the poorest houses offered was hot Chinese tea, regarded as an indispensable accompaniment to opium by all Chinese smokers. The better the house, the higher the quality of the tea it served and the fancier the tea utensils it used. In the more exclusive dens, attractive young women in traditional attire prepared and served tea for the customers. So close was the association between opium and tea in China that during the nineteenth and early twentieth centuries, many of the larger, more renowned teahouses also operated opium dens on their upper floors, so that tea drinkers could go upstairs to smoke a few pipes from time to time while drinking tea and socializing downstairs.

As previously noted, another traditional pastime in Chinese opium dens was mah-jongg (a gambling game played with tiles and dice). This may be the all-time favorite form of gambling and social amusement among the Chinese, similar to the combined roles played by bridge and poker or dominos and backgammon in the West. As these mah-jongg games could continue nonstop for two or three days running, to accommodate this interest, many opium dens set aside special rooms where marathon games could be conducted. The players would pause from time to time to fortify themselves with a few pipes of opium, a bowl of noodles, and a pot of tea, all provided by the house.

Many of the higher-class dens that were equipped with private rooms also offered the services of prostitutes upon request, either from their own stables kept on the premises or by calling in girls from nearby bordellos. All sorts of wild speculation has been made in the Western imagination regarding the association between opium smoking and sex in Asia. Some Westerners, aroused by the myth that opium is a potent aphrodisiac that girds the loins of the smoker for wanton orgies, have eagerly tried the drug only to discover to their great consternation that their organs of pleasure failed to rise to the occasion. That's because for the novice, opium acts as such a powerful sedative to the central nervous system and such a deeply effective relaxant to the muscles that the whole body—unaccustomed to such bone-deep relaxation and languid tranquillity—enters a state of suspended animation in which many vital functions refuse to respond to external stimuli in the usual manner.

On the other hand, for experienced smokers whose systems have grown accustomed to the soft soporific effects of opium, the drug enhances the leisurely enjoyment of all sensual pleasures, including sex. Although opium in fact calms rather than inflames the male libido on the emotional level, it actually increases a man's capacity to savor the nuances of the sexual act by delaying ejaculation while also increasing blood circulation to the sexual organs due to the vasodilating properties of some of the alkaloids, thereby prolonging intercourse. Sometimes, rather than demanding sex, a smoker would simply ask a girl to come in and give him a long, leisurely massage. Thus, for opium smokers in Asia, a few pipes of opium often serve as a pleasure-prolonging prelude to food, sex, massage, and other sensual diversions, inducing a tranquil state of mental and emotional serenity in which all sensory sensitivities are magnified.

So close became the association between sexual amusements and opium smoking in China that, as in teahouses, almost all of the fancier bordellos also offered opium-smoking services to their clients, and thus the girls who worked in these places had to become adept in the art of preparing opium for smoking, as well as in the usual sexual skills. Often their clients invited the girls to share a few pipes as a prelude to the sexual act, and thus many prostitutes themselves became habitual opium smokers.

In places where opium dens were legally licensed, such as Shanghai during the 1930s, they became a significant source of tax revenue for municipal governments. In addition to paying a steep fee for a license to operate, each den was assessed a monthly pipe tax, calculated according to the number of pipes in use on the premises. In places where dens operated illegally, owners bought protection from interference by the authorities through large payoffs to the local coterie of corrupt policemen and district gangsters who provided similar protection to gambling casinos, bordellos, and other illicit activities.

In Asia, recreational activities such as prostitution, gambling, and opium smoking were generally tolerated by society, even when officially declared illegal by government authorities, because they were regarded as so basic to human nature that they were beyond the control of judicial law. As long as such places paid their dues to society, either directly through taxes or indirectly with bribes, the authorities tended to look at them "with one eye open and one eye closed," as the Chinese would say.

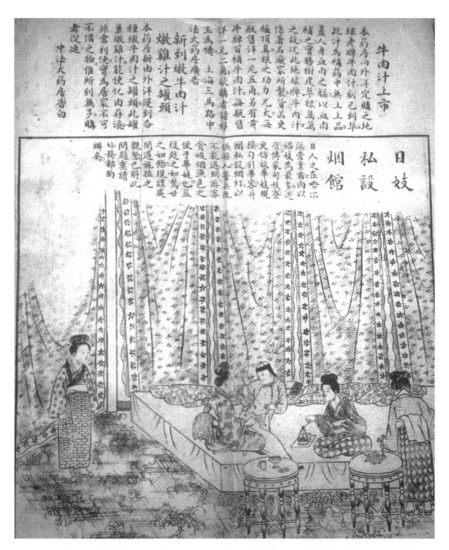

Prostitutes in a brothel having a smoke of opium. Opium preparation was an indispensable skill for prostitutes in nineteenth-century Asia, and many of them also smoked daily. (Courtesy of Wolf K.)

After Japan's defeat in World War II, the Chinese Civil War (1945–1949) broke out between Chiang Kai-shek's Nationalist government and Mao Tse-tung's Chinese Communist Party. During this period, opium consumption continued unabated throughout China, although the price of opium increased tremendously due to disruption of supply sources. As a result, many addicted smokers, particularly the poor, suffered terribly from withdrawal symptoms when their supplies were abruptly terminated by the shifting fortunes of war.

When the Communists finally defeated the Nationalists, driving Chiang Kai-shek and his followers into exile in Taiwan, one of their first orders of business was to enforce a prohibition on the sale and consumption of opium in China. Opium dens were summarily closed, and all of their opium, pipes, and other paraphernalia were burned in huge bonfires. Addicts were given the choice of terminating their habits and re-forming themselves within a specified period of time or facing a firing squad. Many found the latter alternative easier to bear.

In Taiwan, the Nationalists formulated a somewhat different policy on opium addiction. On the one hand, they too enforced a strict prohibition on public sale and consumption of opium, closing all dens and destroying opium pipes and other equipment. On the other hand, among the two million Chinese who followed Chiang into exile in Taiwan were tens of thousands of people addicted to opium. Most of these individuals came from wealthy families who had loyally supported Chiang Kai-shek and his Nationalist regime ever since their triumphant arrival in Shanghai in 1927, and the Nationalists would continue to require their support to develop Taiwan into a bastion of anticommunist resistance. So, after settling in on Taiwan, the Nationalist government permitted opium addicts who had accompanied the exodus from the mainland to continue their habits for the rest of their lives. Addicts were required to register with the government, after which authorities each year provided these registered smokers with the precise amount of opium necessary to sustain their habit for one year, until the end of their lives. After these smokers died, no new addicts were ever allowed to take advantage of this government-sponsored program, and thus the opium-smoking habit gradually disappeared in Taiwan as well.

The Communist victory on the mainland also triggered a major diaspora of Chinese refugees to other parts of Asia, particularly Hong Kong, Singapore, Vietnam, Thailand, Laos, Malaya, and Indonesia. Naturally, it was primarily the wealthy classes who managed to escape, usually with much of their wealth in gold and precious gems. Many of them were also lifelong opium smokers. To accommodate these Chinese immigrants, whose wealth and entrepreneurial skills were badly needed by the weary war-torn nations of Southeast Asia, these countries permitted the establishment of licensed opium dens to cater to the "Chinese habit" of opium smoking. To discourage the spread of the habit to their own populace, however, most of these countries required opium dens to permit entry only to those who could show a Chinese identity card.

This situation continued until the late 1960s and early 1970s, when, due largely to heavy political pressure from the United States, most Asian countries reluctantly illegalized Chinese opium dens and forced them to close down. Apparently, the American government did not want American citizens traveling in Asia to find their way into one of these dens and discover the opium experience, nor did they want American GIs on leave during the Vietnam War to develop a taste for it. In retrospect, it may have been better to allow those with the inclination for this sort of thing to smoke opium, for instead they turned for solace to heroin—a far more addictive and dangerous drug derived from opium. Heroin became the only available opiate on the market when opium itself was banned, just as opium became the only viable option for tobacco smokers three hundred years earlier when tobacco was prohibited in China.

Indeed, since the prohibition on opium smoking went into effect in Asia, an enormous upsurge in heroin addiction swept through the region, as did a rapid growth in poppy production, resulting in a far more dangerous drug problem than before. As Richard Hughes notes in *Foreign Devil,* "When the opium ban applies, they . . . turn to heroin in secret. And that is the killer. Crude. Violent." In the days of legally licensed opium dens, addicts smoked their pipes in peace and quiet, and even the poorest coolie could afford his habit. Now, addicts must prowl the streets to rob and mug others for the money to pay for heroin habits that can easily cost one hundred dollars or more per day. This problem has spread throughout the world and continues to grow.

Today, due to strong pressures from the United Nations, American drug-enforcement agencies, puritan regimes, and other self-appointed watchdogs of human behavior, very few legally condoned opium dens remain in operation. Nevertheless, with some confidential guidance from local acquaintances who know about such things, one can still find the way to the door of an opium den in Laos, Cambodia, Vietnam, India, and a few countries in the Middle East, but they are highly clandestine operations that maintain a low profile and make themselves as difficult to locate as possible. Gone are the days of the brash emporiums with gourmet food and beverage provisions, gambling rooms, and sexual services, and the posh private houses with elegant furnishings and an aesthetically pleasing ambience.

Still, if one is determined to track down the Big Smoke and doesn't mind weaving a roundabout route through littered back alleys and shadowy courtyards in dubious districts of town, one is quite certain—with a dash of luck and a good-natured guide—to find the way to a modest lair where friendly denizens recline by the glow of the Magic Lamp, quietly swallowing clouds and spewing fog from softly gurgling Smoking Guns, the air drenched with the unmistakable bittersweet fragrance of opium and the atmosphere as calm and peaceful as a monastic retreat.

Such places are as difficult to leave as they are to find, and newcomers often discover themselves still reclining comfortably on the smoking mat when the sun rises the next morning.

FLOWER POWER

THE CULTIVATION AND HARVESTING OF OPIUM

While the hill-tribe people who inhabit the highlands of the Golden Triangle have become heirs to the opium-growing tradition of China, considerable quantities are still cultivated within China itself. As noted previously, sprawled across the densely forested regions of northern Burma, Laos, and Thailand, this mountainous area is home to the Hmong, Lahu, Lisu, Tai, Akha, and several other minority tribes, who migrated to this region from their ancestral homes in the southern Chinese province of Yunnan during the late nineteenth and early twentieth centuries. Today, opium remains an important cash crop for many of these tribal peoples, particularly the Hmong, and opium smoking still plays an important role in their traditional way of life.

In the Golden Triangle, the opium poppy grows best at altitudes of one thousand meters or more above sea level, with mountain slopes and ridgelines forming the most favorable terrain for cultivation. Due to stringent campaigns by the central government in Bangkok to suppress opium, only about thirty tons of raw opium are now harvested each year in northern Thailand, while in northern Burma, where central government control is weak and the current military regime in Rangoon profits from the opium trade, annual production is estimated at more than two thousand tons, with about two hundred thousand acres of land under poppy cultivation. In Laos, where opium is still a legal cash crop in some of the northern provinces, about 350 tons per year are produced, most of it for domestic consumption.

During late winter and early spring, planters roam the mountain looking for suitable sites to grow the following season's opium crop. Alkaline soil rich in limestone deposits provides the most fertile ground, and hill-tribe farmers have an interesting way of testing the earth for proper growing conditions. They pick up clods of soil, bite off a chunk, and chew on it for a while, literally tasting the earth for the telltale sweetness of high alkaline content. Chosen sites are then cleared of existing growth by cutting down trees and underbrush—usually in March and early April—leaving the tinder to dry for a month or two, after which it is burned off in late April or early May to produce a deposit of ash rich in potassium, calcium, and phosphates.

Since opium is a winter crop, a fast-growing cover crop is first planted on the cleared sites just as the monsoon rains begin in late May; this prevents the rich soil from eroding and keeps the ground free of weeds. Mountain maize is the crop most often selected for the purpose.

In September, the maize is harvested, and the soil is carefully tilled and raked clear of stones in preparation for planting the opium crop. In October, while the earth is still moist from the last rains of the monsoon, poppy seeds are sown across the prepared surface of the soil. While the hardworking Hmong prefer to sow an entire crop so that it comes into bloom at one time, most tribes stagger the planting so that flowers in different fields mature at different times. This eases the demand on labor during the busy harvest period and provides some insurance against damage to the crop from winter weather during the growing season.

Other crops are planted among the poppies to provide a measure of protection against detection and to further enrich the soil with minerals, and also as a source of extra food for the farmers' families. Spinach and beans, sorghum and taro, and a variety of herbs and spices such as ginger, mustard, mint, coriander, and lemongrass are the most common supplementary crops planted in opium fields. The ever practical Hmong often grow marijuana as border plants around their fields, providing another profitable cash crop.

In November, the poppies are thinned out, leaving only the healthier plants standing, and the fields are carefully weeded. In mid-December, they are selectively thinned again, eliminating all weak and ailing plants, and the vegetables are picked to clear the ground for the remaining poppies to begin their final burst of growth to maturity.

By early January, the plants begin to blossom, creating a beautiful patchwork tapestry of flower petals in various shades of red, purple, and white. As the fields burst into bloom, they are carefully watched every day; all the precious opium latex must be harvested within three to seven days after the last petals drop from the flowers and the egg-shaped capsules turn from a deep green to a lighter shade of grayish green. This change in color signals the beginning of the harvest season, during which the entire crop must be tapped of its valuable latex content in a flurry of labor that continues unabated from dawn till dusk every day for three to six weeks, depending on the size of the crop and how many fields have been planted. For large crops, the workers usually camp out beside the fields to facilitate their labor, sleeping in makeshift shelters and cooking their meals over campfires. Those who smoke also bring along their kits and smoke their daily pipes alfresco.

In small fields grown just for the use of a single household, the harvest is generally done only by the women, but when crops are large and encompass many fields, everyone in the village is recruited for the job— men, women, children, and the elderly. To tap the opium latex contained within them, the ripe capsules are cut with a special knife consisting of three to five razor-sharp blades bound tightly together so that a single stroke of the knife makes a series of parallel incisions along the surface of the pod, each about one millimeter apart from the rest. Holding the capsule gently between the thumb and first two fingers of one hand, the cutter uses the other hand to make a quick clean vertical stroke across the surface of the pod, from the bottom to the top. This process requires speed as well as skill and care, for if the knife cuts too deep, the latex will seep into the interior of the capsule and be lost, or it will ooze to the surface too quickly and drip onto the ground. If the incision is too shallow, the sap congeals inside and seals the wound before it can seep out to the surface.

The cutters move among the poppies walking backward, cutting pods one by one as they go, so that the latex does not stick to their clothing as they cross the fields from one side to the other. Cutting is usually done during the height of midday heat when the pods are warm and the sap is soft, so that the latex trickles out and forms white pearly drops along the lines of the incision. The wounds continue to bleed slowly throughout the afternoon, and the sap gradually congeals and oxidizes, turning from white to yellowish brown. During the night, the cooler air causes the latex to harden and form a sticky gum on the incised surface of the pods.

Very early the next morning, before the sun becomes too hot and bakes the sticky latex gum into a dry crust that can blow away in the wind, the collection phase of the harvest begins. This time, the farmers move forward through the fields to prevent the gum from rubbing off on their clothing. For this task, a single swipe of a large metal spatula attached to a wooden handle is used to scrape the brown gum from the pods. The latex accumulates on the spatula and the sticky gobs of gum are periodically scraped off into a cup that hangs around the collector's neck, or onto a piece of banana leaf.

In their book about opium cultivation in the Golden Triangle, *Opium Fields,* Jon Boyes and S. Piraban interview a sixty-two-year-old Hmong woman named Nabao, who succinctly describes the entire growing and harvesting process:

INTERVIEWER: Please could you explain in detail how to grow opium?

NABAO: It's not difficult, it just takes time. About two weeks after the rains stop, the first thing you have to do is to clear the land and prepare the field. You cut the grass and weeds and clear away any loose rocks. When the field is ready, you sow the poppy seeds, and the seeds for the vegetables. Then you leave it for a week or two. The soil is still damp, so you don't need to water it.

After one or two weeks the seeds start sprouting. When the plants are about thirty centimeters high, you have to look after them a bit. You have to weed them. But you don't have to do much, you needn't go to the fields every day. You can go every four or five days to do a bit of weeding and collect some vegetables. This is wintertime. Normally the fields are on hill slopes. At night the fog helps the poppies to grow well. If it rains just once or twice during the cold season, then the poppies are perfect, and may even grow to head height. You have to take care that insects don't eat them.

After about three months from when you first planted them, the poppies begin to bloom. Two or three days later we start harvesting. We incise the pods on one day, and do the scraping the following day.

INTERVIEWER: What color is the fresh opium?

NABAO: At first it's white, then it changes to brown. After a long time, when it's dry, it goes dark.

INTERVIEWER: How many flowers and pods do you get on a single plant?

NABAO: You get five flowers if it's a perfect plant, but three is more normal.

INTERVIEWER: How long is the harvest period?

NABAO: If three people are working, and it's not a big field, then it takes about two weeks, sometimes more. But not everything is finished after the harvesting. You have to wait for four or five days before you can collect up the poppy seeds for the next season. We choose only the big, perfect pods for the seeds.

After all the latex is collected from a field of incised poppies, the cutters go in and cut the pods again. This alternate cutting and collecting process is repeated three or four times per pod in as many days, until all the precious sap has been milked from the capsules. After an entire field has been fully harvested, the cutters and collectors move on to the next field, always leaving a few of the most robust capsules to fully mature for another four or five days to produce fertile seeds for the following year's crop.

Each day's harvest is brought from the fields to the village, where it is weighed and wrapped in banana leaves or mulberry paper to form packets of one *viss* (1.6 kg) each. In general, about three thousand poppies are needed produce enough raw opium to make a one-viss loaf. In terms of land area, one rai of land (1 acre = 2.47 rai; 1 hectare = 6.75 rai) produces one kilogram (2.2 lbs) of raw opium.

Opium collected for local consumption is wrapped in blocks of one viss each and stored in heavy wicker baskets. If properly wrapped in banana leaves or mulberry paper and kept dry in a cool dark place, raw opium may be stored for up to two years without losing its potency.

Opium harvested for sale is carried by mule or backpack from the mountain villages where it's grown down to designated areas in the plains where buyers, usually Chinese, come to negotiate a price and purchase whatever is available for sale. If the opium is of good quality, the growers may get about two hundred dollars for each 1.6 kg packet, which is far more than they make from any other cash crop but only a small fraction of the amount their buyers receive when they sell it to opium dens and private households, or to illicit factories located in remote jungle regions where Chinese chemists refined opium to produce heroin.

In hill-tribe villages, opium is often smoked raw to make it last longer, but in Chinese opium dens and in the households of more sophisticated smokers in towns and cities, raw opium is carefully refined to produce a pure, smooth smoking essence—a syrup of opium known in China as *yen-gao,* or "smoking paste," and in India and Indochina as chandoo. Before selling their harvest, hill-tribe families keep enough in stock to supply their personal needs until the next growing season.

PAPAVER SOMNIFERUM

THE PHARMACOLOGY OF OPIUM

Opium is one of the most complex and pharmacodynamically active substances on earth. Among the many medicinal plants listed in the herbal pharmacopoeias of the world, few can compare with opium for its biochemical intricacy, its range of alterative effects, its therapeutic potency, and its natural affinity for the human system. Small wonder that Hippocrates, Galen, and Paracelsus—as well as countless lesser-known physicians, alchemists, and shamans of the ancient world—regarded opium as the ultimate heroic remedy and a peerless panacea for all of the aches and pains, diseases and distress, unhappiness and unbalance that render life on earth so miserable for so many human beings.

The biochemical keys that make opium such an effective palliative for pain, and such a reliable remedy for emotional and mental as well as physical distress in the human system, are those potent mysterious bioactive substances found only in what traditional alchemists and shamans refer to as "power plants"—known to modern medical science as alkaloids. Alkaloids are organic bases of highly complex, heterocyclic structure containing nitrogen and usually oxygen and occurring mostly in the form of salts. Many of them decisively influence circulation, respiration, digestion, and other vital functions by acting directly on various tissues and organ systems of the human body, where they exert pronounced and highly specific physiological effects. Others either stimulate or depress the central nervous system, giving rise to associated psychological and emotional responses.

Apparently, alkaloids were created by nature for specific use by humans, for they play no known roles in the metabolism of the plants in which they are found. Many of them are precise biochemical analogs of essential human hormones and neurochemicals that regulate some of the body's most important autonomic responses and govern vital physiological functions throughout the human system. The opium poppy, for example, has no use whatsoever for morphine or codeine, which are the most potent alkaloids in opium. The sap that contains the morphine, codeine, and dozens of other alkaloids appears in the capsule a few days after the last petal falls from the flower, and if it is not harvested within the first week, it simply disappears. It makes no difference to the plant itself whether or not the sap is tapped.

While serving no vital function in the poppy plant, morphine has a molecular structure that mimics an extremely potent class of neurochemicals known as endorphins, which function naturally in the human brain. When certain endorphins are secreted, they attach to specific neuroreceptors in the brain, immediately diminishing sensations of physical pain while producing feelings of euphoria. When someone smokes a pipe of opium, the morphine swiftly enters the bloodstream through the lungs along with all the other alkaloids. It travels to the brain, where it easily crosses the blood–brain barrier and, by virtue of its biochemical similarity to endorphins, attaches to the same receptors in the brain normally reserved exclusively for these euphoric, analgesic neurochemicals. And presto! The same effect is achieved each and every time: awareness of pain is first reduced and finally eliminated; tension dissolves from the whole system and the entire body relaxes; blood pressure decreases and respiration slows down; and an exquisite euphoria spreads like a gentle breeze throughout the body and mind.

Opium contains thirty-six known, and probably many more unknown, alkaloids, of which six have so far been isolated for specific medical uses in humans. No doubt most if not all of the active alkaloids in opium have some potential medical—or recreational—application in the human system, but due to international efforts to suppress public knowledge and use of opium during the latter half of the twentieth century, scientific research on opium has been curtailed, and much of what is already known has been withheld from public view. Following is a list of the alkaloids that have so far been identified in opium:

morphine	gnoscopine
papaveramine	corytuberine
narcotine	hydrocotarnine
porphyroxine	magnoflorine
codeine	lanthopine
pseudo-morphine	coptisine
thebaine	laudanidine
rhoeadine	berberine
papaverine	laudanine
xanthaline	sanguinarine
narceine	mecopidine
scoulerine	glaudine
codamine	narcotoline
coreximine	palaudine
cotarnine	neopine
isocorypalmine	methylcodein
cryptopine	oxynarcotine
salutaridine	meconine

The six main alkaloids that have been isolated from opium for therapeutic use in modern Western medicine are morphine, codeine, thebaine, papaverine, narcotine, and narceine.

Morphine

Morphine, which constitutes anywhere from 3.0 percent to 24.0 percent of the alkaloid content in raw opium, was first isolated in 1803 by the German pharmacist Friedrich Serturner, who named it after Morpheus, the Greek god of dreams. Since then, it has become one of the primary analgesic drugs used for the relief of acute pain in modern medicine. Widely used during the American Civil War, morphine left at least fifty thousand soldiers addicted to the drug, a condition that became known as soldier's disease. Today, approximately seventeen tons of morphine are prescribed for medical use each year in Western Europe alone.

Morphine acts directly upon the central nervous system, occupying the endorphin receptors in the brain and anesthetizing some of the channels in the spinal cord and brain stem. A complex derivative of the phenanthrene group of alkaloids, morphine influences human physiology and psychology with a complicated series of analgesic effects and secondary side effects. Besides its primary properties of eliminating sensations of pain and inducing a luxurious soporific euphoria, it slows respiration, relaxes the bronchial system, suppresses appetite and impedes digestive functions, reduces sexual desire, decreases body temperature, and inhibits perspiration. The most unpleasant side effect of morphine is constipation.

The most notorious derivative of opium is heroin, which is chemically refined from morphine and has become the scourge of the drug world today, contributing to opium's bad name through guilt by association, even though opium and heroin are as different in character and effect as molasses and white sugar. Heroin was first synthesized in 1874 by the English scientist C. Wright, when he boiled and bound morphine with acetic anhydride to produce diacetylmorphine. Twenty years later, German scientists further refined this compound by treating it with ether, alcohol, and hydrochloric acid to produce a white flaky powder known today as Number 4 Heroin. Ironically, the Germans began promoting this new drug as the ideal nonaddictive painkiller and an effective cure for morphine and codeine addiction. It was given the name *heroin* by the German pharmaceutical company Bayer, which manufactured and distributed the drug throughout the world.

While morphine finds legitimate use as an analgesic drug in medicine, heroin serves no purpose other than to produce an intensely soporific intoxication. Even more addictive than morphine, heroin is also more constipating, disrupts and sometimes even stops blood circulation, corrodes and collapses the blood vessels when used intravenously, and demands an ever-increasing dosage in addicts. In short, it has no redeeming value as either a medicinal or a recreational drug.

Codeine

Codeine comprises 0.4 percent to 1.0 percent of opium's alkaloid content and is the most widely used extract of opium in modern medicine. About eighty-five percent of the world's legal opium crop is devoted to the production of codeine. Its primary functions are to suppress coughs and to decongest the bronchial passages, although it also has analgesic properties similar to, though less potent than, morphine. Moderate doses of codeine are also effective sedatives that induce deep, restful sleep, which is why codeine is such a popular remedy for acute respiratory ailments in which painful, uncontrollable coughing and chronic lung congestion keep the patient awake at night. Though codeine itself is less addictive to the central nervous system than is morphine, during withdrawal from opium it is the deprivation of the codeine alkaloid that causes an addict to experience the prolonged and troublesome symptom of persistent insomnia. Codeine is far less constipating than morphine, and, in fact, according to the tenets of traditional Chinese medicine, codeine actually counteracts morphine's binding effects by decongesting and relaxing the bowels.

Thebaine

Like morphine and codeine, thebaine is a complex phenanthrene derivative and the third but least addictive narcotic alkaloid in opium. Comprising 0.4 percent to 0.8 percent of opium's alkaloid content, thebaine acts as a cerebral stimulant and therefore counteracts the soporific effects of morphine and codeine. It also has convulsant properties similar to those of strychnine. While it is sometimes used as a mild analgesic, it is most useful medically as a narcotic antagonist in the treatment of addiction to heroin, morphine, and opium. During withdrawal from these drugs, thebaine is administered in small doses, and owing to its common molecular structure with morphine, it functions as an analog of endorphins and occupies those receptors in the brain, thereby reducing the discomfort and distress of withdrawal and suppressing the craving for opiates. A pharmaceutical derivative of thebaine called buprenorphine is available in the brand-name drug Buprenex or, in tablet form as Subutex, and may be used to ease the discomfort of opiate withdrawal.

Papaverine

Papaverine is a nonaddictive alkaloid first isolated in 1848 and constitutes only 0.4 percent to 0.8 percent of opium's active components. It has virtually no narcotic or analgesic effects on the human system, but rather acts as a relaxant to the involuntary muscles of the body, particularly the smooth muscles that control the walls of blood vessels. It has such powerful relaxing and expanding effects on these vessels that it significantly increases the flow of blood throughout the circulatory system, including the smallest capillaries. Consequently, one of its primary medical uses is to cure male impotence caused by insufficient blood circulation to the sexual organs, a condition for which it has proved effective. For this purpose, papaverine can be administered either orally or by direct injection into the penis, which affords immediate and dramatic results. It is also used to enhance circulation of oxygen and nutrients to the extremities and to the brain, and as a remedy for high blood pressure. In whole opium, papaverine's potent vasodilating properties counteract the inhibiting effects of morphine on circulation and provide a stimulating physiological counterbalance to the soporific effects of morphine and other sedative alkaloids.

Narcotine

One of the most abundant alkaloids in opium is narcotine, which comprises 4.0 percent to 7.0 percent of the total alkaloid content. It functions as a spinal stimulant and accelerates respiration, thereby balancing the soporific and respiratory-suppressant effects of morphine. It has only mild narcotic properties and is not addictive.

Narceine

Narceine constitutes only 0.2 percent to 0.5 percent of the alkaloid content in opium and finds little use in modern medicine. It is an amphoteric compound that can react chemically either as an acid or as a base. It can be extracted either directly from opium or from narcotine. Mildly narcotic but nonaddictive, it has soporific effects similar to those of morphine and codeine, but not nearly as strong.

As the information above clearly indicates, opium is a complex cocktail of active alkaloids, the effects of which work in complementary synergy. For every negative side effect caused by one alkaloid there is another alkaloid with opposite properties to counteract that effect and establish overall balance. Thus it is the sum total of all the essences and energies in opium, working together in synergistic and complementary concert, that gives the Big Smoke its unique character and creates such a smooth harmony of effects in the human system. The net effect produced by this balanced blend of alkaloids when taken together in whole opium is completely different from and far less harmful to the human system than the effects caused by any one of its constituent alkaloids taken alone. Morphine and heroin, for example, have all sorts of dangerous side effects for the habitual user—including chronic constipation, impaired digestion, depressed respiration, sluggish circulation, and diminished alertness—and they contain no other alkaloids with complementary properties to counteract these hazards.

Opium, however, in which morphine usually constitutes less than ten percent of the active components, contains codeine and papaverine to stimulate the bowels and counteract morphine's constipating effects, narcotine to accelerate respiration and counterbalance morphine's inhibitory influence on breathing, papaverine and other vasodilators to increase blood flow and offset morphine's suppressive influence on circulation, and thebaine to stimulate the brain and counteract morphine's soporific effects. Both physiologically and psychologically, the way opium influences the human system is therefore totally different from morphine, codeine, or any other fractional isolate of opium, and consequently opium addiction results in very different behavioral patterns compared with addiction to morphine or heroin.

A basic premise of traditional herbal medicine in China, India, and other Asian cultures is that the various constituents in whole herbs are designed by nature to work together in concert within the human system, and that whole herbs always include specific elements to counteract the toxicity and other negative side effects of the primary active components. This premise, which has been verified by modern biochemical studies, explains why Chinese herbalists always use whole, full-spectrum herbs in their formulas rather than extracted fractional isolates, as in modern Western medicine. Licorice, for example, can be highly toxic to the human system when only the active ingredient is extracted and used. But when the whole herb, with its full spectrum of known as well as unknown constituents, is administered, licorice may be taken in any dosage for any period of time without causing toxicity. Yet some Western medical studies on licorice, which tested only a fractional extract of the primary active component, have condemned it as toxic to the human system. In traditional Chinese medicine, however, licorice is known as the Great Detoxifier because one of its primary medical uses is to detoxify blood and tissues of the human body. This points up just how differently a whole herb like opium functions in the human body compared with the activity of a refined fractional isolate such as morphine or codeine.

The concept of natural balance and harmony in full-spectrum herbs is based on the Great Principle of Yin and Yang, whereby nature complements every element or energy on earth related to yin with an equal measure of yang, thereby maintaining equilibrium. In opium, for example, the two primary effects are sedative, which by virtue of its soft, passive, calming influence belongs to yin, and stimulant, which has the activating, energizing, alert nature of yang. By way of scientific confirmation, modern laboratory analysis has proved what traditional Chinese herbalists and alchemists have known for centuries: that opium is endowed by nature with an equal proportion of both yin and yang activity, and that therefore whole opium, when used properly and in moderation, produces a balanced blend of physical effects that in turn gives rise to a sense of perfect equilibrium in body and mind. Thus it has been shown by modern science that opium contains three major alkaloids endowed with mainly soporific effects—morphine, codeine, and narceine—and three that possess primarily stimulant properties—thebaine, papaverine, and narcotine—providing a six-piece symphony of alkaloidal yin and yang that plays a harmonious alchemical tune in the smoker's system, neither too sedating nor too exciting, not too slow and not too fast, but always achieving just the right balance.

The biochemical complexity and therapeutic diversity of the alkaloids in opium suggest some interesting possibilities whereby modern medical science might render opium into a form that is neither addictive nor toxic, while retaining most of its benefits both as a medicinal drug and as a recreational substance. The writer Jean Cocteau notes in his journal, *Opium, the Diary of His Cure,* kept during a period of temporary withdrawal in a detoxification clinic in St.-Cloud, France, between December 1928 and April 1929: "It's a pity that instead of perfecting curative techniques, medicine does not try to render opium harmless." With the exception of the three addictive phenanthrene alkaloids (morphine, codeine, thebaine), which in most opium constitute only five to ten percent of the alkaloid content, the active constituents of opium are entirely nonaddictive. If these three addictive alkaloids were removed by means of modern laboratory technology, opium might become a medicinal and recreational drug without addictive properties. Furthermore, it is the muscle-relaxing and vasodilating effects of the nonaddictive alkaloids that provide the most pleasant physical relaxation and the most effective therapeutic relief for chronic hypertension, stress, stiff joints, tight muscles, and other "uptight" conditions that plague so many people in these hectic times. Thus, even without the narcotic effects of morphine, codeine, and thebaine, opium could provide a calm, pleasant, relaxing palliative that has both therapeutic and recreational benefits without the risks of addiction and toxic side effects. This is what Cocteau means when he suggests that modern medical science, which is certainly capable of doing so, should "try to render opium harmless."

So why has modern pharmaceutical science failed to do this? By creating such a product, it would provide the public with a relatively harmless, nonaddictive, and inexpensive herbal remedy for many of the chronic conditions for which people now depend on addictive and very expensive pharmaceutical drugs, such as tranquilizers, sedatives, antihypertensives, and muscle relaxants. These drugs, each of which is exclusively patented by the company that manufactures it, earn billions of dollars each year for the pharmaceutical industry. A nonaddictive yet therapeutically effective form of opium, which as a natural herb could be patented by no one, would certainly undermine the profits of the very companies that pharmaceutical science serves. Such a product would also cut deeply into the sale of tobacco and liquor by providing a pleasant, relaxing, and mildly euphoric alternative to alcohol and nicotine. Until the day when modern medical science begins to serve the interests of public health rather than of private corporate interests, Cocteau's vision of a harmless, nonaddictive version of opium will remain nothing more than a pipe dream.

Traditional Medical Uses of Opium

Modern Western medicine uses only extracted fractional isolates of opium, such as morphine, codeine, and papaverine, for therapeutic purposes, but in traditional Eastern medicine, only whole opium, with its full spectrum of active constituents, was administered as an herbal remedy. The medical applications of opium were determined by its basic therapeutic properties as a medicinal herb, calculated according to the standard parameters of traditional herbal medicine.

In traditional Chinese medicine, opium is categorized as a bitter and sour herb, and these flavors correspond respectively to the elemental energies of Fire and Wood, which give opium its analgesic and astringent properties. Opium has what is known in Chinese medicine as a natural affinity for the organ systems of the lungs, large intestine, and kidneys, which means that when ingested, opium's essential energies enter into the energy channels associated with these organs while its basic biochemical effects directly influence those tissues. The Chinese pharmacopoeia describes opium's primary actions as being astringent to lungs and large intestine, analgesic, and antitussive, and lists the main indications for its use: chronic cough, asthma, diarrhea and dysentery, stomachache, prolapse of the rectum, and pains in joints and muscles. Opium may be administered as a tea by dissolving a dose of the purified sap in hot water, as a pill by mixing it with other herbs and binding it with honey, or by smoking. The latter method provides the swiftest relief and leaves the least toxic residue in the system.

Traditionally, opium's main medicinal use was as a remedy for serious cases of diarrhea and dysentery. Its potent astringent properties, which affect primarily the large intestine and lungs, halt uncontrollable purging of the bowels caused by these diseases. Though opium itself does not cure the cause of diarrhea and dysentery, it controls the symptoms long enough for a cure to be effected by other means, and in serious cases, this temporary measure can save the patient's life by preventing critical dehydration.

The second most common use of opium in traditional herbal medicine is to relieve the symptoms of various respiratory ailments, particularly deep chronic coughs, bronchial congestion, and asthma. Codeine has been shown to pacify the cough control center in the brain, which is why opium provides such effective relief from painful coughs. Its astringent powers help eliminate phlegm and other excess fluids from the lungs, bringing quick effective relief from bronchial congestion. It also relaxes the entire bronchial passage, making it easier to breathe in conditions of respiratory distress and providing prompt relief for asthma. Indeed, a few pipes of opium, rapidly administered, have saved the lives of many victims of severe asthma attack.

Among the hill tribes of southern China and Southeast Asia, opium is highly regarded as an effective cure for malaria, which is endemic to these regions. Apparently the potent alkaloids in opium destroy the parasite that causes malaria after it enters a person's body through a bite from an infected mosquito. When he was a young soldier in the Chinese Nationalist Army in 1949, the author's father-in-law contracted malaria while escaping a communist offensive in Yunnan province. Having no drugs to cure the disease, his condition had grown critical by the time he finally stumbled into a remote hill-tribe village. The villagers immediately recognized his condition, took him into one of their huts, and began to prepare opium for him to smoke. Horrified at the prospect of smoking what he regarded as an addictive drug, he at first refused, but they insisted that this was his only hope for a cure. They pointed out that his time was running out, so he finally agreed to try it. As he relates the story, he reluctantly smoked six pipes, then fell into a deep, dreamless sleep that continued for two and a half days. When he awoke, his fever was gone, he was no longer suffering chills and cold sweats, his vitality had returned, and he felt perfectly fine. The cure had worked, and he left the village with his health restored, managing to make good his escape by foot into the rugged mountains of Burma.

Opium is still used to cure malaria in the hill-tribe villages of the Golden Triangle, where, as in many other parts of the world, malaria has once again become a major problem due to the resistance mosquitoes have developed to pesticides and the resistance the parasites have acquired to the chemical drugs used to cure malaria in humans for the past thirty years. Once again, millions of people throughout the world are contracting malaria, and more than two million of them die from it annually due to the failure of pharmaceutical drugs. It may well be time for medical institutions to investigate opium as a potential cure for this killer disease.

In southern China and Southeast Asia, opium has been a traditional cure for tropical fevers besides malaria, including for cholera. Opium seems to be toxic to many infectious agents that cause fevers in the tropics, and many French expatriates assigned to posts in Indochina during the colonial era smoked opium regularly as a preventive as well as a cure for tropical fevers. In addition to destroying microbes responsible for causing fevers, opium brings quick relief from the symptoms of fever by lowering body temperature, inhibiting sweating, decongesting the lungs, and providing analgesic relief from headaches and body pains.

Other common therapeutic applications of opium in traditional medicine are to provide quick relief from toothache, headache, arthritis, and various chronic aches and pains and as a remedy for persistent insomnia. In such cases, opium is taken daily, but in small measured doses, usually during the early part of the day. The body does not develop a tolerance to opium's analgesic and sedative effects, so regardless of how long it is used for these purposes, dosages need not be incrementally increased, as with modern pharmaceutical drugs.

Due to its vasodilating and muscle-relaxing properties, opium frequently served as a palliative for the conditions of old age in traditional Asian societies. In cases of high blood pressure and associated symptoms of hypertension, opium is highly effective in restoring normal blood pressure and relieving tension. Tight muscles and stiff joints also respond well to opium, as does chronic depression. While daily use of opium for these purposes does indeed lead to addiction, only a small dose is required, causing minimal or no negative side effects to the patient. Chemical drugs that doctors prescribe to the elderly for high blood pressure and other hypertensive symptoms, depression, and insomnia are also highly addictive, and all of them have serious negative side effects. In addition, a different drug must be taken for each condition, whereas only a small dose of opium relieves all of them. In the final analysis, the patient experiences more effective relief and suffers less serious side effects from a small daily dose of opium than from a handful of various addictive pharmaceutical drugs, and therefore, when addictive medication is required, whole opium represents a safer medical choice than the synthetic chemical drugs produced today by the pharmaceutical industry.

An important point to note: smoking opium is a significantly safer and more effective way to administer the drug for therapeutic purposes than eating it. Before 1920, when the Dangerous Drugs Act halted all further medical research into the therapeutic benefits of smoking opium, widespread interest existed in British medical circles regarding the advantages of smoking rather than eating opium. Late-nineteenth-century physicians in England referred to a popular pamphlet entitled "Opium Smoking as a Therapeutic Power According to the Latest Medical Authorities" for guidance on the many medical applications of smoking the drug. Smoking opium avoided the problems of upset stomach and liver toxicity frequently experienced by patients who ingest opium orally, and it was described as "an easy, inoffensive, and very efficacious mode of treating chronic and neuralgic affection."

In light of the many dangerous side effects now recognized as a result of long-term use of chemical pharmaceutical drugs, modern medicine might be well advised to once again investigate this (in the words of the above-referenced pamphlet) "inoffensive and very efficacious mode" of administering what amounts to an herbal substitute for tranquilizers, antidepressants, sleeping pills, and antihypertension drugs, all of which are at least as addictive as opium and far more hazardous to human health.

Indeed, this efficacious mode of administering whole herbal opium has more important beneficial applications today than ever before. According to statistics recently published by health authorities at the United Nations—as well as the government health agencies in America, Europe, and Asia—up to eighty-five percent of all new cases of HIV infection today are caused by dirty needles shared by addicts to inject heroin. Allowing addicts to get their daily "fix" of opiate alkaloids by the inoffensive method of inhaling the distilled vapors of whole herbal opium would help to eradicate the primary cause of HIV infection virtually overnight, not to mention eliminating a primary cause of violent crime, official corruption, and pointless imprisonment throughout the world due to the illegal heroin trade.

Many countries are now seriously considering providing legal injector rooms, or shooting galleries, where heroin addicts can go to "shoot up" their daily dose of "smack." Would not an abundantly more sensible solution be to offer confirmed addicts smoking rooms where they could legally get their daily ration of opiate alkaloids by inhaling the distilled vapors of whole herbal opium? Prior to 1920, when whole herbal opium was still legally available, heroin was not a problem, even though pure pharmaceutical heroin could be legally purchased over the counter at only a few dollars an ounce. Given a free choice, most addicts would choose to smoke whole opium rather than inject heroin, a chemically extracted derivative of opium that causes constipation, impotence, digestive failure, and all manner of other unpleasant side effects. This choice alone can do far more to halt the pandemic of HIV infection and reduce the massive crime, corruption, and terrorist activity that feeds off the heroin trade than the so-called War on Drugs, War on Crime, and War on Terrorism can accomplish—and at only a fraction of the cost to society. If the small minority (under two percent) of the general population who cannot function properly without opiates and therefore become addicted to them were permitted to obtain them legally, as they could in the past, then the vast majority (over ninety-eight percent), who don't need or want to use opiates, could once again walk the streets and live their lives free of the constant fear of violent crime motivated by what amounts to a desperate attempt to self-medicate with opiates.

Prior to its prohibition, opium was the most widely prescribed medicinal herb on earth, simply because it is such an effective remedy for a wide range of human ailments and causes relatively few negative side effects, particularly when administered by mode of the traditional Chinese distillation pipe. In his landmark work *Plant Intoxicants: A Classic Text on the Use of Mind-Altering Plants,* published in 1855, Baron Ernst von Bibra gives us a glimpse of just how important whole herbal opium used to be in traditional Western medicine:

> The use of opium in our medicines is so widespread that we can only touch on a few points here; even a partial description is impossible. One of the heroes among our healers, Hufeland, characterizes opium as a wonderful, mysterious, extraordinary drug, whose effects we still do not fully understand. It was no accident that Nature, in all her perfection, put the crown on the seed capsule. He writes that opium is a drug that taps our strength from the life source within and whose effects can mean life and death. It can either save a life at the last moment or bring death when misused. It is a drug that stands alone in its effects and cannot be replaced by any other.
>
> Christoph Wilhelm Hufeland states that, under certain conditions, there is almost no illness for which opium has not been legitimately used. Hufeland considers opium a particularly excellent remedy for local inflammations. He uses it successfully against pleurisy, painful pneumonia, inflammations of the abdominal organs, liver, spleen, stomach, and cholera orientalis, which he treats as a violent inflammation of the stomach. He applies opium against croup, meningitis, ophthalmia, nervous and typhoid fevers, malaria, spasmodic neuropathology, traumatic irritations, cough, and inflammations of the breast. With caution, he administers it in cases of dysentery and diabetes, and finally, in many cases of actual poisoning . . . Opium is thus one of the most important substances in medicine, not only among the vegetable substances dealt with in this book, but generally, among all drugs.

4

ALKALOIDS AND ALCHEMY

PHYSICAL AND CEREBRAL EFFECTS

Due to the complex combination of alkaloids in opium and the broad range of effects it has on the human system, it is difficult to distinguish physical from cerebral effects, and the two must therefore be considered together. While one set of alkaloids influences the brain and nervous system, another group simultaneously affects the muscles, organs, and circulatory system, blurring the boundary between the purely physical sensations that arise in the body and the cerebral effects produced by alterations in brain chemistry. Opium's analgesic effects, for example, come partly from diminished cerebral awareness of pain due to the influence of morphine and codeine at the endorphin receptors in the brain and partly from the deep relaxation of physical tension and improvement of blood flow in the specific tissues where pain resides, due to the effects of the muscle-relaxing and vasodilating alkaloids. Opium's stimulating effects also stem partly from the cerebral excitement caused by thebaine and partly from the physical stimulation caused by papaverine.

Contrary to common misconceptions, the most immediate and tangible effect felt by the opium smoker is one of stimulation, not stupefaction. In "The Big Smoke," the story of her own addiction in Shanghai during the 1930s, Emily Hahn writes:

> The first reaction to a good long pull at the pipe is a stimulating one. I would be full of ideas, and as I lay there I would make plans for all sorts of activity. Drowsiness of a sort came on later, but even then, inside my head, behind my drooping eyes, my mind seethed with exciting thoughts.

It is difficult for the smoker to discriminate between the physical and the cerebral aspects of this stimulation because it arises simultaneously from both the nervous system and the circulatory system. The first of the three primary narcotic alkaloids to influence cerebral functions is thebaine, not morphine, and its effect is distinctly stimulating. At the same time, papaverine and other vasodilators relax and expand the walls of the blood vessels, causing such a significant increase in the flow of blood throughout the body that a strong physical stimulation is felt due to the elevation of available energy resulting from enhanced delivery of oxygen and nutrients to the cells. The degree of stimulation experienced by the smoker depends on two factors: the number of pipes smoked and the amount of dross mixed into the chandoo. The fewer the pipes, the greater the sense of stimulation and the less the soporific effects of opium are felt. On the other hand, the more dross that's added to the smoking mixture, the less become its stimulating effects and the greater grow its soporific qualities. In *Confessions of an English Opium-Eater,* Thomas De Quincey takes particular note of opium's stimulating properties:

> Certainly, opium is classed under the head of narcotics; and some such effect it may produce in the end: but the primary effects of opium are always, and in the highest degree, to excite and stimulate the system: this first stage of its action always lasted with me, during my novitiate, for upwards of eight hours; so that it must be the fault of the opium-eater himself if he does not so time his exhibition of the dose (to speak medically) as that the whole weight of the narcotic influence may descend upon his sleep.

After feeling the initial stimulation of opium in the body and in the brain, the smoker (or eater) gradually begins to notice the more sedative effects, including bone-deep sensations of physical relaxation, the total dissolution of all bodily discomforts, unruffled mental tranquillity, and a sense of complete emotional equanimity. These soft, slack, fluid feelings of relaxation and well-being arise cerebrally as a blissful euphoria produced by the effects of the narcotic alkaloids on the endorphin receptors in the brain and physically as a complete release of all tightness and tension in every tissue of the body due to the effects of the relaxant alkaloids on the autonomic system of smooth muscles and tendons.

The ultimate result of this progressive relaxation of the body and sedation of the nervous system, combined with the initial stimulation of the brain and circulatory system, is a unique sensation of cerebral euphoria, mental alertness, and emotional tranquillity, luxuriously enveloped within a body totally free of discomfort and tension. "A feeling of euphoria usually results after a few pipes," write Boyes and Piraban. "As the smoker continues to smoke, he experiences a general feeling of well-being . . . Many smokers describe a feeling of dreaming whilst awake, with their whole body luxuriating in a greater degree of relaxation with each extra pipe."

In *Le Livre de l'opium,* written during the early twentieth century, the Vietnamese connoisseur of opium Nguyen Te Duc elaborates with obvious enthusiasm on the paradoxical blend of stimulation and sedation, physical satisfaction and cerebral pleasure, internal and external equilibrium, that a few pipes of good opium bestows upon the smoker:

> The first physiological effect felt by the smoker is one of complete satisfaction, a penetrating feeling of warmth through the extremities, an active warmth that arises from the enhanced circulation of blood, a regular rhythmical stimulation that pulses from the heart. This is a uniquely soft and flowing sensation, not an aggressive push, something between stimulation and gentle encouragement. Users of morphine are familiar with this sense of passive stimulation.
>
> For opium addicts, this experience is renewed every time they smoke, and it lasts for as long as the smoker remains aware of himself. Some people experience a sort of tingling in the extremities,

Women smokers imbibing at home. (Courtesy of Wolf K.)

but the smoker's true satisfaction arises from a more profound and deeper source. It is a nobler satisfaction that arises from a sense of perfect balance achieved throughout the entire human system, the nervous system, circulatory system, muscular system, and a supple limberness of the joints, a harmony of all the vital bodily functions, followed immediately by the spontaneous sensation of being in full possession of his body and in complete control of all the tools and motor functions of his body's engine. The smoker may thus be assured of enjoying the full potential of his body's capacities, elevated to the highest degree of sensations, functions, and cerebral impressions. This experience is immediate. All of the senses are instantly clarified and sensitized. Impressions are intensified but more deliberately drawn . . . Eyesight grows sharper and more brilliant, with more penetrating vision. The sense of touch is heightened, and the sense of hearing catches more distant sounds, finer vibrations, even the smallest noises. Indeed, the ears of the reclining smoker hear a veritable symphony of sound. The fingers, especially the tips, acquire an incredible sensitivity. The fingers of a smoker can sense the approach of an object before even touching it, and the tip of the thumb can virtually count the pores on the tip of the index finger. When manipulating the opium skewer, the smoker's fingers can feel the metallic patterns that only a microscope normally reveals. This enhancement of external physical sensitivity is accompanied by an enormous sense of internal rest, imparting a deep quietude to the entire being, and this is the primary source of the euphoria felt by the smoker.

There is also a temporary suppression of various vital functions such as digestion and respiration. In warmer climates, this condition is first noticed by the cessation of perspiration due to the inert state of the pores in the skin. There is also a strong tendency toward inactivity. This arises not so much from inertness of the muscles or physical reluctance to move, but is rather more of a cerebral phenomenon.

Resting tranquilly in the state of physical relaxation, cerebral stimulation, and emotional serenity conjured by opium, the smoker's sensory sensitivities are amplified—heightening his appreciation of all physical sensations—and his awareness of the subtleties of sensual pleasures is greatly enhanced. Opium does not prompt the smoker to wild behavior or extravagant sexual orgies, as many uninitiated Western commentators have reported.

The mistaken view that opium works as a potent aphrodisiac probably stems from the fact that brothels in China often offered opium to their customers on request, while many opium dens provided prostitutes to smokers who asked for them. In fact, men in brothels sometimes smoked a few pipes of opium before sex to cool the heat of their desire, so that they could better control themselves during the act, not to fire up their libido. By delaying ejaculation, they prolonged the pleasure of sex, enhancing their appreciation of the experience and giving them time to enjoy their partner's responses. Rather than thrashing blindly to a quick climax, as those who drink alcohol before sex tend to do, the opium smoker makes love rather than war in bed and conducts the act with a calm and sensitive consideration, even in a brothel. In opium dens where prostitutes were available, a smoker was as likely to request a woman for the cerebral pleasure of her feminine company as he was for the physical pleasures of her body.

The opposite but equally mistaken assumption about opium and sex is that opium makes a man sexually impotent and emotionally indifferent toward sex. This may indeed be temporarily true for the novice or occasional smoker who smokes too many pipes too fast and sinks swiftly into a stupefied state of narcosis. This condition renders his entire system so soft and relaxed, and makes his vital functions respond so slowly, that he would find it difficult to muster sufficient force even to urinate, much less rise to the occasion of sex. But this is a case neither of impotence nor of indifference. It is a case of sheer toxicity and stupefaction caused by the wretched excess of the undisciplined smoker.

Opium influences male sexuality in several ways, with effects that make it an ideal appetizer for men who take a gourmet interest in sex and savor the pleasures of the act itself, rather than merely craving its climax. The sedative and analgesic effects of opium on the central nervous system slow down autonomic responses, permitting men to pace themselves and deliberately delay orgasm, thereby prolonging the act as long as they wish or repeating it as often as they like, either with the same or with multiple partners. The cerebral pleasures of such extended sexual encounters exceed even the physical satisfaction, encouraging men to prolong the act ever more. At the same time, the potent vasodilating properties of papaverine, which has a specific natural affinity for the sexual organs, increase the flow of blood to the penis, enabling men to maintain longstanding erections that last throughout the course of the act.

Opium tames the sexual aggression and predatory behavior of the male libido, balancing the masculine hardness of yang with the feminine softness of yin. This softening influence renders a man more tender and receptive to his partner's feelings in sex and less driven by the need to sexually conquer a woman. Opium cures the male ego of its obsessive preoccupation with the genital aspects of sex and opens his mind to other, more subtle aspects of sexuality as well. As Jean Cocteau remarks in his opium journal, "One cannot say that opium, by removing all sexual obsessions, weakens the smoker, because not only does it not cause impotence, but what is more it replaces those somewhat base obsessions by others which are somewhat lofty, very strange and unknown to a sexually normal organism."

This is why women in traditional Asia, where male dominance is deeply ingrained in society, often preferred men who smoke opium, as long as they used it with caution and moderation. As lovers, experi-

Opium smokers at home in Vietnam. (Courtesy of Wolf K.)

enced opium smokers are usually more considerate of a woman's physical and emotional needs in sex, and better able to perform in a manner that meets those needs. As husbands, such men are less likely to feel the macho drive to bring extra wives or concubines into the household, or to keep extramarital mistresses on the side, and they are far more likely than non-opium-smoking Asian males to find satisfaction in a monogamous marriage.

While actually reclining by the lamp smoking opium, however, men tend to lose interest in all physical activity, including sex.

It simply requires too much initiative and effort. This inertia is due in part to the temporary suspension of motor activity and the slowing of vital functions experienced during the initial stages of smoking and in part to the total cerebral satisfaction provided by the activity of the narcotic alkaloids at the endorphin receptors in the brain, a satisfaction that leaves nothing to be desired. As Nguyen Te Duc observes in *Le Livre de l'opium:*

> There is a total absence of carnal desire when smoking opium. This point must be emphasized because popular misconceptions view the opium smoker as one who inhabits a bawdy paradise of lustful houris and extravagant sexual orgies, whereas in fact the opposite is true. While smoking, the act of love with all of the more or less delicate foreplay it requires seems highly undesirable to the smoker. In thought, attitude, and behavior, there is no one more chaste than the satisfied opium smoker. It must also be noted, however, that this effect does not cause the opium smoker to cease functioning as a man in his daily life, at least not the Asian smoker, as clearly evidenced by the fact that the Asian race, most of whom smoke, is the most prolific on earth.

Opium has a markedly different effect on the sexuality of women from that on men. For men, the softening influence of opium's powerful yin elements and Water energy runs counter to the hard, aggressive yang qualities and Fire energy of male sexuality, thereby cooling the male libido and refining men's sexual expression. For women, however, who are already yin by nature, opium simply reinforces their innate female sexuality and further accents their other feminine qualities. After smoking opium, most women tend to feel rather amorous, and since the female role in sex does not demand the same elaborate effort and strong initiative that it calls for in men, the requirements of the act do not seem as troublesome to the female smoker as they do to the male. Due to the natural resonance between the yin energies of women and opium, it could be said that on the cerebral level, opium serves women as a mild aphrodisiac, or at least as an appetizer for sex.

One of the most immediate and noticeable physical effects of opium on the human body is a rapid dehydration of the tissues. In particular, opium removes a considerable amount of water from the large intestine, leading to a condition of dry bowels that, if not counteracted by drinking plenty of extra water, can cause constipation. For the occasional smoker, this condition passes after about twenty-four hours, when the last traces of opium residues are eliminated from the body, but for the habitual smoker, it is important to compensate for this dehydrating effect with extra rations of water, tea, and other fluids, lest constipation become a chronic condition.

Opium also reduces the flow of gastric juices in the stomach, and tends to dry out the lungs and bronchial passages. Since the skin is also an excretory organ physiologically associated with lung and bowel functions, opium's dehydrating properties affect the skin as well. As a medicinal herb, opium's astringent effects constitute its primary therapeutic value and make it a useful remedy for diarrhea, dysentery, and bronchial congestion, but when used recreationally, opium's dehydrating effects tend to dry out the smoker's body, and this side effect must be counteracted by ingesting sufficient extra amounts of fluids.

Emaciation of the flesh can also be a problem for smokers who smoke more than twenty pipes per day, or who lace their chandoo with excessively high proportions of dross. In his journal, Cocteau quotes a pipe boy as saying, "Good drug makes fat . . . Dross makes sick." This effect may be due to several factors. Highly drossed opium taken daily in large doses tends to create a condition of chronic digestive insufficiency in the smoker's system by constantly suppressing the gastric flow and dehydrating the intestines, which impairs the smoker's capacity to digest food and assimilate nutrients. Dross also drastically reduces the appetite for food, especially for the rich, high-calorie foods required to keep the habitual smoker's body functioning well. Furthermore, heavy consumption of opium that contains a high level of dross leads to a chronic state of elevated toxicity in the blood and tissues, a condition that forces the smoker's body to burn up every available calorie and nutrient in an ongoing effort to process and eliminate these toxic residues from the system.

The state of chronic tissue toxicity that develops as a result of undisciplined smoking habits—especially when further aggravated by negligence to preventive health care and failure to implement periodic intervals of withdrawal from opium—can lead to a wide range of undesirable physiological problems. In *Le Livre de l'opium,* Nguyen Te Duc describes some of these conditions:

> Periods of stimulation above the norm are followed by periods of weakness below the norm. These ups and downs will cause an overall stagnation of the blood circulation, resulting in coldness in the extremities, feelings of heaviness and torpor, pains in the joints, cold sweats, cardiac problems, and so forth. The temporary and partial paralysis of vital functions will also cause congestion of the vital organs, loss of appetite, dyspepsia, nausea, excess acidity, cramps, and the entire range of maladies associated with impaired digestive functions.

Besides the various physical and cerebral effects of opium discussed above, which apply to both habitual and occasional smokers, novices who make the mistake of smoking too much too fast often experience some additional unpleasant side effects, which usually pass four or five hours after their last pipe. The most common of these are nausea and vomiting, along with loss of appetite and digestive stagnation. Other common symptoms of excessive intake and rapid-fire smoking are cold sweat, loss of color in the face, dry throat and dry eyes, inability to concentrate, and deep drowsiness. These side effects are easily prevented if the smoker simply restricts his intake to three to five pipes per session and avoids smoking opium that has been heavily dosed with dross.

One of the most telltale physical signs that someone has been smoking opium is contraction of the pupils into two tiny pinholes, a side effect that identifies the eyes of almost all opium smokers. The eyelids also tend to grow heavier with each successive pipe, and the smoker's limbs move more slowly and deliberately than usual. But the most obvious indication that a person has been indulging in the Big Smoke, especially in the eyes of those who know that person well, is the total relaxation of the more than one hundred muscles of the face, a relaxation that runs so deep that it can completely change the character and composition of a face, particularly in those who normally wear a tight mask in public. This softening and loosening of the autonomic facial muscles, which are normally very taut, results from the same combination of cerebral euphoria and physical relaxation that gives rise to all of opium's effects, and it can cause such a profound change in the smoker's physiognomy that he or she appears to have become an entirely different person. The face that a smoker presents to the world invariably reflects the feelings of profound satisfaction, blissful detachment, and luxuriant relaxation that a few pipes of well-prepared opium produce in the human system.

THE VELVET UNDERGROUND

PSYCHOLOGICAL AND SOCIAL ASPECTS

In her story "The Big Smoke," Emily Hahn writes, "We opium smokers, I reflected, are detached," when she realizes that she's become addicted to opium, "and that is one of our advantages. We aren't troubled with unpleasant emotions." Detachment and the emotional tranquillity it engenders are the primary psychological effects of opium. Both as a short-term effect after each smoking session and as a long-term effect on the smoker's entire approach to life, detachment is the hallmark of the opium smoker. There is no particular alkaloid in opium responsible for causing this sense of detachment. It arises as the net result of the cumulative effects—both cerebral and physical—of all the alkaloids as they work together to create a world within the smoker's mind and body, a tranquil and carefree world that he views as superior to the outside world. But the smoker's preference for the world he finds in opium and for the congenial company of fellow smokers stems more from the pettiness, boredom, and hostility he normally experiences in the society in which he lives than from the attractions of opium itself. The world of opium thus becomes a sort of private club where smokers take refuge from people and places that don't agree with them, and where they find compatible companions. "People who didn't smoke seemed more and more remote," writes Hahn, "whereas smokers always seemed to have tastes and ideas compatible with mine."

Smoking opium together often takes on the trappings of a ritual sacrament, with the lamp serving as a sort of altar light. As the French writer Robert Desnos observed, "Opium unites the souls of smokers who recline around the same lamp. It's a bath in a thick atmosphere, a reunion in one bed with heavy covers, a veritable coupling that one can't resist. It's perhaps because of this that there are so few solitary smokers . . ."

The difference between opium and other drugs that people use to escape an unpleasant and painful world, such as heroin and alcohol, is that the latter merely offer escape by intoxication, while opium offers the added attraction of an alternative world to inhabit, a self-contained world of comfort, contentment, and convivial company, complete with a culture all of its own. "To lie in a quiet room, talking and smoking . . . was delightfully restful and pleasant," recalls Hahn of the time she spent addicted to opium with her Chinese friends in Shanghai. "Reading and music and painting were enough to keep us happy." Such sentiments are rarely expressed by alcoholics or heroin addicts.

Thus the opium smoker not only withdraws himself from the mainstream of society, but he also becomes a member of a congenial fraternity that exists quietly on the outer fringes of society, and from the insular perspective this gives him, he views the world with the detached attitude of a dispassionate observer. Rejecting society's demands on his time and energy, he refuses to conform to conventional morality. Since the mundane machinations of social and political events no longer have any meaning to him, nothing ruffles his emotions. The satisfied smoker rests impervious to disturbance in a sphere of serenity sanctified by the alchemy of opium, and there his body nestles in the cozy privacy of a world whose borders extend no farther than the light cast by the smoking lamp, but within which his mind roams freely beyond all boundaries of time and space.

Society frowns upon such detachment and apathy toward worldly affairs, just as a teacher frowns upon a student who loses interest in his lessons and becomes a truant. And like the teacher does to the truant, society punishes the opium smoker for his indifference and refusal to participate. "Society often forgives the criminal," wrote Oscar Wilde, "but it never forgives the dreamer." Jean Cocteau remarks on society's antagonism toward the opium smoker's alienation as follows:

> Opium desocializes us and removes us from the community. Further, the community takes its revenge. The persecution of opium addicts is an instinctive defense by society against an antisocial gesture.

Society particularly disapproves of the opium smoker's indifference to conventional morality and social values, branding him a threat to the welfare of the community. In fact, however, the smoker poses no threat whatsoever to the community. All he does is retire from society and live aloof in another world defined by opium. As professional law enforcement officers and social scientists know very well, the only time that an addict of opiates becomes a criminal threat to society is when he does *not* have access to his drug, not when he is using it, and the only reason he associates with criminal elements is because society prohibits his drug and thereby obliges him to obtain it from gangsters. If opium were legal, he would purchase it at his local pharmacy, or smoke in an opium den, just as people did all over the world until the early twentieth century, and as they still do when buying alcohol and tobacco, barbiturates and antidepressants, and other socially sanctioned drugs. Prohibition has never deterred people from using drugs, as clearly evidenced by America's abortive attempt to ban the use of alcohol from 1920 to 1933, and today by the government's failed efforts to keep young people from smoking marijuana by declaring it illegal. The only people who profit from laws against recreational drug use are the underworld organizations that supply these drugs whenever they cannot be purchased legally. Nevertheless, though essentially harmless to others, society treats the addict as a criminal and condemns his habit as a threat to the community; this harassment only serves to further alienate the opium smoker from society.

In reality, the smoker who has smoked his pipes is no more inclined to go out and commit a crime than he is to join a parade or compete in a marathon. His dissociation from society is complete, and his lack of interest in participation comprises the full spectrum from social to antisocial behavior. It is this very apathy toward involvement in the world, and the smoker's indifference to values that society holds dear, that most offends society, not the smoker's behavior itself. At least the common criminal cares enough about the same things that society prizes to try to obtain them by any means possible, and thus the criminal becomes a sort of folk hero, glorified in film and fiction. But the opium smoker rejects everything that society values and withdraws entirely from the community, living emotionally detached and psychologically insulated from the world, there in body but not in spirit. Society does not take this rejection well; it views the addict's apathy as an outright insult and retaliates by depriving him of his drug, as though withdrawal from the drug would return him to the fold.

The addict does not reject society because he smokes opium, but rather he smokes opium because he rejects society. The reason that he chooses opium as his vehicle of escape is simply because he has discovered that opium, unlike alcohol and other drugs, not only offers a convenient exit but also provides a comfortable alternative world for him to inhabit. Take away his opium and he will turn to alcohol instead, transforming himself from a harmless hermetic dropout to an obnoxious drunkard and social nuisance who detests society all the more for depriving him of what he likes best. But even the most retrograde drunk is still a social animal who grazes in society's pastures and interacts with the rest of the herd, and so his vice is tolerated as sociable. By contrast, the opium smoker's aloof isolation and emotional detachment from the world are viewed by society as arrogant expressions of disdain and superiority, a rude insult to the entire community, and so his drug is condemned as an antisocial threat.

The opium smoker's only real offense to society is entirely a psychological one, a crime of dispassion, not an overt act of violence or malice. Nevertheless, society brands his habit as the most immoral of all vices. In truth, the addict's behavior is neither moral nor immoral, but rather entirely amoral and neutral, but from society's point of view, this is the worst behavior of all because it does not conform to accepted standards of right and wrong, good and bad, and therefore it allows no room for reform or redemption by society. In *Le Livre de l'opium*, this social paradox is commented on as follows:

The public attributes all manner of vice to the amorality of the opium smoker, and views him as a vicious threat capable of all sorts of crime. This view is an error of excessive simplification. The amorality of the smoker always remains entirely theoretical and inert, just like all of his other states and qualities . . . He is utterly incapable of mustering the will to act upon even his own most personal passions. In his universal indifference, he does not distinguish between right and wrong, good or bad, but he never acts upon his amorality in reality. No, the smoker's amorality is totally spiritual and intellectual.

Despite the stern disapproval and often severe punishment meted out to opium smokers by society since the mid-twentieth century, people continue to use opium, or its derivatives, as they have ever since the dawn of human history, and probably long before that. One has only to note the widespread use of heroin throughout the world today to realize that opiates have a greater following now than ever before. Legal and socially condoned alternatives to opium, such as alcohol and barbiturates, cannot match what De Quincy described as "the divine luxuries of opium." As Cocteau learned from his own experience, "He who has smoked will smoke," regardless of the risks involved. There must therefore be something to opium, besides its narcotic effects, that appeals on a deeper level to those who use it, so let's take a look at some of the ways the world unfolds in the mind of the habitual opium smoker.

In the mind of the smoker, who feels an a priori alienation from society, opium transforms a hostile, sinister world into a warm and friendly place, radiant with familiar feelings. Reminiscing about opium during his second withdrawal, Cocteau recalls:

I had forgotten that opium transforms the world and that, without opium, a sinister room remains a sinister room . . . One of the wonders of opium is to transform instantaneously an unknown room into a room so familiar, so full of memories, that one thinks one has always occupied it. When addicts go away they suffer no hurt because of the certainty that the delicate mechanism will function in one minute, anywhere.

No matter where he goes, as long as the smoker has some opium and a smoking kit, he always feels at home. After deliberately depriving herself of opium for a few days in Shanghai to see if she was really addicted, Emily Hahn noted, "The only really bad thing was the terror I felt of being lost, astray, naked, shivering in a world that seemed imminently brutal." After smoking a few pipes with her friends, that feeling of terror vanished.

The opium smoker grows so accustomed to the velvet underground he inhabits when he's been smoking, and to seeing life through the rose-colored glasses of opium, that without it the world becomes a rough, repugnant prison. Opium insulates the smoker from the unpleasantness of the world with an anesthetic screen that blocks his perception of anything that might bother him. Nguyen Te Duc explains this mechanism in the following passage from *Le Livre de l'opium*:

> Opium does not eliminate pain, but rather it eliminates the sensation of pain. Opium creates a psychic screen between the mind and the body of the smoker, so that pain becomes an abstraction, without the sharpness of physical sensation . . . The anesthesia produced by opium may be described as a sort of cerebral intoxication, a psychic fog between oneself and external reality that diminishes the outer world. The smoker forgets he has a body. His mind escapes the prison of flesh and the material world, and is removed to the periphery of reality by the centrifugal force of opium. He escapes not only his own body, but also the physical world in which his body exists. Opium plays a siren's tune on the piano of his nerves, and as he listens, the smoker forgets the passage of time, and he also forgets about hunger, thirst, fatigue, and sleep.

Over time, the velvet curtain opium draws between the smoker and the physical world completely changes his relationship with the earth. As Cocteau put it, "It is difficult to live without opium after having known it because it is difficult, after knowing opium, to take earth seriously. And unless one is a saint, it is difficult to live without taking earth seriously."

"I would think of the lamp in the shaded room, the coziness, the peace and comfort with great longing," Hahn recalls of the times she strayed too far from the opium tray during her addiction in Shanghai. In the calm and cozy privacy of the smoking room, the soft warm glow of the lamp attracts the smoker like a moth to a flame, and as he puffs clouds of smoke through the pipe, he withdraws into an inner vision of the world conjured by opium while blowing the outer world farther and farther away with each breath. And as he smokes, not only does the world shrink away, but time itself dissolves, leaving the smoker suspended in an artificial eternity. "Time," writes Hahn, "was something that had lost its grip on me. It was amazing how watches varied their rate of running, sometimes galloping, sometimes standing still."

Or as Cocteau describes it, "It is eleven o'clock in the evening. One smokes for five minutes; one looks at one's watch: it is five o'clock in the morning."

In one of the most memorable passages from his opium journal, Cocteau describes how opium halts the race to death in its tracks by making life stand still:

Everything one achieves in life, even love, occurs in an express train racing towards death. To smoke opium is to get out of the train while it is still moving. It is to concern oneself with something other than life or death.

Cocteau was particularly impressed by what he calls "the slow speed of opium," for it allowed him to notice things about life that he had always missed without opium. "Under the influence of opium one becomes the meeting place for the phenomena which art sends to us from outside," he writes. "Opium, which changes our speeds, procures for us a very clear awareness of worlds which are superimposed on each other, which interpenetrate each other, but do not even suspect each other's existence." And again, "Opium is the only vegetable substance which communicates the vegetable state to us. Through it, we get an idea of that other speed of plants." After smoking, "The spirit of the smoker moves without moving, like watered silk."

The English poet Arthur Symons described the experience very well in his poem "The Opium Smoker":

> *I am engulfed, and drown deliciously.*
> *Soft music like a perfume, and sweet light*
> *Golden with audible odours exquisite,*
> *Swathe me with cerements for eternity.*
> *Time is no more, I pause and yet I flee.*
> *A million ages wrap me round with night.*
> *I drain a million ages of delight.*
> *I hold the future in my memory.*

The slow deliberation of perception and endless corridors of dreamy reverie that opium induces explain why opium has always been so popular among writers and poets, painters and musicians. "The opium dream was seen as a kind of waking theater of the imagination," writes Terence McKenna in *Food of the Gods: The Search for the Original Tree of Knowledge: A Radical History of Plants, Drugs, and Human Evolution.* McKenna explains:

Opium exhilarates the spirit; it can produce endlessly unraveling streamers of thought and rhapsodic speculation. The fifty years following Thomas De Quincey's *Confessions* were to see a deep grappling with the impact of opium use on creativity, especially literary creativity. De Quincey pioneered the effort; he was the first writer to study deliberately, from within his personal experience, the way in which dreams and visions are formed, how opium helps form them and intensifies them and how they are then recomposed and used in conscious art, in this case impassioned prose, but the process would also apply to poetry. He learned his waking technique as a writer partly from observation of how the mind works in dreams and reveries under the influence of opium.

It was his belief that opium dreams and reveries could be in themselves a creative process both analogous to, and leading to, literary creation. He used dreams in his writing not as decoration, not as allegory, not as a device to create atmosphere or to forestall and help on the plot, not even as intimations of a higher reality (although he believed they were that) but as a form of art in themselves.

Opium brings a lucid clarity and order to the mind, even as it sedates and anesthetizes the body, and herein lies its most important and distinctive difference from alcohol. "Alcohol provokes fits of madness," writes Cocteau. "Opium provokes fits of wisdom." De Quincey expounds on this distinction in *Confessions of an English Opium-Eater:*

> But the main distinction lies in this, that whereas wine disorders the mental faculties, opium, on the contrary (if taken in a proper manner), introduces amongst them the most exquisite order, legislation, and harmony. Wine robs a man of his self-possession: opium greatly invigorates it. Wine unsettles and clouds the judgment, and gives a preternatural brightness, and a vivid exaltation to the contempts and the admirations, the loves and the hatreds, of the drinker: opium, on the contrary, communicates serenity and equipoise to all the faculties, active or passive: and with respect to the temper and moral feelings in general, it gives simply that sort of vital warmth which is approved by the judgment and would probably always accompany a bodily constitution of primeval and antediluvian health. Thus, for instance, opium, like wine, gives an expansion to the heart and the benevolent affections: but then, with this remarkable difference, that in the sudden development of kindheartedness which accompanies inebriation, there is always more or less of a maudlin character, which exposes it to the contempt of the bystander. Men shake hands, swear eternal friendship, and shed tears, no mortal knows why: and the sensual creature is clearly uppermost. But the expansion of the more benign feelings, incident to opium, is no febrile process, but a healthy restoration to that state which the mind would naturally recover upon the removal of any deep seated irritation of pain that had disturbed and quarreled with the impulses of a heart originally just and good.

It is a serious mistake, however, to suppose that opium itself is a source of creative power to the artist or writer. If creative potential is lacking to start with, then no drug can provide it. Otherwise, all opium smokers would be creative geniuses, which is clearly not the case.

Opium can and often does establish the necessary physiological and psychological conditions of tranquillity and equilibrium that allow an individual's creative potential to fully manifest itself in art or writing, but the talent and inspiration for such creativity can only come from the human heart and mind. Cocteau compares opium's effect on a person's creative imagination with the role of water in bringing a flower to blossom:

> We all carry within us something folded up like those Japanese flowers made of wood, which unfold in water.
>
> Opium plays the same role as the water. None of us carries the same kind of flower. It is possible that a person who does not smoke may never know the kind of flower that opium might have unfolded within him.

Every person has a unique seed of creativity in his or her heart, and the flower to which it gives bloom when the imagination is sufficiently fertile is different in each individual. However, the flower of creative imagination is a delicate plant, and it can blossom only under specific conditions. Those conditions include the sunshine of a happy heart unclouded by stormy emotions; the calm, clear skies of cerebral equilibrium; and the rich loam of a luxuriously relaxed body free of tension and pain. Under these conditions, the flower of creative imagination grows and blooms, unfolding its color and beauty to all the world. For artists and writers, who often feel creatively stultified and emotionally frustrated by conventional society, opium establishes an internal landscape and emotional climate that eases their tension and frees their creative energy to express itself in form. As Cocteau, who used opium as a psychic fertilizer for his own writing, notes, "Opium enables one to give form to the unformed." The writer or artist who once uses opium to release his or her creative spirit from the bondage of worldly cares, the clutch of emotional turmoil, and the cage of physical tension becomes as deeply addicted to the utility and ease of working under the becalming influence of opium as to the opium itself.

The Romantic English poet Samuel Taylor Coleridge—who, like Cocteau and De Quincey, relied on opium for most of his life as a lubricant for his literary creativity—speculated in his *Notebooks* that the:

> . . . drug shall make (the poet) capable of conceiving and bringing forth thoughts, hidden in him before, which shall call forth the deepest feelings of his best, greatest, and sanest contemporaries . . . that the dire poison for a delusive time has made the body . . . a fitter instrument for the all-powerful soul.

The key point here is that whatever thoughts the poet is "bringing forth" under the influence of opium are already there, "hidden in him before," and that the opium serves the poet as a tool for conceiving and expressing his poetically inspired thoughts in words, not as a source of inspiration itself.

Certainly other means besides opium can establish the tranquillity, equanimity, and relaxation required for the flower of creative imagination to unfold. Traditional methods such as meditation, breathing, yoga, and energy work, and more modern techniques like biofeedback and deep-tissue body work, may all be employed to balance the body and harmonize the mind so that creative talent can blossom, but unfortunately few people master these methods sufficiently to achieve the beatific state in which creative energy manifests freely. Opium, however, when properly used, can produce these conditions easily and consistently, and though its positive effects on creative expression are only temporary and artificial and come with negative side effects in physical and spiritual health, for many people opium provides the only opportunity they ever have in life to experience the creative facet of their personalities.

When all is said and done regarding the question of opium, it boils down to a simple matter of the smoker's own volition and will. Nguyen Te Duc states this point clearly in *Le Livre de l'opium*:

> The smoker must never forget to nurture and adore his primary goddess: his own will. Above all, he must scrupulously avoid any

weakness, negligence, and distraction that undermines his will, for diseases of the will are the most dangerous of all. This condition is not really so much a disease per se, but rather a laziness or numbness of the will, although it is not necessarily the case that opium leads to the numbing or atrophy of one's will power. Sometimes this condition is a reflection of other psychological or physical causes, such an atrophy of the nervous system or a chronic state of anemia. It is always important to draw forth and manifest the will in action, but for the opium smoker this becomes increasingly difficult, because the supreme joy of the smoker is not to act. Thus, the problem is not so much a matter of a disease of the will, but rather a total absence of desire.

Nothing forces the smoker to smoke. The only force at work here is the volitional force of the smoker's own free will. For all the various reasons and rationalizations that opium smokers might cite to justify their decision to adopt an addictive and toxic substance as a mainstay of their daily lives, the bottom line still remains their own volition and will. And at the heart of the matter, the volition that prompts one to smoke opium is the self-indulgent imperative of the hedonist, the persistent pleasure principle by which the sensualist lives his life. For all the convoluted complexities and manifold manifestations of opium, it is still the sheer physical pleasure and exquisite cerebral satisfaction bestowed by it that motivates the smoker each time he presses his lips to the mouth of an opium pipe. The price the smoker pays for this luxury in terms of physical health and spiritual integrity is a mandatory but variable cost that fluctuates in direct proportion to the discipline and willpower he exercises when using opium.

Opium itself is neither good nor bad, and using it is neither right nor wrong. As Cocteau so succinctly summarized the situation, "Opium is a decision to be taken." The decision to smoke or not to smoke can only be made by each individual as a conscious act of volition and a deliberate exercise of free will, guided by a mind fully informed of the facts. And while that decision may be driven by a longing for the carefree detachment, timeless euphoria, and bodily comfort that opium so readily provides, it must always be tempered with a thorough and honest understanding of the truth and full responsibility for the consequences involved in such a choice.

6

A DECISION TO BE TAKEN

ADDICTION AND WITHDRAWAL

Addiction is the scarlet letter of opium smoking. The very word *addict* has become a social stigma throughout the modern world, even though people today are, by definition, addicted to all sorts of things, many of which are at least as detrimental to health as opium. The dictionary defines the word *addict* as "one who has become dependent on something," a definition that certainly includes those who depend on their daily dose of coffee or tea, sugar or chocolate, television or sex, as well as recreational drugs like alcohol and tobacco and prescription drugs such as sleeping pills, antidepressants, and antihypertensives.

Legality often seems to define the border between addictions that are socially condoned (e.g., cigarettes and prescription drugs) and those that are socially unacceptable (e.g., opiates), but even people who are addicted to legal substances such as tobacco and coffee usually cringe at the suggestion that they are addicts. Such sensitivity is particularly true of opium smokers, who are loath to admit that they've become slaves to their habit. Even those who have lived with their habit for many years tend to deny their addiction when someone who is not addicted confronts them with it. For example, in *The City of Lingering Splendor*, John Blofeld expresses surprise when his friend Chu informs him that a famous opera singer they both know smokes several dozen pipes of opium daily:

> "That's odd," I said without much conviction. "The Singing-Master assured me he rarely smokes opium, and yet . . ."
>
> Chu stared at me in amazement. "Surely you didn't believe him? You say he's fat and jolly looking, but I think it likely he smokes a whole liang [Chinese ounce] every day. Whoever heard of a singing-master who doesn't smoke?"
>
> "Then why . . ."
>
> "Smokers are like that. My father used to be the same. They always pretend, even to themselves if possible, that they are not addicted. A few of them really aren't, but more often they are just trying to convince you or themselves that they are still their own masters."

"I can stop whenever I want," is one of the most common statements made by opium addicts in reply to questions about their smoking habits, but in fact they cannot, at least not without facing the extremely unpleasant ordeal of withdrawal, for opium is without question one of the most addictive substances on earth. In "The Big Smoke," Emily Hahn made note of the contradictory attitude expressed by her opium-smoking friends about their addiction:

> During such talks, Heh-ven sometimes spoke of himself frankly as an addict but at other times he still said he wasn't. I never knew what sort of statement he was going to make on the subject . . .
>
> One day, after he had been even more contradictory than was his custom, I drew up a table of the smoker's creed:
>
> 1. I will never be an addict.
> 2. I can't become addicted. I am one of those people who take it or let it alone.
> 3. I'm not badly addicted.
> 4. It's a matter of will power, and I can stop any time.

On the other hand, some smokers, albeit a small minority, are not the least bit fazed by the fact of their addiction and happily admit to it. Hahn herself was such a person, for she opens her frank account of her addiction in "The Big Smoke" with the startling line: "Though I had always wanted to be an opium addict, I can't claim that as the reason I went to China. The opium ambition dates back to that obscure period of childhood when I wanted to be a lot of other things, too . . ." A few pages further she states, with undisguised pleasure, "I was an addict. I admitted it now, and was pleased that I could feel detached."

Jean Cocteau was another writer and opium smoker who readily admitted to his addiction and took obvious delight in it. In his journal, he gives us an unabashed account of his addiction to opium. Subsequently published in book form, the journal constitutes one of the most candid and incisive accounts of addiction to opium smoking ever recorded. Significantly, both Hahn and Cocteau, who speak directly from personal experience, write about their addiction without a trace of regret or moral diatribe, and neither of them in any way condemns opium. Their observations provide many valuable insights on various aspects and practical issues involved in both the addiction to and the withdrawal from opium smoking.

While modern Western literature on the subject of opium addiction usually cites Thomas De Quincey's famous work *Confessions of an English Opium-Eater* as a standard reference, it is not entirely pertinent to the topic of opium smoking, for as the title clearly states, De Quincey was an opium eater, not a smoker, and the two habits—despite employing the same substance—are very different. Cocteau takes note of this fact in his diary: "Never confuse the opium smoker with the opium eater. Quite different phenomena." In *Foreign Devil,* Richard Hughes also remarks on this distinction:

De Quincey suffered his monstrous dreams because he drank laudanum and ate opium; that is just as barbarous as smoking opium by yourself; if you smoke, you must always smoke in agreeable company.

The first question that arises is: What exactly constitutes addiction to opium? We are speaking here of actual physiological addiction to the drug, not psychological craving for it, which is a different matter. This is easy to tell: You know you're addicted when you skip a day or two of smoking and experience the discomfort of withdrawal symptoms as a result. Hahn decided to test herself for addiction by accepting an invitation to spend the weekend on a houseboat upriver from Shanghai, where she would not be able to get opium, with the following results: "I had an awful cold, and didn't sleep much. My stomach was upset and my legs hurt . . . On the way home, my cold got rapidly worse." These are all typical symptoms of opium withdrawal. Half an hour after returning to Shanghai, she rushes over to her friend's house, and, "snuggling luxuriously on a pillow," she announces to her curious friends, "[t]here won't be a next time." Cocteau describes the feeling even more explicitly:

> Without opium I am cold, I catch cold, I do not feel hungry . . . Imagine a silence equivalent to the crying of thousands of children whose mothers do not return to give them the breast. The lover's anxiety transposed into nervous awareness. An absence which dominates, a negative despotism.
>
> The phenomena become clearer. Flashes like moire before the eyes, champagne in the veins, frozen siphons, cramps, sweating at the root of the hair, dryness in the mouth, sniffling, tears. Do not persist. Your courage is to no purpose. If you delay too long, you will no longer be able to take your equipment and roll your pipe. Smoke. Your body was waiting only for a sign. One pipe is enough.

The next question usually asked by those who toy with opium is: How long does it take to get addicted? This of course varies from person to person, depending on one's health and basic constitution as well as one's daily dose and the quality of the opium being smoked. Generally speaking, at a rate of three to seven pipes per day, using good opium that has not been excessively fortified with dross, one can smoke for one or two or even three days in a row without experiencing any serious withdrawal symptoms the following day, as long as one then abstains for a few days thereafter. Smoke this way for a week or two, and you will acquire a mild habit that is relatively easy, though somewhat uncomfortable, to break. Continue for a month or two, and you will have become addicted, requiring a major effort and substantial willpower to detoxify and withdraw without stumbling back into the habit by the third day of abstinence. A year or two of daily smoking without a break will turn virtually anyone into a confirmed opium addict, after which only a major health crisis or spiritual illumination will prompt one to attempt quitting, and even then it will be an uphill battle, one a person is likely to lose without help from professionals experienced in these matters.

Opium can, of course, be smoked and enjoyed without addiction; one can have one's cake and eat it without getting hooked on the cake, but it takes discipline to do this, at least for those who enjoy opium. The cardinal rule here is: Never smoke two days in a row, and never smoke more than ten pipes in a day. But if you push this rule to the limit by smoking ten pipes every other day, after a month or two you will find that you cannot endure two days of abstinence without experiencing withdrawal symptoms, which means you've become addicted. So the way to follow this rule without becoming addicted is to exercise strict restraint.

Opium can be smoked daily without triggering addiction, but the only way to accomplish that is to limit yourself to just one or two small pipes a day and no more. According to traditional Chinese herbal medicine manuals, if a smoker keeps his daily ration of opium below half a gram, he will not become physically addicted to it. Very few opium smokers have the discipline to smoke just one or two pipes a day, but those few who do may enjoy their daily pipe year after year without addiction, and they can stop whenever they want to without experiencing the distress of withdrawal symptoms. In *Poppies, Pipes, and People,* Joseph Westermeyer tells of a Laotian medical colleague who for many years smoked just one pipe of opium at home each night after dinner as a way of relaxing after work, but whenever he traveled out of town he simply abstained until his return home, without any discomfort or craving for a pipe, and without addiction.

Another system some smokers use to avoid addiction is to smoke only once a week—usually on Sunday—or even once a month. As Hughes points out in his essay in *Foreign Devil* on opium dens:

> Nor need a moderate opium smoker necessarily become a hopeless and uncontrollable addict. In the old permissive days, the white bankers and taipans (English trading tycoons in Hong Kong), in Chinese cities like Shanghai and Hong Kong enjoyed a few pipes of opium once a week—or month—in relaxed company in eminently respectable and indeed exclusive surroundings. Those few who became addicts would have become alcoholics had they stuck to liquor.

Of course, this regimen lends itself readily to liberalization and soon one might find oneself lying hip by the lamp twice a week, then every other day, and finally each and every day. But as Hughes notes, such individuals would otherwise become addicted to alcohol or other drugs anyway, usually with far more hazardous effects on their health and lifestyles than those caused by opium.

After his first withdrawal from opium addiction, which lasted five months, Jean Cocteau explains how he became addicted again:

> I therefore became an opium addict again because the doctors who cure, one should really say, quite simply, purge—do not seek to cure the troubles which first cause the addiction; I had found again my unbalanced state of mind; and I preferred an artificial equilibrium to no equilibrium at all . . . I never exceeded ten pipes. I smoked them at the rate of three in the morning (at nine o'clock), four in the afternoon (at five o'clock), three in the evening (at eleven o'clock). I believed that, in this way, I was reducing the chances of addiction.

On the other hand, one of Emily Hahn's Chinese friends, with whom she smoked almost daily in Shanghai, and as discussed in her story "The

Big Smoke," believed that addiction could be prevented by not smoking at the same time every day:

> Hua-ching had a theory that addiction lay not so much in the smoking itself as in the time pattern one got used to. "If you vary your smoking every day, you have far less strong a habit," he assured us earnestly. "The great mistake is to do it at the same hour day after day. I'm careful to vary my smoking times. You see, it's all in the head."

Another friend and fellow smoker in her circle disputed this theory. "It's the drug itself," he said. "If it's all in the head, why do I feel it in my body?"

"All these little points we discussed at great length," Hahn recalls, "lying around the tray . . . A smoker loves semantics." But after all is said and done about addiction, the addicted smoker continues to smoke, and a lot more gets said than done. So the only fail-safe and foolproof way to avoid addiction to smoking opium is not to smoke it at all.

Having clarified that point, let us take a closer look at the habitual opium smoker, assuming that the smoker has already become addicted. A question of particular interest—and endless debate—among opium smokers is how many pipes to smoke per day. Among Chinese smokers, odd numbers are always preferred to even, such as three or five, seven or eleven, because odd numbers are regarded as yang, which represents strength and light, while even numbers are yin, which is passive and dark. Very few addicted smokers take fewer than seven pipes per day, while most smoke an average of fifteen. The general rule, however, is to smoke only as many pipes each day as one requires to achieve satisfaction and satiation, and, for the habitual smoker, not to exceed one's optimum daily measure.

An interesting aspect of opium smoking, and one that distinguishes it clearly from other addictive drug habits such as alcohol, amphetamines, and cocaine, as well as opium derivatives like morphine and heroin, is that the opium smoker can easily maintain the same daily dosage year after year without developing a tolerance that requires constantly increasing doses over time. As Cocteau notes:

> Let no one say to me: "Habit forces the smoker to increase the dose." One of the riddles of opium is that the smoker never has to increase his dose.

Opium remains unique among drugs in this respect. Moreover, the smoker whose daily measure is, for example, seven pipes may from time to time splurge and smoke fifteen to twenty pipes, then go right back to seven pipes the next day without experiencing any discomfort or craving for more. This also applies to opium eating, as evidenced by Thomas De Quincey's observation in his *Confessions* that the opium eater, after a period of excessive indulgence, may gradually reduce his daily dosage from as much as two hundred drops per day down to as little as twenty drops, often with better effects at the lower dosage than the higher. Even cigarette and coffee addicts are unable to do this without significant discomfort, while the need for ever-increasing dosages among addicts of cocaine and heroin, barbiturates, and amphetamines is a well known phenomenon.

What, then, might be the ultimate limit in terms of pipes per day for an opium addict? The limit seems to be defined only by the amount of time it takes to prepare and smoke the pipes, and of course by access to a reliable and steady source of opium. There are still smokers in Laos and Cambodia today who routinely puff down fifty to sixty pipes per day, but that is almost a full-time job that requires the smoker to spend most of the day and much of the night lying beside the opium lamp preparing pipes.

The greatest number of pipes per day that this writer has ever heard of is 150, a figure confirmed by Graham Greene, who himself enjoyed smoking opium during his frequent visits to Southeast Asia. In his novel *The Quiet American,* set in Vietnam during the 1950s, we find the following vignette:

> A Chinese of extreme emaciation came into the room. He seemed to take up no room at all: he was like the piece of greaseproof paper

that divides the biscuits in a tin. The only thickness he had was in his striped flannel pajamas.

"Monsieur Chou?" I asked.

He looked at me with the indifferent gaze of a smoker: the sunken cheeks, the baby wrists, the arms of a small girl. Many years and many pipes had been needed to whittle him down to these dimensions . . .

He began to cough, and under his pajama jacket, which had lost two buttons, the tight skin twanged like a native drum.

A newcomer joined us . . . He said in English, "Mr. Chou has only one lung . . . He smokes one hundred and fifty pipes every day."

Opium addiction tends to trim fat and muscle from the body in direct proportion to the number of pipes smoked per day, as well as to the amount of dross added to the smoking mixture. At fewer than twenty pipes per day, a normal healthy physique is easily maintained, assuming that one takes care to eat well and get sufficient exercise. Beyond that number, opium tends to shrink the body to its minimum proportions. The same principle applies to the amount of dross consumed. Cocteau notes this point in his opium diary:

Some people will say to you: "The discriminating throw away the dross." Others: "The discriminating make their boys smoke while they smoke only the dross." If one questions a boy about the drug's dangers, "Good drug make fat," he replies. "Dross make sick."

The vice of opium smoking is to smoke the dross.

The question often arises, "Why do some people get addicted to opium and others do not?" Indeed, the very smell of opium makes some people feel nauseous and only a pipe or two suffices to make them sick for days, while for others it provides instantaneous euphoria and tastes like manna from heaven. It all depends upon a person's physiological constitution and psychological disposition. For some people, opium provides precisely the elements their bodies require to correct inherent or acquired biochemical imbalances and thereby achieve functional equilibrium, and these are the people most likely to become addicted to it, for no other drug compares to opium for restoring balance and harmony to a disordered system. For those who lack normal equilibrium and are thus predisposed to addiction, smoking a few pipes of opium provides immediate physical comfort and emotional equanimity, grounding them with a soothing feeling of well-being. "The amateurs feel nothing," writes Cocteau, "they wait for dreams and risk being seasick . . ."

In America today, as well as in many other parts of the world where the natural rhythms of life have been disrupted by modern technology, millions of people have become totally dependent on various pharmaceutical drugs such as sleeping pills and painkillers, antihypertensives and antidepressants, stimulants and muscle relaxants. People often take these drugs in dangerous combinations for chronic conditions that have become endemic to modern societies: insomnia and fatigue, hypertension, depression, and chronic pain. Opium alone, even in small doses, provides immediate and reliable relief for all of these conditions, with far fewer harmful side effects than chemical drugs. No doubt this is the reason that, as Cocteau puts it, "[o]pium perpetuates itself across the centuries," particularly in times of turmoil, despite all efforts to suppress it.

There is no typical social profile of the opium addict. People who become addicted to opium cut across all classes and categories—men and women, young and old, rich and poor, merchants and mendicants, scholars and farmers, artists and technicians. The reason for such diversity is the fact that opium addiction is not a socially or economically determined phenomenon. Most people who use opium or its derivatives on a long-term daily basis do so mainly as a form of self-medication. The condition for which they use opium as a remedy is a basic imbalance in their neurochemistry, an imbalance that, if not corrected, manifests itself as mental and emotional disturbance, impaired ability to perform well at work, unstable personal relationships, depression and irritability, hypertension and insomnia, and other disruptions in their daily lives. Such conditions can affect anyone in any walk of life and of any social class. They can be caused genetically or they can be acquired through lifestyle factors. In the past, when opium was legally available for medical use, it was the medicine of choice for these chronic conditions, first and foremost because opium is such an effective remedy for disorders of the nervous system, and second because it is also a pleasant relaxant. Today, most people who need such medicine must resort to the toxic chemical drugs that the pharmaceutical industry produces, but the few who manage to discover the superior therapeutic efficacy of smoking opium, and who are able to gain consistent access to it, invariably choose to become addicted to opium as their medicine of choice.

Of course, there are some people who become addicted to opium by abusing it as a crutch for mental and emotional malaise that is caused not by neurological factors, but rather by failures and frustrations in their personal lives. Such individuals are no different from alcoholics who drink to drown their sorrows, but they represent only a small minority of those who use opium on a regular basis, and they do less harm to themselves with opium than do those who resort to alcohol for such purposes. In the final analysis, it doesn't really matter whether the root cause of the chronic mental and emotional disturbance that drives one to opium addiction is physiologically or psychologically based. Either way, the condition must be corrected somehow, or the individual will sooner or later become socially dysfunctional. For some people, only opium or its derivatives can restore them to functional equilibrium. Such people constitute a small minority of the general population, but for them opium is the only remedy that works. Cocteau describes people who gravitate toward opium as follows:

> Certain organisms are born to become prey to drugs. They demand a corrective, without which they can have no contact with the outside world. They float. They vegetate in the half-light. The world remains unreal, until some substance has given it body. It does happen that these unfortunates can live without ever finding the slightest remedy. It does happen, too, that the remedy they find kills them.
>
> It is a matter of luck when opium steadies them and provides these souls of cork with a diver's suit. For the harm done by opium will be less than that caused by other substances and less than the infirmity which they try to heal.

In China, as well as in England, Europe, and America during the nineteenth century, when the use of opium was legally and socially condoned, opium addiction was most common among the literati and leisure classes, not the poor and underprivileged. At the turn of the century, a survey in San Francisco revealed that middle-class white American women were the most common opium addicts, not the Chinese, blacks, or poor inhabitants of the city. At the time, about one in four hundred Americans was estimated to have some sort of opium habit, and without manifesting any serious health problems or antisocial behavior. Only when morphine and heroin appeared on the scene did serious problems arise, for opium itself, as a full-spectrum herb, has built-in safeguards in the form of specific alkaloids that counteract the negative side effects of the addictive alkaloids.

The opium-smoking habit in particular requires abundant leisure time to cultivate, and therefore is not suitable for a high-pressure, eat-and-run style of life. "Opium is a living substance," writes Cocteau. "It does not like to be rushed." Writers and poets, artists and musicians have always lived somewhat apart from the mainstream of society, aloof from rigid schedules and inflexible social conventions, and these are precisely the sort of people who were, and still are, most attracted to the opium-smoking habit. As Mick Jagger put it in an interview with *Esquire* magazine in April 1993, "It's hard to have a nine-to-five job as an opium addict; but if all you've got to do is to toss off a chapter of a novel every month, you could find that lifestyle suits you."

The opium-smoking habit is also unsuitable for young people, with all their budding energy and hasty impatience. Their minds as well as their bodies are far too overactive to focus on the slow, deliberate rituals and intricate minutiae involved in such a leisurely, languorous activity, and the sort of subdued energy and introspective mood that opium imparts to the smoker invariably conflicts with the robust bloom of youth. What usually happens when young people get addicted to smoking opium is that they lose patience with the elaborate rituals and detailed procedures, the regularity and the restraint required by the habit, while the subtleties of the drug itself, and the complex tapestry of cerebral effects it weaves, soon lose their appeal to their young minds. Before long, they begin experimenting with faster-acting drugs like morphine and heroin, mixing them haphazardly with cocaine and amphetamines, and switching from the ponderous pipe to the swift, scintillating syringe. For these reasons, one should never cultivate an opium smoking habit until reaching at least the age of thirty-six years. As Nguyen Te Duc warns in *Le Livre de l'opium,* "It is absolutely essential not to smoke opium during one's youth."

Opium smoking requires time and patience. One must learn to slow down, both physically and psychologically, which is why the habit has lost its appeal and is overlooked in the mad rush of today's world. That is also why heroin has become so popular instead, because for those who require opiates to achieve balance, heroin provides a convenient quick-fix solution. But heroin, stripped bare of all the other counterbalancing alkaloids and cofactors contained in whole opium, provides instant relief at long-term expense to health, wreaking havoc on the human system and debilitating body and mind alike. This seems to be the fate of opiate users who insist on living in the fast lane, for opium by nature rejects such users. "Opium cannot bear impatient addicts, bunglers," notes Cocteau in his journal. "It moves away, leaving them morphine, heroin, suicide, and death." And yet Cocteau believes that those who are willing to take the time to get acquainted with opium in its proper context will certainly benefit from its soft, civilizing influence:

> It seems to me that on an earth so old, so wrinkled, so painted, where so many compromises and laughable conventions are rife, opium (if its harmful effects could be eliminated) would soften people's manners and would cause more good than the fever of activity causes harm.

It was not only in the big cities of China and Southeast Asia that opium smoking became such a popular pastime: People in rural villages and hill-tribe settlements also found great pleasure in the habit, particularly as they grew older. Back in the days when they were free to grow their own opium along with other crops, the opium-smoking habit did not cause social or economic hardship for rural and tribal communities. Beside growing sufficient supplies for their own personal use, opium was also a valuable cash crop that provided extra income for rural villages, and many minority tribal people look back wistfully to the days when they could enjoy the opium habit without fear of raids and arrest by police, and without having to spend their entire income to buy expensive contraband opium, as those who still smoke opium today must do. In *Opium Fields,* authors Boyes and Piraban interview an ex-Nationalist Chinese soldier named Pai Chi-sha, who escaped the turmoil of the Chinese civil war in 1948 and found his way down to Burma, Laos, and finally the northern hills of Thailand, where he became an opium addict. In the interview, he explains the opium situation past and present:

> We used to keep some to smoke, and some we sold. We'd have top quality opium to smoke for the whole year . . .
>
> When I first started smoking opium, I smoked whenever I felt ill. Opium was our medicine, it was all we had. We used it for toothache, headaches, and for fever. I didn't smoke many pipes a day . . .
>
> Then I started to smoke more and more every day. I began smoking three times a day, after breakfast, in the late afternoon, and at night before I went to bed . . .
>
> Now I have very good quality opium and smoke about nine pipes every session, so that's about thirty pipes a day . . .
>
> When I was younger, I smoked to stay healthy. Opium was good for my body. Now that I am old, I smoke to give myself pleasure and to make myself a little bit stronger. Because I smoke I can do many things, I have much more get-up-and-go. After smoking opium I feel stronger, and I'm in a good mood and like to talk with many people, and I don't get tired. Now I smoke to keep my body ticking over. I've been smoking for thirty years, so if I stopped now I would die.

Another addict interviewed in the book, a woman named Najia, tells much the same story:

> In the past, when I was much younger, I tried opium just for fun. We live in the mountains, in the jungle there is nowhere to go. I liked to smoke a bit of opium. In those days there wasn't really anything wrong with smoking. It wasn't breaking the law. You could smoke

opium out in the open. And it was cheap. Anybody could grow it, anybody could smoke it. But now it is illegal to grow or smoke it. Now the police are cutting the fields everywhere. That's why opium is so expensive. The price goes up every year . . .

Oh, in the past it was so easy. I could carry my pipe with me to the fields. Whenever I got tired from working, I could lie down and smoke in the field . . .

For the last two or three years, it's been difficult to get any. It's harder than it used to be. It's difficult for my husband to make enough money to buy it now . . . When I can't get enough, I have to use the scrapings [dross], the stuff that has already been burnt once. I mix it with a little bit of pure opium.

In *Plants and People of the Golden Triangle,* by Edward F. Anderson, a similar story is told:

Older tribal people remember the pleasures of opium smoking and how it helped them relax after a long walk or a hard day in the fields. Some claim that opium smoking made a person mild and gentle; women especially liked this aspect because their husbands treated them less harshly and did not seek a second wife. Addicts often became the dreamers and thinkers in the village. Some of the elders even believe that opium smokers contracted illnesses less frequently. They also thought that opium was an effective treatment when someone was bitten by a snake or stung by a scorpion or by wild bees. Years ago, many addicts were arrogant, believing that one could not be "fully a man until you are able to smoke opium."

Today, however, the once simple pleasure of opium smoking, which for many tribal people was their only pleasure, has become an enormously expensive habit that also involves the risk of imprisonment. Moreover, the strict suppression of opium smoking in Asia today has caused a far worse problem—heroin. While opium is still grown abundantly in many parts of Asia and the Middle East—protected by underworld organizations and corrupt government officials—almost all of it is now refined into heroin rather than smoked, and heroin has become readily available at very low prices throughout these regions. Heroin, without the distinctive telltale smell of opium, can be easily transported and used without detection, and many who formerly smoked opium for pleasure or relief of pain have turned to heroin instead, with far more harmful consequences. The world would have been much better off if opium had remained a legal commodity.

In China, during the eighteenth, nineteenth, and early twentieth centuries, monks and martial artists, who, like the literati and leisure classes, lived a relatively independent lifestyle free from schedules and social conventions, sometimes took up the opium-smoking habit as well. While Western readers with culturally conditioned biases against opium might be surprised that Buddhist monks and Taoist priests in China sometimes smoked opium, Asians were equally shocked to discover that Christian clergymen were permitted to drink liquor, which throughout Asia and the Middle East has always been regarded as the most dangerous of drugs and the greatest threat to moral discipline, particularly because of the uninhibited sexual behavior it often arouses. The widespread sexual scandals so frequently exposed among ordained clergymen in Europe and America today have only served to reinforce this traditional view.

As for Chinese martial artists, they sometimes smoked opium, albeit sparingly, to facilitate the practice of soft, internal schools of martial arts, such as Tai Chi Chuan and Pa Kua. The deeply relaxing effect of the alkaloids on muscles and tendons enhances the long stretching and slow, rhythmic movements involved in these practices, while also promoting deep abdominal breathing by relaxing the diaphragm and dilating the bronchial passages. Compared to the chemical steroids and amphetamines so commonly used today by modern athletes to enhance their performances in field sports, opium used in this moderate manner by Chinese martial artists was relatively benign.

Perhaps the most devoted, and addicted, smokers of opium in China during these ages were Chinese opera singers, particularly those who sang female roles, such as the Singing-Master described in John Blofeld's memoirs of old Peking, *City of Lingering Splendor*. In fact, smoking opium was an integral part of a Chinese opera singer's training and lifestyle, because opium permitted the singer's voice to reach and sustain the prolonged, extremely high-pitched tones so frequently heard in Chinese opera. Indeed, by the time Chinese opera—referred to as *jing-hsi,* or Capital Opera—was born in Peking as a special form of entertainment for the emperor during the late eighteenth century, opium smoking had already become a popular habit in China, especially among actors and the literati. The distinctive high-pitched warbling that characterizes Chinese opera may quite possibly have developed as a direct result of the wide range of voice pitch with which opium smoking endowed Chinese singers.

In the 1993 movie *Farewell, My Concubine,* the lead opera singer of female roles was depicted as a chronic opium smoker, as was typical in that profession. Even after opium smoking was banned in Hong Kong during the 1960s, famous Chinese opera singers who had escaped there from the Communist revolution on the mainland were issued special permits that allowed them to continue smoking opium so that they could go on performing.

In all of these examples of people who cultivate the opium-smoking habit, the common denominator is a slow, leisurely pace of life, free from rigid schedules and aloof from high-pressure social commitments. Factory workers and corporate executives, with their nine-to-five jobs, their rush-hour commuting, and their frenzied weekend sprees, are poorly suited for the unhurried style of life that opium smoking induces. If such people become addicted to the habit, either the habit will force them to change their way of life or their way of life will quickly lead them away from opium and into heroin or other quick-fix drugs, such as cocaine and amphetamines. As Cocteau observes, these are the people "who pass from the pipe to the syringe and from morphine to heroin." For people who hurry through life, it is best never to get involved in the opium habit, because "opium cannot bear impatient addicts."

Opium seems to enchant other species of animals also, and habitual smokers have observed how easily and happily most animals become addicted to its aromatic vapors. The ever-observant Cocteau remarks on this phenomenon in his opium diary:

> All animals are charmed by opium. Addicts in the colonies know
> the danger of this bait for wild beasts and reptiles.

Flies gather round the tray and dream, the lizards with their little
mittens swoon on the ceiling above the lamp and wait for the night,
mice come close and nibble the dross. I do not speak of the dogs and
monkeys who become addicted like their masters.

At the opium factories in India, the world's largest producer of legal
opium for the medical industry, wild monkeys gather eagerly at the drain
spouts where the water used to swab the floors and wash the pots runs
out into the surrounding fields. There they drink their fill and feed their
habit, in strict order of seniority, and on days when the factory is closed
and no opiated water appears at the drain, a terrible hue and cry erupts as
entire bands of addicted monkeys experience the throes of withdrawal.

In *The City of Lingering Splendor,* John Blofeld tells of a Chinese
gentleman who, after smoking opium daily for fifteen years, is advised
by his doctor to give up the habit for reasons of health. The man takes
his doctor's advice and enters a Chinese clinic for a month in order to
withdraw under the doctor's supervision. When he returns home cured
of his habit, he is distraught to discover that his pet parrot had died less
than a week after his departure. As it turned out, the gentleman had kept
his beloved parrot for company in his private smoking room, where for
fifteen years he had smoked opium twice a day, every day, engulfing the
bird in clouds of opium fumes. The parrot had thus become as addicted
to opium as his master, and when the man left to quit his habit, he had
neglected to instruct his servants to blow some opium smoke at the parrot each day, and so the hapless bird died of withdrawal.

Another topic of great concern and endless debate among opium
smokers is the issue of addiction and health. The typical tabloid image of
the opium smoker as dope fiend—emaciated and pale, with sunken eyes
and hollow cheeks, shivering and desperate—is no more true of the average opium smoker than the image of the skid-row wino is of the connoisseur of fine wine, or the obese glutton is of the gourmet of haute cuisine.
The fact is that opium addiction need not be debilitating, especially when
the habit is conducted with care and self-discipline. In Asia, most opium
addicts report that a small daily dose of opium, such as two or three pipes,
increases their energy, sharpens their minds, and improves their perfor-

mance at work. In *Pipes, Poppies, and People,* Westermeyer interviews a Hmong tribal woman in Laos who tells him, "A little opium, and strength flows into my arms, my mind becomes sharp and quick, and my food tastes good. It's been like that for the last few years." This woman was well muscled and alert, known for her robust strength and diligence, and worked twice as hard as the other women in the village, and her example is the rule rather than the exception in countries such as Laos, where the judicious use of opium is part of the traditional culture.

As with all pleasures, particularly intoxicants, whether one is able to enjoy smoking opium without ruining one's health depends entirely on how one handles the habit. In *Le Livre de l'opium,* Nguyen Te Duc lists the following basic measures as indispensable to cultivating the opium-smoking habit without ruining one's health:

- Never surpass the normal limits, even out of curiosity, of your initial satiation and simple satisfaction.
- Learn the art of smoking in Asia, from Asians.
- Always procure good quality opium from a known and reliable source.
- Always prepare the drug properly for smoking.
- When preparing the drug for smoking, as well as when actually smoking it, be careful not to lose the volatile thebaine content.
- Never smoke during your youth.
- Do not smoke too many times each day. Smoke only at your regular set times.
- Under no circumstances, for reasons of poverty or economy, should one ever smoke the dross.
- Always exercise wisdom when smoking opium, and swiftly learn the wisest ways to conduct the habit.

Cocteau firmly believes that it is the misuse of opium rather than opium itself that causes problems:

I remain convinced, despite my failures, that opium can be good and that it is entirely up to us to make it well disposed. We must know how to handle it. Nothing is worse than clumsiness on our part. A strict regime . . . would permit the use of a remedy jeopardized by half-wits . . . If he takes care of himself, an addict who inhales twelve pipes a day all his life will not only be fortified against influenza, colds, and sore throats, but will also be far less in danger than a man who drinks a glass of brandy or who smokes four cigars. I know people who have smoked one, three, seven, up to twelve pipes a day for forty years.

Probably the single most important preventive against ruining one's health when addicted to smoking opium, other than carefully regulating the habit itself, is to eat properly. This means not only eating highly nutritious foods and strictly avoiding junk foods such as refined sugar and starch, but it means also eating greater quantities of food than one normally would. As has already been noted, opium tends to trim down the body, especially in heavy smokers, because the body burns up calories and nutrients processing the toxic residues of opium and restoring itself. If an opium smoker does not eat sufficient quantities of high-quality, high-calorie foods, the body burns its own fat, then breaks down its own flesh to obtain calories and nutrients to keep itself in proper working order. If they could afford it, Chinese opium smokers not only ate well, as evidenced in Blofeld's description of the Te I Lou in Peking, but they also used various herbal tonics to counteract the toxicity of opium and boost vital bodily functions. Today, high-potency vitamin and mineral supplements may also be used to help protect the health of opium smokers.

Drinking plenty of water is also important when smoking opium, even more than one might normally drink, for opium dehydrates the system, particularly the bowels and skin. Without sufficient water to counteract this effect, opium smokers tend to become constipated from dry bowels and develop dry skin. Note, however, that the opium itself does not constipate the bowels; it is the insufficient intake of fluids.

Another preventive measure traditionally taken by Chinese smokers is to drink plenty of oolong tea. Oolong is a semi-fermented Chinese tea, halfway between a green tea and a black tea, and it has remarkable purification properties. Oolong tea quickly enters the bloodstream and removes toxic residues, excreting them through the kidneys. In fact, it is so effective in this respect that if someone who is unaccustomed to opium smokes a few pipes and then drinks a pot or two of oolong tea, he will experience such a rapid detoxification that he is likely to become nauseated and vomit. But for habitual smokers, high-quality oolong tea, when properly prepared, provides significant protection from excessive blood toxicity due to smoking, especially when they smoke more than ten pipes per day, as so many addicts do.

Another benefit of oolong tea is that the volatile aromatic elements, which as a gas are expelled from the blood via the lungs along with other gases, have been shown by recent studies in Japan to drive toxic residues out of the alveoli, thereby purging the tissue of sticky resins that accumulate in the lungs of opium smokers. These resins are excreted in dark wads of phlegm that are coughed up and spat into spittoons provided for this purpose. No doubt tea is one reason that the Chinese, who today rank among the world's heaviest smokers of tobacco as well as of opium, suffer a relatively low rate of lung cancer compared to other populations who smoke heavily.

Virtually all opium smokers testify that when they are smoking opium, they rarely suffer from colds, influenza, fevers, or digestive ailments. Opium seems to confer protection against many types of common infectious disease that normally spread like wildfire, particularly respiratory and digestive ailments. This might be due to the toxic effects of opium on certain infectious agents, or else to conditions created in the human system that are antagonistic to such infections. But this does not exempt opium smokers from other forms of discomfort and disease. Smokers suffer their own peculiar ailments, which are exclusively related to the drug itself. As Cocteau puts it:

Opium is a season. The smoker no longer suffers from changes in the weather. He never catches cold. He suffers only from the changes in drugs, doses, and hours, in everything in fact which influences the barometer of opium.

Opium has its colds, shivers and fevers, which do not coincide with cold and heat.

Indeed, prolonged use of opium, without occasional spells of withdrawal and abstinence, invariably gives rise to health problems, and if the smoker fails to detoxify from time to time and permit his body a period of recovery, his health will gradually deteriorate, resulting in chronic debility. How long one can smoke without taking a break depends on many factors, including the basic state of one's health, how well one handles the various facets of the habit, the number of pipes smoked per day, whether one fortifies the opium with dross, and daily diet. Generally speaking, six months to a year of smoking followed by three to six months of abstinence is a fairly safe regimen for most habitual smokers. Those who don't want to stop must simply accept the consequences to their health, and many such confirmed smokers live well into their nineties, albeit in a weakened state of health. Both the misery of withdrawal and the risks of continuous smoking could be avoided if medical science were to develop a way to alter opium so that it was neither addictive nor harmful.

Detoxification and Withdrawal

If addiction is the scarlet letter of opium smoking, then detoxification is doomsday. Until medical science comes up with a way to remove the addictive alkaloids from opium, periodic detoxification is the only recourse available to the habitual opium smoker to preserve health and vitality. Due to the unpleasant nature of the detox process, many smokers procrastinate or put it off indefinitely—but the longer one delays, the more difficult it becomes. Fortunately, the means exist to cushion discomfort and ease the distress of withdrawal, although it's never a pleasant experience. When you play with fire, not only do you get smoke; sometimes you get burned as well. Thus, unless you have the discipline to put out the fire and put away your toys from time to time and stop smoking, you have no business playing with the fire of opium in the first place.

Two basic approaches address detoxification and withdrawal: One is to quit permanently, which is the path usually taken by those who get hooked on opium inadvertently and want to stop, and by those who have already ruined their health after a prolonged period of excessive abuse and must quit; the other is to approach detox as a temporary period of withdrawal and abstinence, after which the habit is resumed in a moderate way. The latter approach is taken by the confirmed smoker who wants to continue smoking for life without running the risk of ruining his or her health. But either way, the process and the experience of withdrawal are the same.

First, let's review the basic physiological and psychological symptoms of classic cold-turkey withdrawal—unaided by substitute drugs, supplementary herbs, or other palliative measures. Then we'll take a look at some methods, both traditional and modern, that can help alleviate the discomfort and distress of detoxification.

Physiological Symptoms

About twenty-four hours after the last smoke has been taken, detox announces itself to the addicted smoker with a mighty shudder that runs up and down the spine. This is followed quickly by alternate bouts of hot and cold sweats and chills. "They spend their time making me sweat day and night," writes Jean Cocteau about his experience in a detox clinic. "Opium takes its revenge. It does not like its secrets to be sweated out."

"Then my nose would start running," Emily Hahn notes. Runny nose, watery eyes, big wet sneezes, deep phlegmy coughs, and huge gaping yawns—these are the invariable symptoms that quickly follow the initial bout of sweats and chills. As Cocteau puts it, "The reawakening of one's senses . . . is accompanied by sneezes, yawns, sniffling, and tears." This is the "cold" that both Hahn and Cocteau, as well as other smokers, refer to whenever they go more than a day without a smoke. In fact, it is a sort of cold, inasmuch as it is the body's most basic way of ridding itself of accumulated toxins. But with opium detox, that's just the beginning.

By the second day, an overwhelming, bone-deep fatigue sets in, and yet one finds it difficult, if not impossible, to sleep. In some people, this insomnia can last up to three or four weeks, and often it's the symptom that addicts find most intolerable and which drives them prematurely back to opium—or, worse, onto sleeping pills. Any such drug used for relief during withdrawal halts the detoxification process.

Next come cramps and body pains, as well as intermittent headaches. "Cramps are a well-known withdrawal symptom," Hahn writes of her own detox experience. "They might make themselves felt anywhere in the addict's body, but most people get them in the arms, they feel as if all the bones have broken. I had mine in the legs, all the way up the hips." In Chinese, this feeling of deep discomfort in the muscles, tendons, ligaments, and bones is called *suan-tung,* literally "sour pain," a sensation that makes it extremely difficult to sit or lie still. These aches and pains are caused by the residues of opium metabolites leaving the cellular matrix of tissues for excretion via the bloodstream and kidneys, and sometimes they get so bad that a person will fling himself repeatedly against a wall or onto the floor, thrashing around like a beached fish or a decapitated chicken. Such thrashing actually provides considerable relief, for it accelerates the excretion of residues from tissues, though it can also leave the body bruised and battered. Headaches, too, are caused by the opium toxins gradually seeping out of the brain cells, causing dizziness and inhibiting mental clarity.

By the second or third day, the digestive system begins to detoxify, which usually causes severe diarrhea that can last up to a week. It becomes difficult to digest food, intestinal gas erupts with a volcanic resonance, and the appetite for food is lost, although there is an intense feeling of hunger and a deep need for nutrition. The radical purging of the bowels, difficulty in eating and digesting food, profuse sweating and urination, chronic insomnia, and the enormous amount of energy expended in detoxifying tissues all combine to create a feeling of great weakness and lethargy throughout the body, a hollowness that permeates every bone down to the marrow. As one anonymous addict described the experience, "It feels as though your whole body were a dirty old rag that's been wrung dry and flung out into the garbage."

No matter how bad it gets, the entire process usually takes only seven days to complete, no more and no less, although it seems more like seven weeks. Seven days is exactly how long it takes the human system to rid the blood, tissues, and nervous system of residual opium toxins. It takes a lot longer than that to detoxify the body of barbiturates, amphetamines, and other synthetic drugs, so if one can tolerate that first week of misery, the rest is relatively tolerable. However, the process leaves the body feeling weak and depleted, so it is necessary to spend a period of time and effort rebuilding strength and restoring vitality after the worst is over. For most people, however, the psychological aspect of withdrawal takes a lot longer than a week.

Psychological Symptoms

Both body and mind are kept so busy with the intensive, relentless process of physiological detox during the first seven days of withdrawal that the psychological symptoms usually don't begin to manifest until the eighth day. Mental malaise, depression, nightmares, a deep sense of alienation, feelings of deprivation, nostalgia for the habit, and craving for the drug are all part of the process of psychological withdrawal from opium. Depending on one's strength of mind and emotional balance, the process can last anywhere from six weeks to six months, and until it's complete, it is essential to abstain from the drug. "The symptoms of the craving are of so strange a kind," writes Cocteau, "that they cannot be described . . . Imagine that the earth is turning a little less fast, that the moon is coming a little closer."

Most opium smokers manage to tolerate the physical discomforts of withdrawal well enough, but the psychological symptoms can be difficult to bear, especially when compounded by the mental fatigue of prolonged insomnia. When Hahn wrote of her opium deprivation experience, she described feeling "lost, astray, shivering in a world that seemed imminently brutal." When smoking, the opium smoker feels so safe and secure and physically comfortable that he does not worry the least bit about the long-range consequences of his habit. Then when he stops, his whole world comes tumbling down. Here's how Cocteau describes some of the symptoms and feelings that suddenly arise on the eighth day of withdrawal:

Opium leads the organism towards death in a euphoric mood. The tortures arise from the process of returning to life against one's wish. A whole springtime excites the veins to madness, bringing with it ice and fiery lava.

I recommend the patient who has been deprived for eight days to bury his head in his arm, to glue his ear to that arm, and wait.

Catastrophe, riots, factories blowing up, armies in flight, flood, the ear can detect a whole apocalypse in the starry night of the human body.

One of the most enervating psychological symptoms of the withdrawal process is what Cocteau describes as "[t]he mortal boredom of the smoker who is cured!" Time crawls by like a snail, or just stops dead. "My watch simply refused to run," writes Hahn. The feeling is similar, though far more intense, to what happens when fasting: One misses not only the food itself, but also the time spent handling food, the ritual of preparing and eating it, the camaraderie of sharing meals with friends and family, the pots and pans and dining table and eating utensils. Suddenly, all of this is gone, leaving a huge psychic vacuum, with nothing to replace it and nothing else to do.

There is an old Vietnamese saying that what the opium smoker misses most when he quits is the lamp. Hahn agrees with this observation: "I would think of the lamp in the shaded room, the coziness, the peace and comfort with great longing." When her friend Heh-ven tries to quit, inspired by Hahn's successful effort, he fails, explaining wistfully to her, "It didn't last more than about thirty six hours. I missed the lamp most of all. I find the lamp very nice." Somehow the lamp, with its soft warm glow, symbolizes the entire setting of opium smoking and all its happy comfort, and of course the first step one takes each day when getting ready to smoke opium is to light the lamp. Indeed in China, the term *dian-deng* ("light the lamp") came to mean "Let's have a smoke."

Former, or temporarily cured, opium addicts all over the world seem to look back on their old habit with great affection, recalling it fondly as the ultimate, incomparable luxury. Cocteau writes:

Do not expect me to be a traitor. Of course opium remains unique and the euphoria it induces superior to health. I owe it my perfect hours . . .

I am not one of the cured who is proud of his effort. I am ashamed to have been expelled from that world, compared with which the world of health resembles those revolting films in which ministers unveil statues.

In *Confessions of an English Opium-Eater,* Thomas De Quincey says basically the same thing in one of his most often quoted lines:

I do not readily believe that any man, having once tasted the divine luxuries of opium, will afterward descend to the gross and mortal enjoyments of alcohol.

And yet, time and time again the observation is made that after withdrawal from opium or heroin, many former addicts who are unwilling or unable to return to their habits turn instead to alcohol for comfort and end up becoming chronic alcoholics. Rolling Stones guitarist Keith Richards, after finally quitting an extremely heavy heroin habit that spanned more than a decade, spent the next few years drinking several bottles of whiskey every day, starting in the morning and continuing until he dropped drunk into bed at night. Many others have done the same.

How does this phenomenon accord with the claims of De Quincey and other opium addicts in that, to paraphrase Cocteau, opium and alcohol are opposed to each other, and alcohol is no substitute for the divine luxuries of opium? The answer to this puzzle was finally discovered during the 1970s, when autopsies performed on destitute winos who had died of alcohol poisoning revealed the presence of a heroin-like substance in their brains. Curious researchers pursued these studies until they were able to demonstrate that when the alcohol metabolite called acetaldehyde crosses the blood–brain barrier and enters the fluids of the brain, it combines with a naturally occurring neurochemical to form a compound belonging to a family of chemicals known as *isoquinolines.* These substances have properties similar to those of opiates, and

Cooking pan fitted to a glass chimney.

they can attach to the same receptors in the brain affected by opiates, thereby producing similar effects. This explains why so many former opiate addicts find comfort in alcohol, even though they hate its primary effects. Unfortunately, in order to produce enough acetaldehyde to cross the blood–brain barrier and create this opiate-like compound, an enormous amount of alcohol must be consumed, not just a simple drink or two, and those who seek solace in this manner end up doing far more damage to their bodies than they did with their original opiate habit.

This finding is also significant in understanding extreme cases of alcohol abuse, for it indicates that the effect alcoholics are really seeking may be an opiate effect, and that an initial cure for such extreme cases of alcohol abuse might be a mild daily dose of opium—the lesser of two evils—after which the resulting opium habit, which does far less damage to the body, could also be cured.

Palliatives for Detoxification

Now let's take a brief look at some of the methods that may be used to help alleviate the physical discomfort and reduce the psychological distress of opium withdrawal so that the detoxification process can be successfully completed without slipping into a relapse. We'll start with the methods that are, according to this writer's research and experience, the least effective supports for opium withdrawal and conclude on a more upbeat note with the most successful methods.

Drug Replacement Therapy

This involves the substitution of other addictive drugs to wean the addict off opium without experiencing the intensive discomfort and malaise of cold-turkey withdrawal. In effect, this method constitutes a sort of chemical bribe by the therapist. While it provides a relatively easy way to stop using opium, the addict never really detoxifies—the body remains in a state of addictive toxicity due to the effects of the substitute drug. In the end, the addict usually returns to his old habit because he never experiences the healing crisis of detoxification and finally decides that if he's going use drugs anyway, he may as well use the one he likes most. Typically, this method is highly favored today by modern Western medicine, especially in America, even though the relapse rate is well over fifty percent.

Methadone, which is a synthetic chemical similar to morphine but without morphine's euphoric properties, is the most commonly used drug for this purpose, but once the patient becomes addicted to methadone, an even longer period is needed to break that habit than the opium (or heroin) habit he or she had in the first place. Another drug sometimes used for withdrawal from opium or heroin is buprenorphine, which is refined from thebaine, one of the three addictive alkaloids in opium. (As noted earlier, buprenorphine is available as a sublingual under the Buprenex label, or as Subutex in tablet form.) In both these cases, the substitute drug attaches to opiate receptors in the brain, giving the addict the physiological and psychological satisfaction of an opiate but without the euphoria. Unless this is done with great discipline and under strict supervision to ensure that the substitute drug is gradually decreased rather than increased, it usually degenerates swiftly into abuse and then relapse. The dubious practice of using morphine to wean addicts off opium began as early as the mid-nineteenth century in China,

as evidenced in the following passage from *Chinese Materia Medica:
Vegetable Kingdom,* by G. A. Stuart, published in Shanghai in 1911:

> The substitution of decreasing doses of morphia may also be prac-
> ticed, but should only be done under supervision of a competent
> and conscientious physician or dispenser, lest a morphia-eating
> habit be substituted for that of opium smoking. The indiscriminate
> sale or distribution of anti-opium pills, most of which contain mor-
> phia, is reprehensible.

Gradual Withdrawal Therapy

During the nineteenth and early twentieth centuries, when much of
Indochina was under French colonial rule, opium-smoking French expatriates developed a simple method of withdrawal they used whenever
they returned to France and had to give up their habit. They added two
or three ounces of diluted liquid opium to a bottle of cognac and took
this bottle with them on board the ships on which they traveled back to
France, a journey that took a month or more. Smoking their last pipes
at their residence or in an opium den on the day of departure, they
embarked for the long journey home.

The next day, on an empty stomach, they drank one ounce of the opiated cognac, then replaced that ounce in the bottle with an ounce of pure
cognac from another bottle, thereby slightly diluting the mixture. On the
second day, they drank a second dose, and then replaced that with straight
cognac, further diluting the blend. In this manner, the bottle remained full
throughout the journey, but each day the dose of opium was reduced, and
their bodies inched that much closer to detoxification. By the time they
arrived back in France, they were drinking pure cognac, and theoretically,
at least, they would have completed withdrawal and detoxification.

This method works well up to a point. It allows the body to adjust
gradually to the deprivation from addictive alkaloids, thereby reducing
the abruptness and intensity of withdrawal symptoms. But at a certain
stage toward the end of the program, the discomfort and distress of
detoxification symptoms begin to make themselves felt, and an overwhelming temptation arises to assuage the misery with an extra dose

of the drug, or a substitute drug, which of course undermines the process. De Quincey used a similar method when he decided to give up his opium-eating habit, and he notes that while it's quite effective at first in alleviating the physical discomfort of withdrawal, in the end the addict must deal with a considerable degree of pain. In addition, the mental and emotional distress struck with full impact when the daily dosage reached a critical level of reduction. This method is suitable, then, only for those who can exercise great self-discipline and tolerate a prolonged period of chronic discomfort.

Physical Therapy

Physical therapy helps distract the addict from the misery of detox, and it usually accelerates the elimination of toxic residues from tissues, but it does little to reduce the actual physical discomfort, nor does it do much to ease the psychological distress. But by occupying the addict's attention and giving him something to do, it helps pass the time more quickly and thereby reduces the chance of relapse during the withdrawal process.

Massage is often used to help knead the toxins from tissues and facilitate circulation of blood and lymph, thereby accelerating excretion. De Quincey extols the benefits of long, vigorous hikes in the woods and hills, and recent research has confirmed that jogging helps promote the secretion of endorphins into the brain. Endorphins are the body's natural opiates, some of which are two hundred times more potent than morphine, and their secretion at the site of opiate receptors in the brain helps eliminate a craving for the drug itself.

A wealthy Japanese woman who smoked opium periodically from the age of thirty-eight until her death at ninety-three, and who remained fit and healthy until the very end of her life despite her habit, used a unique method of physical therapy during detoxification: After smoking for a period of eight to twelve months, she would withdraw from the habit by practicing an ancient Tibetan exercise known as Grand Prostrations, whereby the body is flung to the floor and stretched fully prostrate, then swiftly pushed back up to an erect standing posture, over and over again, at least a thousand times per session. The practice constitutes one of the most intensive physical regimens ever devised—

exercising virtually every muscle and tendon in the body—and according to her, it cleared her tissues of residual opium toxins in less than a week while enabling her to continue eating and sleeping normally and swiftly restoring physical stamina.

According to Cocteau, the most effective form of physical therapy for opium detoxification is vibratory, due to its soothing effects on the nerves and vital organs:

> A car can massage organs, which no masseur can reach. It is the only remedy for the disorders of the great sympathetic nervous system. The craving for opium can be endured in a car.

Hot baths heavily laced with Epsom salts or mineral salts from the sea can also be soothing, and they help the body excrete toxins rapidly through the pores of the skin. This is particularly effective if followed by deep-tissue or vibratory massage and a nap.

Herbal and Nutritional Therapy

Herbs can be helpful in relieving some of the physical discomfort of opium withdrawal and in facilitating the detoxification process, although they do not do much on the psychological level. The herb most frequently employed to aid detoxification in traditional Chinese medicine is the dried, empty capsule of the opium poppy, after it has been milked of its opium latex. The dried capsule itself contains a few traces of some alkaloids of opium, although not in sufficient concentrations to provide a narcotic effect. These trace elements affect the opiate receptors in the brain and relax the smooth muscles of the body just enough to make withdrawal more tolerable. The capsules are crushed and ground, then boiled with water and reduced to a decoction that is administered three times daily, on an empty stomach. The dosage is gradually reduced over a period of seven to ten days, after which it is no longer given.

In the traditional ayurvedic medicine of India, physicians have for centuries successfully used a tincture of oat seeds *(Avena sativa)* to cure the opium habit. Contemporary research in the West has confirmed the anti-addictive and calming properties of oat seed, which is often used in combination with other sedative herbs. In the Andaman Islands west of India, as well as in Pakistan, seeds of the Tula tree *(Pterygota alata)* are employed as a substitute for opium during the withdrawal process—with considerable success, according to those who have tried it. In Thailand, Burma, and Assam, as well as northern Malaysia, the leaves of the bush *Mitragyna speciosa,* known in local dialects as *kratom,* were traditionally used as a palliative during opium withdrawal, either by grinding them into a paste for oral administration or by smoking the dried leaves. Kratom is said to have mild hallucinogenic properties, which provide a measure of relief from the psychological as well as the physical distress of opium withdrawal and help distract the addict from his craving.

In 1898, the journal *American Pharmacist* published a report from San Francisco describing how whole sow thistle plant *(Sonchus oleraceus)* was boiled to produce an herbal brew that proved quite effective in getting local Chinese opium addicts to quit their habit. In light of the widespread abuse of heroin in America today, and the proven failure of drug-substitution programs such as methadone to cure addiction, it seems incredible that modern medicine has failed to investigate such traditional herbal remedies.

De Quincey reports in his *Confessions* that the only thing that provided him with a significant measure of relief during his withdrawal from opium was a highly concentrated extract of valerian *(Valerian officinalis),* which is well known for its antispasmodic, sedative, and nervine properties. The calming nervine effects of valerian when used for opium withdrawal may be enhanced when used in combination with skullcap *(Scutellaria laterifolia),* passionflower *(Passiflora incarnata),* hops *(Humulus lupulus),* and/or chamomile *(Chamaemelum nobile).*

Recent research in nutritional therapy has demonstrated that certain nutrients, particularly amino acids that function as precursors for the production of neurochemicals, when taken in proper combination with synergistic co-factors, not only provide significant relief from opiate withdrawal but also help correct neurochemical imbalances that are often the original cause of drug addiction. These nutrients are even more effective for this purpose when taken in conjunction with some of the herbal therapies outlined above.

For example, a common cause of chronic depression, which drives many people to become addicted to either illegal opiates or legal anti-depressant drugs such as Prozac, is insufficient supply in the brain of the neurochemical serotonin. This deficiency is caused either by insufficient production of serotonin itself or by overactivity of the enzyme responsible for breaking down serotonin. Prozac works by inhibiting the enzyme that breaks down serotonin, but in doing so, it severely interferes with normal brain chemistry and sometimes causes episodes of psychosis. The amino acid L-tryptophan, when taken in combination with vitamin B_6, is converted into serotonin in the brain, thereby increasing available supplies of this calming neurotransmitter in a natural, nutritional way, without negative side effects.

L-phenylalanine in combination with vitamin B_6 converts into norepinephrine, a brain chemical that increases alertness and effectively counteracts depression in people who are undergoing withdrawal from addictive drugs. Perhaps the most useful of all such neuroactive nutrients in drug withdrawal programs is a form of phenylalanine called dl-phenylalanine, which counteracts the enzyme that inhibits enkephalins and endorphins—the so-called natural opiates of the brain—from attaching to the brain's opiate receptors. This amino acid thus increases enkephalin and endorphin activity at these receptor sites, which in turn reduces the craving for opiates and diminishes awareness of pain in recovering addicts.

This aspect of nutritional therapy as a support for addictive-drug withdrawal holds great potential for developing effective remedies for both the physical discomfort and the psychological distress of withdrawal; it also holds promise for developing permanent cures for some of the basic causes of drug addiction. However, this field of research remains in its infancy, and like herbal therapy, it is not well received by mainstream modern medicine due to the threat it poses to patented pharmaceuticals.

Hypnosis

This technique is helpful only in those individuals who are receptive to hypnosis and who truly want to quit their habit permanently. It's the method that Emily Hahn resorted to for her addiction, and it seemed to work well for her. First, the physician gave her a mild sedative and then he hypnotized her, all on the first day of withdrawal, before any serious symptoms set in. After she had entered a hypnotic state, the physician did some basic psychoanalysis to pinpoint the underlying cause of her addiction and to program her subconscious self to muster the intention and will to withdraw from opium. The most important function of the hypnosis was to eliminate her craving for the drug itself, for after she came out of the trance, she still had to face a week of unpleasant withdrawal symptoms. As she reports in her story:

> It was true that the picture of the tray and the lighted lamp was no longer there in the middle of my mind . . . Why should I want to smoke? . . . Never through the week that was worst did I have the thought that I would feel a lot better if only I could get to a pipe. That was where the hypnotism came in, I realized. Knowing it, however, didn't spoil the effect. It worked . . . Of all my urges, that one was missing . . .

Nevertheless, Hahn had to endure all of the classic symptoms of opium detox, which she tolerated quite well. Certainly having had her attraction to opium psychologically unraveled—and her craving for the lamp and tray, the pipe and smoke, erased under hypnotic trance—enabled her to go through the entire process without faltering. This method merits further study, but it can be administered safely and successfully only by someone who is not just highly qualified in hypnotism, but who also has a thorough understanding of the drug itself as well as the phenomena associated with addiction to it.

Acupuncture

Acupuncture is another technique used with considerable success in traditional Chinese medicine to facilitate withdrawal from opium addiction. Modern Western medical research has demonstrated that one of the primary effects of acupuncture is stimulation of endorphin secretions in the brain, thereby providing effective relief from chronic pain, which has become the main condition for which Western medicine uses acupuncture today. This analgesic effect makes acupuncture a reliable support for addictive-drug withdrawal, particularly effective in cases of cocaine addiction. Studies have shown that the analgesic effects of acupuncture are fifty-five to eighty-five percent effective in providing relief from chronic pain in all patients tested, which compares favorably with the average seventy percent efficacy achieved with morphine. When traditional acupuncture is further enhanced by attaching electrodes to the needles and running a pulsed microcurrent through them, the analgesic effects are considerably amplified, rendering this technique even more effective for addictive-drug withdrawal. At Lincoln Hospital in the South Bronx in New York City, where up to 250 addicts are treated every day, resident psychiatrist Michael O. Smith reports, "In many cases, acupuncture is considered the treatment of choice. It's more highly touted all the time."

In *The Shambhala Guide to Traditional Chinese Medicine,* Daniel Reid explains another reason that acupuncture has proved to be such a highly effective treatment for addictive drug withdrawal:

> One of the reasons for the success of acupuncture in the treatment of drug abuse is that acupuncture always has both psychological and physiological benefits, a phenomenon that most western physicians find difficult to understand. That is because western medicine deals only with the body and the mind, separating them into two mutually exclusive departments, whereas Chinese medicine recognizes a third system, the human energy system that functions as a bridge between the physical body and the psychological mind. Any treatment that works directly to balance the human energy system, such as acupuncture, balances the body as well as the mind, providing the patient with a sense of wholeness and organic integration that neither Western physiology nor psychology alone can ever achieve . . . These combined psychic and physical effects make acupuncture a superior form of therapy in all cases where the patient's state of mind, emotional condition, and patterns of thought are closely associated with his or her physiological problems, such as in drug addiction.

Neuro-electric Therapy (NET)

Electrically enhanced acupuncture provided the inspiration for the development of a method of addictive-drug withdrawal therapy that has become the most effective medical technique for relieving the distress of drug withdrawal, as well as for effecting a lasting cure for addiction. While working in a hospital in Hong Kong, the Scottish surgeon Margaret Patterson observed a Chinese doctor treating surgery patients with electro-acupuncture to facilitate their recovery from postsurgical trauma, a form of therapy that provided significant relief from postsurgical pain while accelerating the healing of surgical wounds. As it turned out, some of these patients were also opium or heroin addicts, and much of the postsurgical trauma experienced by these patients was caused not by surgery but by the painful symptoms of withdrawal from their drug habits that were interrupted by surgery. Finally, some of these addicted patients admitted their condition to the doctor and pleaded with him to increase the electro-acupuncture therapy because it provided them with so much relief from withdrawal symptoms. Significantly, these patients reported that regardless of which points on the body were used for stimulation, they always experienced the same relief.

Working in conjunction with the American medical scientist Dr. Robert Becker, one of the world's leading authorities on innate human healing responses, Dr. Patterson concluded that electrical stimulation entering the body through the acupuncture needles, rather than the needles themselves or the point of insertion, was the agent that prompted the observed analgesic effects. Based on this observation, Dr. Patterson developed a technique called neuro-electric therapy (NET), whereby a pulsed micro-current is delivered to the brain from a small battery-operated device—about the size of a handheld tape recorder—via electrodes taped over the mastoid bone behind each ear. The genius to her method was her analysis of the precise characteristics of electromagnetic wave patterns produced by the brain when addicted to various drugs. She then produced a programmable key that, when plugged into the device, caused it to simulate that frequency and wave pattern and deliver it to the brain, thereby producing the cerebral effects of the drug without the presence of the drug. This enables the body to undergo detoxification without the pain and distress of withdrawal symptoms. Dr. Patterson has produced specific keys for withdrawal from heroin and opium, amphetamines, barbiturates, alcohol, and cocaine. Her NET treatment has shown a success rate of over ninety percent in effecting cures for addiction to all of these drugs, without relapse—a far better record than the chemical drug–substitution therapies favored by conventional medicine in most countries today.

Despite the scientifically proved success of her NET method, however, Dr. Patterson is struggling to gain approval for its use in drug addiction programs in America, and it remains virtually unknown in all but a few European countries, another example of how the medical mafia conspires to suppress therapies that threaten its profitable monopolies.

Spiritual Healing with "Clear Light"

This is a method that transcends all conventional medical therapies, both physiological and psychological, providing a cure for drug addiction that is highly effective and relatively painless without the use of any drugs or devices. No schools teach this technique; the only people who can practice it are psychically gifted individuals with clairvoyant powers and the capacity to transmit the powerful healing energy of the universe, known in spiritual circles as Clear Light, or universal free energy. While the mention of this method in the context of drug-withdrawal therapy may strike the reader as far-fetched and scientifically unsound, results in even the most stubborn cases of drug addiction are often so effective that only those who have personally experienced them can testify to this method's unparalleled success.

Since no scientific studies exist to verify this technique, let's listen to the testimony of an artist who was addicted to opium smoking for seven years, during which time he tried repeatedly but without success to quit the habit, using most of the methods described above, until he had the good fortune to meet a gifted psychic healer and clairvoyant in San Francisco:

> I had tried just about everything to give up my habit, including neuro-electric therapy, but even that, which worked very well for

several friends of mine, failed to do the trick for me. Every time I tried to stop, I ended up going back to it, and the longest I ever lasted without opium was about one month, though usually I'd end up smoking again after only a week or two.

Then I met this amazing healer in California, who billed herself as a clairvoyant and luminary mystic. I must admit that I really had my doubts when I went to see her, but she came very highly recommended by someone I trust, so I thought I'd give it a try. There was absolutely no "faith healing" involved here, because frankly I did not believe it would work. In fact, before starting her treatment, I made sure that I had a plentiful supply of opium at home, but I never needed it.

She worked on me for about two hours one afternoon, all the while intoning some high-pitched sounds and making strange gurgling noises deep inside her gut, and pointing her fingertips at various parts of my body. Then she made me lie down on the floor and gently touched a few points on my body, mostly on my legs and the back of my neck, continuously uttering those strange gurgles and whispering what sounded like prayers. Finally, she made me sit and stare at a translucent spinning wheel with colored lights behind it, and told me to tell the opium to leave my body and return to the cosmos for recycling. After that I went home and waited for the usual shit to hit the fan, but absolutely nothing happened! I had a great appetite that night, ate a big dinner, and slept soundly. The next morning I woke up feeling fine. Had I not experienced it myself, I would never have believed it possible to detoxify so painlessly.

And this was after three years of continuous smoking, doing an average of 15 pipes of strong opium every day. The only symptoms I felt were a mild fatigue and a slight weakness in my legs, but they were barely noticeable. I went back to see her again four days later, and she made some final adjustments on my system, using basically the same methods she'd applied the first time. When I walked out of there that afternoon, not only was I completely rid of my habit, I felt better than I had for many years. This method really works,

I can testify to that, but it's very difficult to meet healers like her. If there were more of them around and they were willing to work with addicts, I'm sure that a lot more people would be willing to give up their addictions, because what prevents most drug addicts from quitting their habits is the intolerable discomfort of the withdrawal process. With this method, it's a breeze!

Regarding opium addiction, the bottom line is that, as Cocteau put it, "Opium is a decision to be taken." Only the individual can make such a decision, and he or she has no one else to blame for it. Moral considerations are irrelevant here, although medical and sometimes spiritual factors should certainly be taken into account. The only way to truly enjoy opium, whether it be for just one afternoon or for a whole year, is not to take it too seriously, and to approach it as a sort of hobby, not as a crutch. All hobbies, regardless of how much one enjoys them, can be set aside from time to time when circumstances demand, whereas crutches— i.e., addictions—hobble the addict, interfering with the normal course of life and ultimately undermining health and eroding willpower.

If a person chooses to become physically addicted to opium for a period of time while fully aware that sooner or later he must quit and then he actually does quit, that person is not psychically addicted and remains free. And if such a person is willing to endure the process of withdrawal and recovery, it doesn't really matter whether he smokes again later or quits forever. Only in this manner may a person cultivate opium as an art and become its master, rather than succumbing to it as an addiction and becoming its slave.

The same holds true for alcohol and alcoholics. If a former alcoholic believes that he may never again drink a single drop of alcohol without falling back into alcoholism, that person will always be an alcoholic, even if he never touches the stuff again, for it means that the addiction has not been cured. On the other hand, if an addiction to alcohol is truly cured and the former alcoholic once again becomes his own master, he has nothing more to fear from alcohol and is able to enjoy a drink from time to time, without worrying about becoming hooked again. Thus it is that the opium smoker who has the will to quit whenever he wishes, and knows how to do so, has nothing to fear from addiction, regardless how often he becomes addicted. Cocteau analyzes this situation very succinctly in his journal *Opium:*

> About 1909 there were artists who smoked without talking about it and who no longer smoke. Many young couples smoke without anyone suspecting it; colonials smoke to combat fever and stop smoking when circumstances force them to stop. They then experience the discomforts of a heavy dose of influenza. Opium spares all these addicts because they did not and do not take it seriously.
>
> Opium becomes serious to the extent to which it affects the nerve centers that control the soul. Otherwise, it is an antidote, a pleasure, an ultimate siesta.
>
> The danger is smoking as a defense against some moral disequilibrium. Then it is difficult to approach the drug in the way it must be approached, as wild beasts should be approached—without fear.

As long as one does not take opium too seriously, one has nothing to fear from it. Most important of all, one must never use opium as a psychic crutch to compensate for some spiritual malaise or emotional imbalance, for that is how the master ends up becoming a slave to the servant. Opium should always be approached with courage, confidence, and complete nonchalance—or not at all.

SWALLOWING CLOUDS, SPEWING FOG

OPIUM SMOKERS—PAST AND PRESENT

The human affinity for opium transcends all national boundaries and cultural contexts. As Jean Cocteau notes, "Opium perpetuates itself across the centuries." No other substance has exerted such a powerful, consistent, and enduring influence on the bodies and minds of men and women throughout the world, spanning the globe from the sands of ancient Egypt to the concrete jungles of contemporary New York and Paris.

No typical profile of the opium smoker can be drawn, based on social or economic status, education, occupation, age, or gender. They come from all walks of life, in search of the missing piece of their neurochemical complex, and once they have discovered it in opium, nothing else will do.

An important point to note is that even when opium was legal and socially condoned, readily available at little cost in licensed opium dens and pharmacies in every city of the world, only a small fraction of society ever became addicted to it, and indeed relatively few people ever tried it. For example, in China during the early twentieth century, when opium smoking and poppy production reached their zenith there, approximately twenty million people were confirmed opium addicts out of a population of about 450 million, which comes to less than five percent of the population. During the same period in America, when opium was legally available and constituted the active ingredient in dozens of common patent remedies sold over the counter, only .25 percent of the American people regularly used opium products.

For that reason, the claim that legalizing opium would inevitably give rise to massive addiction is unfounded and does not accord with historical experience. Nevertheless, in large countries like China and America, the small fraction of society that needs opium alkaloids to achieve the cerebral and physiological equilibrium required to function normally still amounts to millions of people, and one way or another their needs must be met. Forcing such people to rely on alcohol and pharmaceutical drugs, or to resort to illegal and dangerous opium derivatives like morphine and heroin, may not be a wise policy, particularly when whole opium can readily meet such people's needs with far less risk.

Basically, people smoke opium because it provides them with the fundamental balance and equanimity that is missing in their lives. The imbalance that opium redresses may be caused by physical, psychological, or emotional factors, and it may be congenital or acquired, temporary or permanent, but regardless of the cause, the effects of the basic imbalance are the same: emotional instability, mental malaise, ill health, chronic discomfort, and functional disharmony between the individual and society. Something must be done to restore balance and harmony to the disordered human system lest life be wasted wallowing in a hopeless funk of pain and depression.

Today, many people try to drink their way into a semblance of balance and happiness, but always at great cost to health and with real hazard to their families and fellow citizens. Others take pills prescribed by their doctors, quickly becoming addicted to drugs that disrupt the delicate biorhythm of nature and have severe side effects that often lead to even worse conditions. Some practice meditation and deep breathing with varying degrees of success, and while this is no doubt the best solution, the fact remains that relatively few people have the discipline and motivation to cultivate such practices. And a few rediscover by happenstance the one thing in the world that, for thousands of years and millions of people, has provided proven, reliable relief from chronic pain and depression while restoring functional balance to the disordered human system. That ancient remedy, which today has been declared a forbidden fruit, is opium. Taking a brief look at some of the lives, past and present, in which opium has played a prominent restorative role will therefore be instructive.

Vignettes of Smokers Past

The following vignettes represent a small sample of some of the famous figures in history who smoked opium—either habitually or occasionally—and reflect the broad spectrum of personalities and professions among which opium smokers were commonly found. Opium eaters were even more prevalent than smokers for a much longer period of history, but since this book deals predominantly with opium smoking, we shall discuss only smokers here.

Sir Richard Burton

This celebrated Victorian explorer and Oriental scholar who discovered the headwaters of the Nile River in Africa and translated the erotic Hindu classic Kama-sutra in India was a confirmed opium smoker for most of his adult life. He picked up the habit while living in India, after discovering that opium effectively counterbalanced certain disorders of the nervous system that had been troubling him since his youth. Thereafter, wherever he went in the world, he brought along opium and a portable smoking kit, even during his exploits in the wilderness of Africa. Indeed, among his retinue of porters and servants while searching for the source of the Nile, he included a skilled pipe boy from India, whose sole responsibility was to prepare his pipes and look after his opium paraphernalia. Whenever Burton's party of explorers halted for the day to pitch camp, his first and foremost priority was to have his boy set up his tray in a tent, where he would lie down to savor what he described in his journals as "that sweetest of all smokes."

Jean Cocteau

The French intellectual and avant-garde writer attributed his life's "most perfect hours" to the exquisite equilibrium and reveries he experienced after smoking opium. The journal he kept during one of his periodic withdrawals from opium addiction has become one of the most insightful, frank, and lucid discussions of opium ever recorded in Western literature. Unlike most habitual opium smokers, Cocteau preferred to smoke alone. In his journal he wrote, "Smoking *à deux* is already crowded. Smoking *à trois* is difficult. Smoking *à quatre* is impossible." Despite repeated efforts to give up the habit, Cocteau continued to smoke opium for most of his life, for he realized that what he called the "artificial equilibrium" it provided him was better than no equilibrium at all, and that without a basic equilibrium, no artist could express his creative energy in any art form.

Claude Farrère

Farrère was the author of the notorious book *Fumée d'opium (Black Opium)*, which described every aspect of the opium smoker's life in lurid detail. Renowned as a grand connoisseur of opium smoking who sometimes puffed down twenty to thirty pipes at a session, Farrère introduced many of his contemporary French literati, artists, and musicians to the pleasures of "fumée d'opium." Toward the end of his life, he claimed that over the years he had smoked his own weight in opium, which was no small feat for a man of his considerable size. It didn't seem to do him much harm, for he lived to the ripe old age of ninety and continued enjoying his pipes to the very end.

Graham Greene

Greene was known to be fond of smoking opium, although no one really knows the extent to which he indulged this affinity. He was probably more of an occasional than a habitual smoker. Greene paid frequent visits to friends in Vietnam during the 1950s and 1960s, when opium smoking was still an integral part of social life in that part of the world, and there he enjoyed excellent-quality opium in congenial company, surrounded by Oriental luxury. His views on opium, and the feelings a few pipes of the Big Smoke gave him, are revealed in the narrator's voice in his novel *The Quiet American.*

Pablo Picasso

Picasso often smoked opium during his years in Paris, where he was very much part of the "hip" avant-garde world of artists and writers. The influence of opium on Picasso's style of artistic expression has never been properly researched, but it may well account for his prodigious productivity and unique vision, for all artists and writers who smoke opium are well aware of opium's capacity to focus undivided attention and energy on creative work.

Billie Holiday

The popular black American blues singer whose music and way of life served as a model of inspiration for Janis Joplin was a prominent figure in the American jazz underworld during the 1930s. This was the world that first coined the word *hip* to indicate someone who smoked opium. In those days, musicians like Holiday preferred smoking opium to using morphine or heroin, and resorted to the latter only when the former was unavailable or inconvenient to use due to the telltale smell. Holiday's habitual use of opiates caused her great trouble with the police for most of her life, and during her final days, as she lay dying in pain in a hospital bed, the police spitefully posted guards at the door to prevent anyone— doctor or friend—from providing her with any form of opiate to relieve her agony, forcing her to endure an excruciating withdrawal from her lifelong drug habit in addition to her death throes. As Cocteau notes in his opium journal, "The community takes its revenge" against the opium smoker for rejecting society's values. For Holiday, this experience must surely have been something "that only the blues can explain."

Lin Piao

Lin Piao was the brilliant Chinese army general who masterminded many of Mao Tse-tung's most important victories in China, both against Japan during World War II and later against Chiang Kai-shek's forces in the ensuing civil war. Throughout the tumultuous two decades of constant warfare in China that preceded the Communist victory in 1949, Lin continued to cultivate a daily opium habit, smoking in tents and caves, mountains and deserts, rain or shine; he no doubt would have continued to smoke for the rest of his life if Chairman Mao (who did not smoke opium) had not decreed that all traces of the opium-smoking habit be stamped out in China. In 1950, Lin was sent to the Soviet Union to undergo a radical cure for his opium addiction. No one knows now what sort of treatment he received there, but when he returned to China he was a completely different person—emaciated and weak, hypersensitive to both sun and wind, moody, reclusive, compulsive, and unpredictable. In the end, he hatched a plot to overthrow Mao and was killed when the airplane in which he tried to escape to the Soviet Union ran out of fuel and crashed.

Yu Shu-yen

Regarded as one of the greatest Chinese opera singers of the early twentieth century, Yu Shu-yen specialized in singing female roles, much like the male actor who played the role of the concubine in the movie *Farewell, My Concubine*. Like all such actors in those days, Yu smoked opium daily to enable his voice to reach and sustain the high-pitched warbling tones that characterize female arias in traditional Chinese opera. Whenever he toured overseas, he brought along his travel kit, and even in countries that generally did not condone opium smoking, Chinese opera singers like Yu were permitted to smoke as part of their professional regimen.

Count Eric Stenbock

Scion of a prominent aristocratic German family who settled in England during the 1890s, Stenbock became one of the Western world's leading literary exponents of opium smoking. Highly theatrical and notoriously decadent, this flamboyant character flaunted his opium-smoking habit at a time when Victorian England was beginning to clamp down on the practice, and he enthusiastically recommended it to his fellow literati as a sort of artistic sacrament and potent fuel for creative expression.

Interviews with Contemporary Opium Smokers

To give the reader an idea of who still smokes opium today and why anyone does so, excerpts from interviews conducted with several contemporary opium smokers are presented below. With the exception of hill-tribe villages in remote opium-growing regions of Southeast Asia and semi-legal opium dens in a few Asian cities such as Bombay, Vientiane, Hanoi, and Phnom Penh, opium smoking has become a clandestine affair conducted with the utmost discretion in private salons at the homes of connoisseurs throughout the world. Those who smoke at home come from all walks of life—artists and writers, businessmen and diplomats—but they all share a fond appreciation for the power and pleasure of opium and for the art and craft involved in the traditional Chinese way of smoking it.

The individuals interviewed below are identified only by their age, nationality, and profession. For obvious reasons, their names are withheld, lest they end up lying on an iron cot in jail rather than reclining comfortably on their hips in the intimate ambience of their own smoking rooms, swallowing clouds and spewing fog with their closest friends. That such a peaceful, personal pursuit of happiness can so easily land a person in prison these days is stark testimony to the severity and legal strictures of contemporary times. Those who have developed a taste for the Big Smoke often manage, against all odds, to cultivate it as either a daily habit or an occasional hobby. These contemporary cosmopolitan connoisseurs are few and far between, and needless to say, they keep a low profile.

Mr. L: age 50; American; writer

Q: *When and where did you first smoke opium?*

A: At an old Chinese opium den in Bombay, in 1969.

Q: *Do you smoke regularly now?*

A: Usually I do. But it was not until I moved to Southeast Asia in 1987 that I was able to start smoking regularly at home. Since then, it's become one of my favorite things in life. It also really helps me with my writing work.

Q: *What is your smoking schedule?*

A: When I'm smoking daily, I usually have five or six pipes early in the morning and no more. I never smoke in the afternoon or at night. Generally, I only smoke daily when I'm working on a book, sometimes for up to a year at a time, and when I'm finished with the writing, I stop and withdraw. At other times, when I'm not involved in a writing project, I only smoke about once or twice a week, sort of as a hobby rather than a habit. It's very important to keep it under control and not let it control you, to consume opium rather than be consumed by it.

Q: *Why do you smoke opium?*

A: Because I like it. It's by far the most relaxing thing I've ever found, and these days we all need to find a way to relax, although opium is not necessarily the best way for everyone. Beyond that aspect, I also find that a few pipes of opium in the morning really enhances my capacity to sustain prolonged periods of focused writing. Opium certainly does not provide creative inspiration itself, but it definitely establishes the ideal state of physical relaxation and cerebral balance required to let whatever creative ideas you might have to express themselves, whether it be in writing or painting or music or whatever. I even know a few gourmet chefs who say that they cook their best food after smoking some opium in the afternoon. I doubt that it works this way for all artists, but it does for most of those who I know, including myself. With opium, a book that might otherwise take me eighteen months to write only requires about eight months of work.

Q: *Why is that?*

A: I think that it compensates for imbalances in neurochemistry and corrects emotional instability, which are conditions that many artists and writers seem to have. Without opium, not only does it take me a lot longer to write a book, it's also an uphill struggle all the way. With opium, it becomes a labor of love. It annoys me that government authorities, particularly those busybody Americans, try so hard to eradicate something that I find so useful for my work, and that also provides such soothing satisfaction.

Opium poses no threat to society. That's one reason I no longer live in America. It's not really a free country anymore. Here in Asia, the laws against opium smoking were imposed only after heavy political pressure from the American government, as well historical hypocrisy of Western missionaries, so there is no deeply ingrained stigma against it. Still, you must be very careful about using opium here, because if you get caught, you are in a heap of trouble, and the only way to get off the hook is to pay a fortune in bribes.

Q: *Do you recommend that everyone smoke opium?*

A: Certainly not! I'm what you might call "pro-choice" regarding opium. Just as women should have the free choice to decide whether to terminate a pregnancy, people should have the free choice to decide what they consume. This certainly applies to tobacco and alcohol, which are legal but far more hazardous to health than opium. Those who need or want it should have the right to use it, especially in the privacy of their own homes. It's nobody else's business.

Q: *Do you have any suggestions for a novice who wants to try smoking opium?*

A: Yes, I do. First of all, always start slowly and carefully. Don't jump into a daily habit right away, and if possible, avoid addiction altogether. Try it once or twice and see how it suits your system. Find your own level: most beginners smoke way too much and get sick from it. Three pipes is usually the perfect measure for an occasional smoker.

Also, it's very important to smoke only pure, properly prepared opium. Stay away from opium that's been heavily dosed with dross! If you decide to try smoking daily, then make your first run a short and well-disciplined one, no longer than three months and no more than three to five pipes a day. That way, the withdrawal won't be so rough. If you are not prepared to deal with detox, then by no means should you cultivate a habit! Also, if you decide to smoke daily, then be sure to have some sort of project to work on so that you can put the energy to good use. Write a book, learn a foreign language, play music, paint, teach—whatever you like—but don't just loll around all day long.

Finally, I suggest smoking in the morning, before noon, the earlier the better, and never at night. That way you'll stay in harmony with opium's own natural rhythms. And always treat opium with great respect. It's not a toy to be trifled with. It's very beautiful and very powerful, like a goddess. Without due respect, it can utterly destroy you, but it can also become your best friend and closest ally. It all depends on cultivating the proper attitude toward it.

Ms. C: age 39; Chinese; herbalist

Q: *When and where did you first smoke opium?*

A: About eight years ago, in Thailand.

Q: *Do you still smoke now?*

A: No.

Q: *Why not?*

A: Because I don't need it anymore. I got what I wanted from it. It served me very well, but eight years of smoking was enough to do what I wanted to do with it.

Q: *When you were smoking, how often and how much did you smoke?*

A: In the beginning, I'd smoke once a week, usually on Sunday afternoon, but with no set limit on how many pipes. Sometimes I'd start at noon and still be lying there at midnight, having smoked at least a dozen pipes. After four or five months of this, I started to manage it more carefully. I smoked twice a week but only two or three pipes per session. That gave me very good results.

I also started to study the therapeutic value of smoking opium based on some old Chinese herbal manuscripts that I found. And that gave me a lot of insight about how to use it.

Q: *What did you learn about it from traditional Chinese medical resources?*

A: To begin with, I discovered that it really helps to drive dampness and mucus out of my body. It's quite humid in Thailand, and women especially tend to absorb dampness from the environment like a sponge absorbs water. It can cause women a lot of discomfort, especially menstrual problems. I found that a few pipes of opium effectively drove the dampness right out of my system. It also helped to regulate my menstrual cycles and completely eliminated the discomfort I'd always experienced during that time of month. I noticed that it increased my resistance to infection and contagious diseases as well, which is a big advantage in a tropical climate.

Another benefit I discovered was that it helped me focus my mind and concentration on my work in herbal medicine. After a few pipes, I could sit and read complicated Chinese herbal manuals for hours at a time and remember almost everything. It really seems to boost memory and retention of detail.

Q: *What advice would you offer to people who smoke opium or to someone who would like to try it?*

A: First, it's best not to smoke opium at all, unless you really need it for a specific therapeutic function or other practical purpose. Second, if you do smoke, it's definitely a good idea not to get addicted. Smoke only occasionally, never more than twice a week, and smoke only as much as you need to get the basic effects you want. Third, find a good teacher, someone who has been smoking for a while and can teach you how to properly prepare it, how to handle it, how to control it. That's very important.

Q: *Do you think you'll ever smoke opium again?*

A: No. I smoked on and off for about eight years and due to my background in Chinese herbal medicine, I was able to use it to maximum advantage to balance my body and regulate my vital functions. No other herb on earth is as potent and useful as opium for correcting basic imbalances in my system. I don't need opium anymore, so there's really no point in smoking it again.

Q: *Is there anything else you want to say about it?*

A: Yes, I think that opium should be legally available to doctors and herbalists as a therapeutic tool. It is far superior to any pharmaceutical drug and, as an herbalist, I can tell you for sure that it is the most useful medicinal herb in the entire pharmacopoeia. This used to be common knowledge in the West as well as in the East, prior to the twentieth century. Just because some people abuse it is no reason to ban it; people abuse alcohol and tobacco, meat and sugar, and all sorts of other things, and those are not banned. I also believe that there should be legally licensed opium dens where people who need or want it can go to smoke a few pipes.

There will always be a small minority of people in every society who need or want to use opiates, and the way things are today, such people have no other choice except heroin, which is very dangerous and therapeutically useless. Or else they become alcoholics, or turn to amphetamines and barbiturates, all of which are far more hazardous than opium. There is absolutely no question in my mind that licensed opium dens would eliminate the heroin problem overnight and that many alcoholics would also switch over to opium.

Mr. P: age 49; American; photojournalist

Q: *When and where did you first smoke opium?*

A: In northern Thailand, in 1997. I had a chance to smoke opium in Istanbul back in 1971, but I was afraid to try it then due to all the negative propaganda I'd heard in America. If I'd known then what I know today about it, I would not have hesitated to try it.

Q: *How do you like smoking opium and what effects does it have on you?*

A: I love it! I regard it to be a wonderful herbal medicine with very profound and positive therapeutic benefits. The first thing I noticed after a few pipes is a complete recalibration of my entire system, very much like tuning up the motor of a car, except in this case I'd say it's more a matter of "tuning down." Nothing else I've ever tried has given me such a deep sense of relaxation and perfect balance. When I smoke, I become very still and peaceful inside, while my mind becomes very clear and well focused. It slows down my metabolic rate, but at the same time it sharpens my senses, especially my sense of hearing. In fact, it heightens all forms of sense perception. Mental static stops completely, allowing great clarity of thought.

Any kind of physical, mental, and emotional stress instantly dissolves, like ice in the sun. I can actually feel it unraveling all the knots and kinks in my muscles and tendons.

It was not until I had my first smoke of opium that I actually realized how much tension I usually carry around in my body. I'd say the best words to describe the feeling of opium are *soft and smooth, warm and glowing.* Opium makes me feel the way I imagine it must have felt to be in Mama's womb—all safe and secure, warm and happy, floating in utter bliss. Unless I smoke too much.

Q: *What happens if you smoke too much?*

A: I get a sort of toxic reaction and feel incapacitated. Rather than the usual light and buoyant feeling, I feel heavy and sluggish. Also, rather nauseous. There seems to be a very fine line between the perfect dosage and too much, and it's very important for each person to find out where that line is for him or her.

Q: *For you, what's the perfect number of pipes?*

A: Between three and five. More than five is always too much for me. Once I tried smoking seven and it made me feel like a zombie. But when I smoke just three I feel very well balanced and highly energized. I get elated and very talkative, bubbling up with all kinds of great ideas. That's why it's best to smoke with a few compatible, intelligent friends. The conversation gets incredibly interesting, very satisfying, and friendships really blossom.

When I smoke alone, I tend to get inner visions. Entire worlds and beautiful dreamscapes unfold in my mind and that too is very rewarding. I can understand why writers and artists and musicians have always been so strongly attracted to opium—it really helps to release creative potential and allow creative energy to express itself. I also love the taste of opium smoke. It's fantastic! An earthy, nutty taste that you'll never forget.

Q: *How do you feel the day after smoking opium?*

Boxed collector's set of eight rare porcelain opium bowls. Bowls like these were used only by wealthy smokers and were usually custom-made on order from the smoker. (Courtesy of Wolf K.)

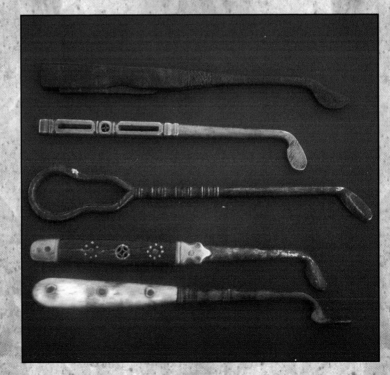

Various opium pipe–cleaning tools required to maintain a smoker's equipment in good working order.

Bamboo pipe with silver saddle and antique Chinese I-Hsing clay bowl with ceramic box for *chandoo* syrup.

Chinese woman in Laos enjoying an afternoon smoke of opium in her salon.

Details of silver saddles on antique Chinese opium pipes. (Courtesy of Wolf K.)

Classical-style Chinese opium lamp, gold-plated, on ceramic lamp stand.

Wooden stand holding ten fine-quality Chinese bowls for smoking opium.

Four antique opium
bowls with tradi-
tional cobalt blue
enameled motifs.
(Courtesy of Wolf K.)

An exquisitely detailed gold-plated, wrought-silver opium box in the "Inro" shape, shown front and back. Such quality utensils were commonly used by wealthy opium smokers and are now highly prized collectors' pieces. (Courtesy of Wolf K.)

An enameled silver opium box, shown top and side views. The animals depicted are from the Chinese zodiac, separated by a motif of Chinese characters, each one of which mean "long life," a recurring theme in Chinese culture through the ages. (Courtesy of Wolf K.)

A silver traveling lamp styled as an ornate birdcage.

Two opium bowls decorated with I Ching divination symbols. Note that the bowl on the right has two apertures set within the yin-yang design for double-barreled enjoyment. (Courtesy of Wolf K.)

"Gun rack" with a variety of different-caliber "smoking guns."

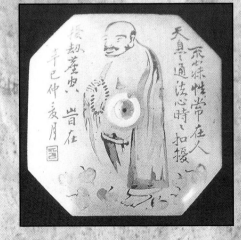

Antique opium bowl with a figure of Boddhidharma engraved on the surface. Buddhist and Taoist motifs were common on opium paraphernalia. (Courtesy of Wolf K.)

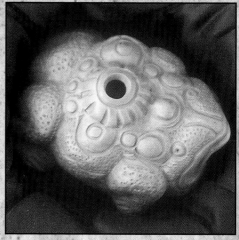

Opium bowls shaped in the forms of an opium pod and a toad. (Courtesy of Wolf K.)

Wooden stand, inlaid with mother-of-pearl, used to display opium bowls.

TONKIN — Fumeur d'Opium fumant la pipe

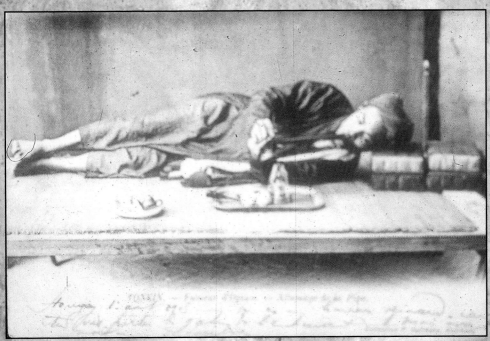

Chinese opium smokers smoking at home. (Courtesy of Wolf K.)

A servant brings his master a bowl of tea as he enjoys his afternoon smoke at home in nineteenth-century China. (Courtesy of Wolf K.)

Opium poppies growing in the mountains of Southeast Asia. (Courtesy of Jim Goodman)

Fresh sap collected from an incised poppy pod during the annual harvest in the northern hills of Southeast Asia. (Courtesy of Jim Goodman)

Three ripe poppy pods, freshly incised and ready for sap to be collected. (Courtesy of Jim Goodman)

Beautiful purple poppies bobbing over a ripe pod ready for harvest. (Courtesy of Jim Goodman)

Knife scrapers for scraping dross residue, from the inner surface of a metal collar on an opium bowl, after smoking. (Courtesy of Wolf K.)

Document from the Opium Suppression Bureau in northeastern China. (Courtesy of Wolf K.)

財收字第 No. 0032128 號

收

據

財務總署華北禁煙總局

發給收據事茲據 班永文 繳納執照費 ○萬 ○千

○百○十○元○角業經如數收訖合行發給收據存執

中華民國 卅 年

收款人

月

日

Details of silver saddles on antique Chinese opium pipes. The pipes of wealthy smokers were often studded with precious gemstones. (Courtesy of Wolf K.)

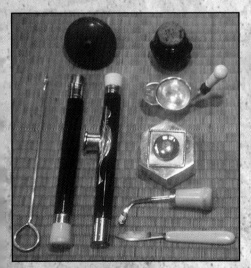

Complete "traveling kit" pipe and paraphernalia, hand-crafted in Laos in silver.

An elaborately engraved, self-contained traveling opium kit that includes a compartment for a breakdown pipe and tools, lamp, and dross box. (Courtesy of Wolf K.)

Detail of a silver saddle on an old Chinese opium pipe, with "Eight Immortals" motif in high relief. (Courtesy of Wolf K.)

Old Chinese opium pipe with "Eight Immortals" motif and attached bowl. (Courtesy of Wolf K.)

A bamboo opium tray set with smoking utensils: crystal-domed, gold-plated Chinese lamp, black lacquered breakdown traveling pipe with silver and ivory fittings, skewers on their ivory rest, opium jar, dross box, and cooking pan.

Complete "breakfast-in-bed" tray of scraper, dross box, opium box, and opium tools, including lamp, spindles, and lacquered pipe with silver saddle.

Liquid chandoo boiling in a copper pot over the lamp slowly reduced to treacle.

Spinning the cooked chandoo treacle from the copper pot with the tip of a spindle.

Rolling a shaped pellet of chandoo into a cone against the smooth, warmed surface of the bowl to prepare it for smoking

A rolled pellet of chandoo inserted into the aperture of the pipe bowl.

A complete smoking kit arranged for smoking on an antique Chinese smoking bed.

Examples of aesthetically pleasing opium bowls.

Fine, old, hand-painted glazed porcelain bowls. During the late Ching dynasty, China was the undisputed king of the ceramic-making arts. No one in the world could surpass their artistry and craftsmanship. (Courtesy of Wolf K.)

Government tax stamps for legal retail opium sales in China. (Courtesy of Wolf K.)

Wad of chandoo spun with two spindles over the lamp to form a "Black Gold" pellet for smoking.

The bowl is held at an angle over the lamp to vaporize the inserted pellet for smoking.

A tray with all requisite opium paraphernalia for a smoking session, including a Vietnamese-style opium lamp with glass oil well and base shaped like a poppy pod.

A: Great! I wake up feeling thoroughly refreshed and very happy, perfectly balanced, and that feeling lasts all day long. There's no hangover, no blues. I've also noticed that it makes my skin very smooth and lustrous, which might have something to do with the enhancement of microcirculation in the skin. Another aftereffect that I always notice the next day is that I feel erotically charged up and quite horny. That feeling never occurs while I'm actually smoking, but always the next day. I also notice that the next day I'm always full of creative inspiration and enthusiasm for my work and I can really write well.

Q: *Do you think smoking is dangerous?*

A: Not if you smoke in moderation. Properly handled, I believe it has great benefits, especially in today's tense, hectic, stressed-out world. There is simply no better way to unwind, relax, and counteract all the stress and strain of daily life in this hyperactive world. In that respect, I believe that it can really work to sustain mental and physical health, and prolong life.

It's really an extraordinary medicine. It's hard to believe that it's prohibited. It just doesn't make sense. Smoking a bit of opium once in a while would be especially beneficial for people in the Western world, particularly America, where stress has become an epidemic and causes all kinds of health problems. I can say for sure that it is infinitely superior to Prozac, Valium, sleeping pills, and all the other "downers" that Americans take so much of these days, in terms of both therapeutic efficacy and safety. For one thing, opium has built-in safeguards. You cannot die of an overdose from smoking opium because if you smoke too much, it gives you a spanking by making you sick to your stomach.

Q: *How often do you like to smoke opium?*

A: Two or three times a month is perfect for me. It's a myth that everyone who smokes opium automatically gets addicted. Only a very small minority of opium smokers ever become addicted to it, and those are the ones who need it to correct serious imbalances in their systems. If they didn't smoke opium, they'd be drinking booze all day long or popping pills like candy. But most people who smoke opium never get addicted to it. After all, how many wine drinkers in the world become winos? Maybe one out of ten thousand? It's the same with opium smokers.

Q: *What else do you like about it?*

A: I love the art of smoking opium the old Chinese way. The beautiful equipment, the skill involved in cooking and preparing the pellets for the pipe. The soft warm glow of the lamp. It's a connoisseur's delight in every respect. I would never use opium if the only way to take it is by eating it. The art and craft of smoking opium the traditional Chinese way constitutes at least half the pleasure. The rest of it is the wonderful relaxation it provides. And I cannot think of anything else the world needs more of today than plain old relaxation.

Q: *Who introduced you to this art?*

A: I was very lucky. I was first introduced to it by a true master of the art. He refined his opium paste at home and got it so pure and clean that it would turn a beautiful golden color when he cooked the pellets over the lamp. He had a fantastic collection of pipes, lamps, and other utensils and a beautiful smoking room, and he was a very skillful pipe master.

He introduced me to the art of Chinese tea at the same time, and he taught me to approach the whole experience as a sort of sacrament. Learning about opium from someone like that can make all the difference in the world.

Q: *Anything else you would like to say about it?*

A: Yes. Chinese culture is without question the oldest and most sophisticated show on earth. They have a particular genius for blending practical function and beautiful form into high art so that virtually every aspect of life becomes a richly rewarding aesthetic experience. The Chinese art of smoking opium is one of the best examples of this genius and it's right up there with Chinese food and Chinese medicine. It's just incredible to me that such a beautiful and useful thing would be banned.

Mr. H: age 45; Scandinavian; corporate executive

Q: *How long have you smoked opium?*

A: About four years, although it's something that I've wanted to do for at least twenty years but never had the chance until four years ago.

Q: *How did it start?*

A: A good friend of mine in Thailand introduced me to it one afternoon at his house. I liked it from the very first pipe.

Q: *How often and how much do you smoke?*

A: I like to smoke about three or four times a month. Generally, I smoke three pipes each session, sometimes four. The most I've ever smoked was six pipes, but that proved to be too much for me.

Q: *What effects does it have on you?*

A: Primarily, it has a very deep relaxing effect on me both in body and in mind. It also gives me a feeling of complete contentment. In addition, I always notice a heightened sense of perception.

Another thing that I really like about smoking opium is the feeling of intimacy that comes from sharing a few pipes with good friends who also like to smoke. It really produces a deep feeling of spiritual communion with fellow smokers.

Q: *How does it affect your work in the office?*

A: I can say for certain that it has no negative impact on my work. In fact, it seems to make me far more mellow and equitable at the office. After smoking a few pipes of opium, I never get annoyed or flustered at work regardless of what happens. Things that normally might stress or anger me simply do not bother me at all. I also seem to get my work done more efficiently because I'm able to focus better on the business at hand. I find it particularly useful to smoke a few pipes before long, tedious meetings. Even the most boring affairs can become rather interesting after smoking opium.

Q: *Do you think opium is a dangerous drug?*

A: I'm not really qualified to judge that, but according to my own personal experience I would certainly say that it is not dangerous. I imagine that it might become harmful if one were to smoke too much and too often, but that's true of almost everything, especially alcohol.

For me, opium is a mild and extremely pleasant relaxant that has no negative side effects and doesn't leave me with a hangover of any kind. I've never felt threatened by it, nor have I ever felt tempted to become addicted to it. I've gone four or five months without a smoke and it's no problem for me. I've also smoked opium four or five times a week when I'm on holiday and had no trouble cutting back again afterward.

Q: *Besides work and leisure time, are there any other particular times that you like to smoke opium?*

A: Yes, I really like to smoke a few pipes prior to boarding an airplane for long intercontinental flights. It completely eliminates all symptoms of jet lag on arrival. It also makes the flight itself a lot more pleasant. Also, if I feel a cold or flu coming on, a few pipes of opium either prevents it entirely from developing or else greatly reduces the severity and duration of the symptoms.

Q: *Does smoking opium have any negative effects on you?*

A: No, none at all, not as long as I don't smoke more than my normal measure. However, if I smoke too much, then it makes me feel heavy and sometimes irritable, and also I find it difficult to fall asleep at night. But if I smoke just three pipes, I always sleep very well and wake up the next morning feeling great. That sense of well being usually lasts all day long, so I actually get two full days of pleasure from smoking a few pipes of opium. I cannot think of anything else that works quite like that.

Q: *Is there anything else you'd like to say about smoking opium?*

A: Yes, but not about its actual effects. What I'd like to say is that I really do not like the stigma that has become attached to smoking opium these days. I don't like not being able to talk about it openly

with people, and I don't like always having to be so secretive and fur-
tive about smoking it. It seems to me that this is something that one
should be able to enjoy as freely and casually as having a drink in a
bar or a coffee in a café. The prohibition on smoking opium is totally
unjustified and unfair. And I must say that I rather resent that.

Mr. N: age 62; Australian; teacher

Q: *When and where did you first smoke opium?*

A: In Malaysia, while I was living there for two years, from 1972 to '74.

Q: *How were you introduced to it?*

A: Before coming to Malaysia, I had been traveling for about eighteen
months in Afghanistan, Pakistan, and India, where I developed a very
serious bronchial infection that just kept getting worse and worse. I
went to all sorts of hospitals and doctors, but none of the medication
they gave me ever did any good, it just kept getting worse. By the time
I got to Malaysia, I could hardly breathe without coughing up big gobs
of phlegm. It got so bad that sometimes I could not sleep at night. One
evening, I was in my favorite little restaurant having a bowl of noodles,
and the old man who ran it—who was Chinese—heard me hacking
and wheezing. So he came over, sat down at my table, and told me that
the only thing that would ever cure me was to smoke opium for a year
or two. At first I thought he was kidding, but he wasn't. He told me to
come back the next day at noon to join him for a smoke at his favorite
opium den.

Q: *What happened?*

A: At first I was a bit nervous about it, but I was also very curious
to visit an opium den, so the next day I went with him. Dens were
legal there in those days, so I wasn't worried about getting arrested or
anything like that. I watched him smoke a few pipes, then he finally
coaxed me into trying it myself.

Q: *How was it?*

A: Beautiful! After a couple of pipes, I could feel my lungs clearing up, and I was able to breathe freely again for the first time in nearly two years. The effect lasted for about five days, then my lungs got congested again, so I went back to the same den for a few more pipes, and pretty soon I was smoking every day.

I had found a job teaching English, so I had enough money to support myself, including my daily visit to the den, which became like a second home to me. I went there at exactly the same time each day—noon—and I smoked exactly five pipes each time, no more and no less.

Q: *Did it cure your bronchial disease?*

A: It sure did! My lungs cleared up completely and I was breathing normally again, exactly as the old man said. It also cured me of a chronic case of amebic dysentery that I'd picked up in India and never really managed to get rid of with pharmacy drugs.

Q: *How long did you continue smoking?*

A: About two years. Then my father died, and I had to go back to Australia to take care of my mother, so I had to give it up.

Q: *Was it difficult to quit?*

A: Not really, not nearly as difficult as it is to quit tobacco. The owner of the den was very helpful. He told me to gradually cut back from five pipes a day to just one pipe over a period of three weeks, after which I just stopped. He suggested I drink lots of water, have a very hot bath with sea salt in it every day, followed by a two-hour massage, and plenty of Chinese tea. I followed all of his advice, and two weeks after stopping I was fine.

Q: *After you stopped, did your bronchial problem return?*

A: No, the cure was permanent; I've never had a sign of it since.

Q: *Do you still smoke opium today?*

A: Only when I visit friends in Asia. It's not available in Australia, and that's where I live now.

Q: *Would you smoke again if it were available in Australia?*

A: Definitely! Especially at my age. It's the best thing for all those nagging aches and pains that come with age—stiff joints, high blood pressure, depression, insomnia; you name it, opium fixes it. That's why I always look for a place to smoke whenever I travel to Asia, but it's very difficult to find such places these days, unless you know someone who smokes at home.

After they banned opium dens in Malaysia in the late 1970s, they passed a law allowing anyone over the age of fifty-five to apply for a legal license to smoke opium privately at home. The old Chinese man from the noodle shop got one of those licenses, and whenever I came back to visit him in Malaysia, he invited me to join him for a few pipes at home. The last time I saw him he was nearly eighty and still in excellent health, happy as can be. Now that's what I call a civilized way of life. I wish they had such a law in Australia. If they did, I'd be the first one to apply!

Mr. K: age 76; Laotian-Chinese; opium den proprietor

Q: *Please tell us a bit about your background.*

A: I was born in Cambodia. My mother was Chinese, my father was Cambodian. We were so poor that sometimes the only thing we had to feed the entire family was some water in which a handful of rice had been briefly boiled. I came to Laos in 1950 and have been living here since then. I have seven children; the youngest is my ten-year-old son and the oldest is a daughter who lives in Thailand.

Q: *How long have you been smoking opium?*

A: Since I was thirty.

Q: *How did you start?*

A: I first started for sex. To play with young ladies. I heard that if a man smokes three pipes of opium before sex, he can continue all night with the same girl, or with many different girls, because it is very easy to control himself. Well, it was true, so I did that a few times a week for a while, but then soon I was smoking every day and I haven't gone a day without it since. Opium was legal in Laos then and very cheap and easy to get, so I decided to go into the business myself and opened a small opium den. I've been doing this for a living ever since.

Q: *How much opium is smoked each month in your den?*

A: About two kilos.

Q: *And how much do you smoke?*

A: I smoke about forty pipes per day, more or less.

Q: *That's quite a lot, especially after forty-six years of continuous smoking. How do you mange to stay healthy?*

A: You have to know what you're doing to smoke every day for that long. Food is very important. I try to eat some kind of fish every day. Fish is very good for the nervous system, so it helps to balance the effects of opium on the nerves.

I also try to drink a glass or two of liquor every night to keep my blood circulation strong. Opium tends to slow down the circulation. My favorite drink is French cognac. Chinese tea is also very important because it helps clean the blood and stimulates the internal organs.

Most important, you must be married and have a good wife in order to smoke opium all your life. This is absolutely essential. A smoker must have a family to take care of him and create a happy household. And a smoker must have a family to take care of, a responsibility that prevents him from losing his spirit to opium. That's why it's a very bad idea for young unmarried men to start smoking opium. It can easily lead to their destruction because they will tend not to eat properly, not bathe, not to do anything except smoke. Also, they will become impotent from not eating properly and from not having a woman to sleep with, and that is very bad for a man's energy.

It's important for a smoker to stay sexually active, even when you're older, because it keeps the body functioning properly and is good for the hormones. My youngest son there (pointing proudly across the room) is only ten and I'm seventy-six!

I would also say that someone who wants to smoke opium for a long time should always try to smoke only good, properly prepared opium. It should never contain more than ten percent dross and by no means should you ever start smoking dross by itself!

Q: *Is that what your pipe boy is smoking over there in the corner?*

A: Yes. Once you start smoking that, you can never stop. He mixes it with morphine tablets and a narcotic headache powder to make it even stronger. Then he smokes the dross from that again, and then again, and each time it gets stronger. Look at him! He's only thirty years old and weighs less than forty kilos. He won't live very long doing that, but that's what some people like to do.

Q: *Do you ever smoke that dross mix?*

A: Never! Absolutely not!

Q: *What's your daily schedule?*

A: I get up about ten o'clock in the morning. First I have a few cups of strong coffee with milk and sugar and smoke a few cigarettes. By the time I'm done with that, I'm awake and the children and grandchildren have all gone off to school or work. So then I smoke eight or nine pipes, either by myself or with any customers who come in that early. After that my wife prepares my first meal. I cannot eat anything in the morning until I've had my first pipes.

After eating, I prepare the place for a day of business, making sure there are enough opium wafers cooked, oil in the lamps, the pipes are clean, tea is prepared, and so forth. If we are running low on opium, I send the pipe boy out to buy a kilo of raw opium and have him cook it down in the kitchen. Most of my customers start showing up in mid-afternoon, and the busiest time is around sunset. Around seven o'clock in the evening, the whole family gathers together for dinner and I try to eat as much as I can then. I usually have half a dozen pipes or so just before dinner and again right after because it seems to stimulate my digestion. Then there are usually some more customers who come in to smoke after dinner, and by around ten P.M. they're all gone. So then I smoke a few more pipes, watch TV until about midnight, eat a bowl or two of rice if I get hungry, and go to sleep.

Q: *Does anyone else in your family smoke opium?*

A: No, not a single one. None of them seems the least bit interested in opium. Sometimes my wife and children help with the business in various ways, but none of them has ever even tried it. It's not for everyone, that's for sure, but for those who like it, it's the best thing in life. In fact, I just got some very special stuff in from the highlands, very pure and aromatic. Would you like to try some?

Q: *Yes, thank you.*

8

"PIPE DREAMS" AND "THE ALCHEMIST'S SONG"

OPIUM POETRY BY MARTIN MATZ

An Introduction to Martin Matz

Martin Matz is one of the most original, inventive, and eloquent American poets of the post–World War II era. A bona fide Beat poet who, along with friends such as Kerouac, Ginsberg, and Burroughs, appeared like a comet in the blank literary skies of 1960s America, Matz went on to create his own unique and highly exotic style of poetic expression. His startling imagery and beautifully bejeweled metaphors leap sparkling from the page to command the reader's complete attention. With each successive reading, his words reveal yet another subtle nuance that lay previously hidden, like the facets of a gemstone seen from various angles, until finally the entire richly brocaded tapestry of his vision manifests its intricate patterns to the reader's mind. Matz combines threadbare reality with the most marvelously embroidered dreams, weaves decadence and epiphany into the seamless veil of paradox through which the human mind experiences the world, and blends the deepest nihilistic despair with the most exalted visions of salvation. Like most poets in late-twentieth-century America, his work has gone virtually unnoticed by a public mesmerized by television, film, and sensational fiction, but for those who know the man and his work, he is respectfully regarded as a "poet's poet," a literary star shining in the benighted sky of modern civilization.

The late Herbert Hunke, another eloquent voice of the Beat generation and a longtime friend of Martin Matz, described the poet and his work as follows in an introduction he wrote to Matz's *Pipe Dreams* in 1989:

> How fine and beautiful are the opium drenched lines in his *Pipe Dreams*, exquisitely presented in manner: delicate, mysterious, and wondrous. He succeeds in developing an awareness of the strength and awesome beauty, the hidden power and intricate structure in the heart of stone; the intangible mystique beheld in the flight of a hummingbird, the wing of a dragonfly or exotic butterfly kissing and drawing the sweet nectar from each flower. His demanding retentive memory . . . fuses into revelation . . . a vibrancy we can instinctively recognize: the perfection of the moment.
>
> There exist certain people of strange, mysterious bent who see the palest colors of each day. The eyes see what is not there . . . thought moving steadily through the inner being, alerting our senses to the charm and almost imperceptible awareness of the inspiring beauty, the outpouring of energy pulsing within a scene unfolding before one unexpectedly. Mr. Matz can successfully blend the strange and fascinating dream-level reality with the mundane daily experience most perfectly, weaving perfect magic.
>
> When I think of his poetry I think particularly of his words . . . or should I say his choice of words, words that he has rolled around in his thoughts, perhaps tasting their sounds in his head, his mouth. His lines are strong yet tinged with a touch of pathos. His world of color and ancient life . . . makes dreams unfold before him. There is a "force" at work within the whole of his poetry, very nearly in every one of the poems I've read.
>
> And he draws support for the solidity of his statements from the earth, all of nature; trees, rocks, and gems—upheaval and rest-

less winds, strange dream producing flowers. His is an awareness of the endless mystery we are all so much a part of.

Pipe Dreams is a collection of eleven poems that Matz wrote during his six-year sojourn in northern Thailand, most of which he spent living in a hill-tribe village with his wife, Barbara. Opium drenched though they are, it is clear that the opium only serves the poet as a cerebral springboard to a much greater vision, a vision that should by rights be perfectly clear to any poet without resort to opium. But with all the floss and gloss of modern civilization, with its neon lights and loud sounds, its trashy entertainment and constant distractions, the global malaise and colossal waste, perhaps the poet today needs something like opium to override the morass of artifice imposed on our senses by contemporary times and thereby reveal to his mind the underlying patterns of eternal nature and universal truth from which humanity has strayed so far. In *Pipe Dreams,* Matz uses opium as a door through which to gain entry into the ancient realms of nature and the cosmos that have been all but forgotten in today's mad-dash world, and so powerful is his art that we, as readers, can share the awe and wondrous beauty of what he finds in those hidden realms simply by reading his words, even without the lubricant of opium to loosen the hinges of our rusty doors.

In *The Alchemist's Song*, Matz commemorates an afternoon he spent at the home of a friend living along the banks of the Ping River in Chiang Mai, shortly before the poet's reluctant departure from Thailand. His friend, the "Alchemist" to whom this poem is dedicated, introduced Matz for the first time to the highly refined art and craft of smoking opium the traditional Chinese way, which, after his experience with the cruder techniques he encountered among the less cultured hill tribes of northern Thailand, impressed Matz as an aesthetic revelation of the first order and inspired him to coin the term "Black Gold" to describe the perfect purity and fragrance of the homemade chandoo his friend offered him. Thus he wrote this poem as a literary memorial to his experience that afternoon.

Neither *Pipe Dreams* nor *The Alchemist's Song* is really about opium, per se. They are all about life and art, dreams and reality, psyche and soma, and all the incredible, complex paradoxes that the human spirit must deal with in its corporeal existence on earth. In Matz's paradigm of human life, opium is like a magical flower in the Garden of Eden, a flower with the power to fertilize the garden of the human imagination and make it blossom with beautiful dreams. As those dreams unfold, we realize that the boundaries between dreams and reality, Eden and Mammon, are nothing more substantial than gossamer veils of perception, mere "smoke screens" in the mind. It is the powers of perception that opium unlocks, not the drug itself, of which these poems sing.

To view more of Martin's work, visit www.MartyMatz.com.

Pipe Dream 1

There are sacrificial whispers
    to the North
    beyond the river Ping
        where elephant dreams
      dress in yellow leaves
and ancient spirits
wing down the barrel of my pipe
    the hills are drenched
        with poppy blood
    and a red moon
        drowns
      at the edge of my molten eye
This is the land
        of the reclining Buddha
      the little wheel
    the water buffalo's last dance
This is the place
        of green legends
      of silk and silver teak
    where incense mingles
        with a cobra's breath
    and in these hills alone
      the chef
        with his lamp
        is King

Pipe Dream 2

It must be fate
          that moves a man
     to Bogota or Bangkok
          tripping past
a blood clawed sky at dawn
          remembering
          all the border crossings
     in a smuggler's dream
               gone wrong
     the smell of tropic rivers
          the stink of mangrove swamps
          the custom inspector's fatuous smile
          a golden cheddi
pressed against the pearlescent intaglio
          of another summer's guile
     the ivory fingered keys
          of a life
          played long and hard
54 years of going up
and an eternity coming down

Pipe Dream 3

I am

no longer there

under a coca cola sky

when the ticking of the puppet master's hand

stops singing

as all the strings get caught

in a surreal frenzy of creation

on the horns

of a blue bull at dusk

and the only thing that's left

is the sinking sun

like a fried orange in a fish shop window

Siam

is no longer Siam

the blue bull has become

just another dung colored water buffalo

mewling at the moon

and there I am again

walking a twisted horizon

while lying on my hip

in search of

what?

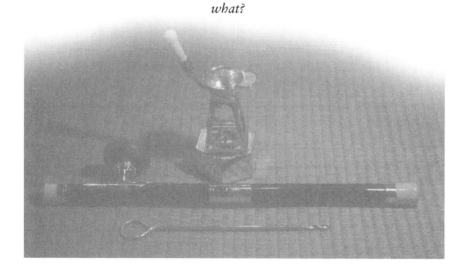

Pipe Dream 4

The ivory pipe is still warm in the hands of time
the chefing lamp flickers
casting deep shadows on the wall
from the cricket's bamboo cage
and everyone can see
by its buttery light
poverty's tin smile
pasted on the thin lips
of this century's dreams betrayed
and every mouth is filled
with the cold taste
of December's white ashes
just as each of us knows
by the empty echo
in our planetary hearts
beating across these barren hills
that no elephant remains
to dance a final dance
beneath the mystic Burmese moon
no ultimate bird is left
to sing a final song
The purple poppies
have all nodded their final goodnights
and the last pill has been smoked

Pipe Dream 5

I have trekked
        beyond the borders
                of this world
past all the bejeweled imagery
        delusions and illusions
                on the far side of moonlit mirrors
        in search of a sign or a sound
I have wandered aimlessly through soulless mists
                my rusting tongue
                probing restlessly
        dark pools of agony
                for a single taste
        of that simple spot behind the line
                which is the origin of all things
                and come up empty
        I have sought
                answers for failures & successes
for unknowable truths and knowable lies
                walked strange byways of madness
        ambled hand in hand with death
                welcomed with open arms
                        all the twisted demons
                of the heart
                        that others shun
hoping for a glimpse of solitary plains
                where rise the mountains
        of deepest dissipation
                and most wretched excesses
        and come up empty
        I have seen a sky of lemon whispers
        and beat it black and blue
                with baboon bones

I have vomited vast seas of silence
             on the dawn
opened with sure fingers
             the flower of my soul
    and come out singing
             along plains and prairies
singing praises of all the planets, the galaxies, the cosmos
             I have never seen
        nor ever hope to see
    For this is poetry
         and wheresoever poetry leads
             I shall follow
    and still I'll come up empty

Pipe Dream 6

The rains of Thailand
                    are not like California rains
           there is no soft pattern
                              no song of life
                    no warm breath of air
only callused stillbirths at dawn
                    only oppressive sheets of living water
           that dampen the quickest spirit
                    brings down the highest mind
           If monsoons even bear at all
                    they bear children of rapacious natures
                                        and deep depression
                    that only 15 pipes can cure
I remember hilly San Francisco streets
           whose cobblestones
           glisten with magnolia
Here
                    one is always alone
           caught in a fishnet of time
remembering south side Chicago 1930 alleyways
           that only the blues can explain
Here one wears the rain
                    Like some ancient ceremonial shroud
                    with no shock of death allowed
only oppressive sheets of living water
                    to dampen the quickest spirit
                    bring down the highest mind
           The monsoons
                    the monsoons
                              the monsoons I say
                    if they ever bear at all

bear the children of darkest depression
that only 15 pipes
15 pipes at least
15 pipes and many more
can ever hope to cure

Pipe Dream 7

It may be smoke
> that rings my head
yet nonetheless
> these bamboo poles
frame a cosmic roof
> with surgical precision
and it may be smoke
> that weaves a hat of thatch
to rub against the rain
and so it seems
> it must be smoke
to make me see
> > a black and orange spider
come dropping down a silken thread
> that's hanging from the moon
for I have danced thru Lahu nights
> > and beat the stars
with mummy bones
to open the roads of dawn
I have drank and cackled
> with shamen of my choice
and smoked my 20 penny pipes
and yes it may be smoke
> that brought me to these shores
For I have always been
> > the jigsaw puzzle piece
just slightly out of whack
for any kind of fit
I am the month of Limember
> in a calendar of 13 months

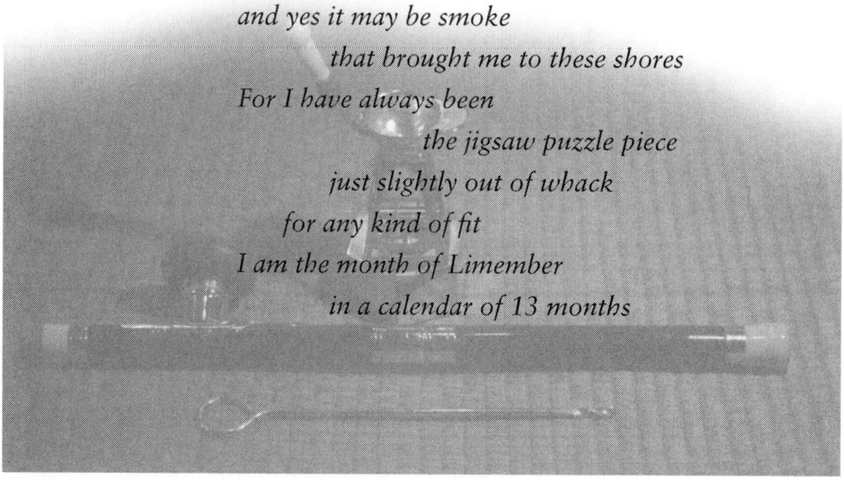

I am that total weirdo
           whose treasure lies
      in planetary observation
      not in interest rates
I sometimes wish
      that like some magic chrysalis
           I too could emerge
      from green cocoons
           of my own making
      Transmogrify
into a pastel seahorse
           who spends all day
      just browsing along arbors
and fields of strange unholy dreams

Pipe Dream 8

Less spiders and more porcupines
                would make a better world
      the porcupine quill
            is good to eat
      sews a neat stitch
                  makes a fine pen
      spreads opium evenly
                over any surface
      picks up a perfect pill
as for spiders
                  everytime I smoke
      the holy gum of poppies
      in a well carved ebony pipe
they appear
                  as horrid hairy bags of fear
      or silent shadowy poisonous shapes
            like flags of death unfurled
      Less spiders I say
                  and more porcupines
      would make a hell of a better world

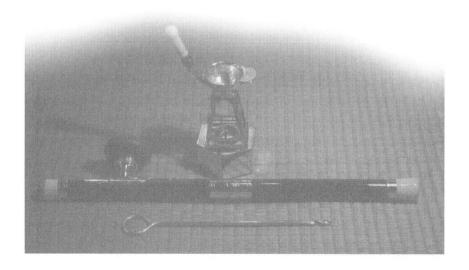

Pipe Dream 9

Tonight I have twice
             maligned great Egypt
       told lies about Osirus
             put Anubis the dog faced
                   in his kennel
For here in old Siam
             I have smoked the holy pipe
       rode elephant charges
             against the Burmese hordes
       and yes
             I have eaten the flesh
                   of an ancient cobra moon
             with the builders of Angkor Wat
                   that
       sister city of the Mayan dead
                   from the Americas
             whence I came
             I tell you
       I have an appetite for death
       a taste for her mouth
             kissed her dark lips
             sought the other side
                   of her most enigmatic smile
                   and been denied
       But soon
                   soon
                         soon
       no symphony shall play for me
             only a band of maggots & worms
       playing the fifes and drums
             Pain Agony Suffering
             this is the world my friends

the son kills his father
the upright Christian
cheats his mistress
The old ones
the wise ones
all considered useless
are given a fast shuffle
to a pauper's grave
The planet dies
and there is no place
for man or woman
who would walk in the rain
and rub their aching shoulders
against a velvet rainbow
or just sit beneath a rock and dream
So here I stand
amongst magnificent fields of poppies
white and purple
as they nod their heads in agreement
to my shouting joy
They drop their petals
exposing their pregnant pods
which swell with buttermilk
the true gift of god
that for a time sustains and soothes
until
they too
become pain and suffering
just another cosmic joke
another minor irritant
on madness road
the one I walk from birth
a twisted path
to hell

Pipe Dream 10

I would love
>to look down
one more time
>and watch the fog
enshroud the Golden Gate
>yet time
>who once was my closest friend
seems like all the others
>to have run out
and I shall never
>leave this strange land
where the closest thing to fog
>I shall ever see again
is perhaps
>a mountain mist
>or the smoke that comes
rolling out of my long stemmed pipe
>to cover all my dreams
>with loneliness and pain
The pipe like time
>I once did see
as a true friend
>who would always
bring me joy
>and visions true
Yet like time
>the pipe too
has moved on to richer fields
>and left an aching hollow
where once
>a heart beat strong

Pipe Dream 11

A wounded poppy
            and a wounded pipe
        gives a wounded high
    but when all is right
when the poppy sheds her petals
                by herself
    and the pods allowed to swell
when the 3-bladed knife
        cuts bold and true
when the mellow smoking tube
        is in tune
    with chefing needle and lamp
and when a shaman of the pipe
    builds his perfect cone
oh my friends then
    you walk amongst the gods
for nothing beats the poppy juice
            perfectly prepared
    It brings the true magic of dreams
in fact
        It is the emperor of highs

The Alchemist's Song

FRIEND
AN UNEXPECTED WIND HAS BLOWN
    AN UNEXPECTED FLOWER
ACROSS THE LOTUS OF MY MIND
    AND I WISH
THAT YOU AND I
    COULD SHARE RIGHT NOW
THE MIDNIGHT CAMEL'S FULGUROUS DANCE
    OR THE RUPTURED ECLIPSE
            OF AN AGING STAR
YOU KNOW I WAS BORN
    ONE HOT SUMMER NIGHT
IN THE SIGN OF A STEAMING DRAGON
    WITH A VAGRANT TATTOO RISING
    AND A BLACKJACK MOON ABOVE
IT WAS DESTINY
    THAT ROLLED THE DICE
    AND A GAMBLER'S LUCK
THAT WRAPPED ME UP
    IN A SMOKER'S COBWEB SMILE
    AND DROPPED ME ON SOME HIDDEN
    BURMESE EDGE
WITH BAMBOO PIPE AND TINY LAMP
        AT HAND
MY SILVER BEARD
            WAS TANGLED IN THE DAWN
    AND SO I PASSED AWAY
        THE SEAMLESS YEARS
    CAREFULLY OBSERVING
HOW NEON CATERPILLARS GREW FAT
    BY EATING STOLEN DREAMS

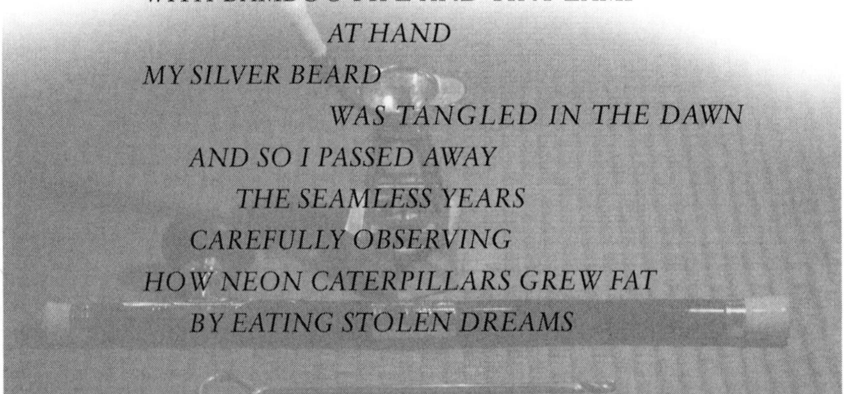

WHICH REVEALED THE OCCULT
   SECRETS
THAT ENABLED THOSE
   HAIRY EARTHBOUND CRAWLERS
TO GROW A PAIR OF WINGS
BUT THE MEMORY GROWS DIM
   HOWEVER
      I SHALL NEVER FORGET
THAT AFTERNOON
   I SPENT
   IN YOUR HOUSE ON THE BANKS OF THE PING
IN EACH HAND YOU HELD
   A SILVER TOOL DIPPED IN POPPY BLOOD
   ABOVE THE JADE LAMP'S RUBY FLAME
YOUR NEEDLES
   TWIRLED AND SPUN
      WEAVING MAGIC PATTERNS
   LIKE SOME FABLED PERSIAN CARPET
   MASTER WIZARD
YOU WORKED THE PUNGENT SAP
AS IT BUBBLED AS IT SWELLED
   YOU TURNED MECHANICAL TECHNIQUE
   INTO GREAT ART
   FORCED THE SACRED PEARLS OF
   WISDOM
TO SING THE ALCHEMIST'S GREAT SONG
   BEFORE MY EYES
I WATCHED YOU TRANSMUTE
TWO PILLS OF BLACK MUD
   INTO THE PUREST GOLD
IF I COULD HAVE ONE WISH
   IT WOULD BE TO MEET
YOU TOMORROW IF I COULD

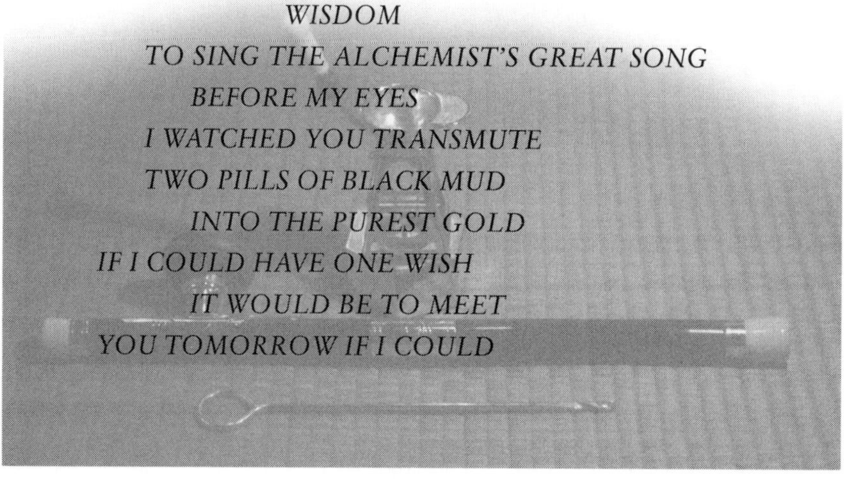

IN DOWNTOWN VIENTIANE
AT THE OLD WOMAN'S SHOP
OR BETTER YET
AT THE CHINESE MASTER'S DEN
WHERE WE COULD
TALK AND SMOKE BLACK GOLD
UNTIL THE
WORLD COMES TO AN END

—MARTIN MATZ, OCTOBER 1997

9

TO SMOKE OR NOT TO SMOKE

REVIEWING THE EVIDENCE

The question remains: Is opium basically a good thing or a bad thing? Is using opium for medicinal purposes right or wrong? Is the Chinese art and craft of smoking opium for pleasure a positive or a negative contribution to human civilization?

As in all such dualistic debates, cogent arguments can be devised to support both sides of the question, while the real truth lies somewhere in between. Yet, this sort of philosophical neutrality leaves most people dissatisfied, particularly when it comes to controversial issues such as opium. Most people prefer to pass unequivocal judgment in such matters, to declare one side the winner and the other side the loser, and to conclude whether the defendant is guilty or not guilty. In order to assist readers in reaching their own verdicts on the question of opium, some of the most relevant issues and indisputable evidence is briefly reviewed below.

Opium is fundamentally a medicinal herb that for thousands of years has been used primarily as a remedy for human ailments, so we must judge it first and foremost on the basis of its medicinal merits. Prior to its prohibition for medical use in America during the first half of the twentieth century, and the subsequent extension of this ban throughout

169

the rest of the world by political and economic pressure from the U.S. government, opium was the single most widely used medicinal substance on earth, and it appeared in some form in the majority of medical compounds in both Eastern and Western medicine. Its recorded history as a peerless medicine and a pleasant relaxant stretches back at least five thousand years to the very beginnings of human civilization. The ancient medical archives of Sumeria, Egypt, India, and China all mention opium repeatedly as an indispensable item for treating a broad range of common ailments, both chronic and acute, in men as well as women and from infants to the elderly. Soon after Arab traders introduced it to the Western world, opium quickly became a primary component in traditional Greek and Roman medicine, and from there its therapeutic use spread rapidly throughout Western Europe, where it continued to play a central role in medicine well into the twentieth century.

Christopher Hufeland (1762–1836), widely acclaimed as one of the greatest healers and most learned physicians in the history of traditional Western medicine, declared opium to be the single most important and therapeutically effective medication on earth. He used it successfully as a treatment for pneumonia, pleurisy, and other acute respiratory diseases; for inflammations of the liver, spleen, stomach, and kidneys; for malaria, typhoid, cholera, and other infectious fevers; for all types of nervous system disorders; for dysentery, colitis, and other bowel problems; and as an effective treatment for diabetes.

Opium was always the most essential ingredient in both Eastern and Western medical prescriptions until the U.S. government began strictly enforcing its worldwide prohibition during the 1940s. By then, approximately eighty percent of all medications sold in America and Europe contained some form of opium or opium derivative. Pharmacists and physicians throughout the world regarded opium as an indispensable component in blending most medicinal compounds. Thus for thousands of years, the world's medical profession unanimously judged opium to be the best of all medicines and the most important constituent in medicinal prescriptions. If we allow this professional medical testimony to guide us, then we can only conclude that as a medicine for treating human disease opium is, beyond doubt, a good thing.

That brings us to the next questions: Is opium good or bad in its role as a recreational relaxant, and how does it compare, for example, with alcohol? We've already heard the unequivocal and often quoted view of the famous nineteenth-century opium connoisseur Thomas De Quincey, author of *Confessions of an English Opium-Eater,* who stated, "I do not readily believe that any man, having once tasted the divine luxuries of opium, will afterward descend to the gross and mortal enjoyments of alcohol." Let's listen now to a testimonial from a more contemporary source, the New York novelist Nick Tosches. In his lengthy and lovingly crafted article for the September 2000 issue of *Vanity Fair,* "Confessions of an Opium Seeker" (later published in a slim volume by Bloomsbury as *The Last Opium Den*), Tosches writes, "I am not going to rhapsodize here about opium. But I will say this: it is the perfect drug. There is nothing else like it. In this age of pharmaceutical-pill pushing, it delivers all that drugs such as Prozac promise."

The experienced opium smokers interviewed in chapter 7 all say basically the same thing—that opium is "by far the most relaxing thing on earth," that it provides "a feeling of complete contentment," and that nothing else on earth can compare with it. Jean Cocteau, Emily Hahn, Thomas De Quincey, Arthur Symons, Sir Richard Burton, and other Western aficionados whose testimony on opium we've heard in the foregoing chapters—not to mention supporting evidence from countless Chinese, Vietnamese, and other Asian smokers over the past three centuries—all agree with the conclusion Tosches reached after smoking opium just a few times: It is the perfect drug. If "perfect" may be taken to mean "good," and if we accept the evidence provided by those who've tried it, then the verdict on opium as a pleasant relaxant is obvious: It must be very good indeed!

Generally, people who condemn opium as bad, and who therefore insist that it must remain strictly prohibited, are people who have never tried it. They often base their judgment on the fact that opium is addictive. No one—least of all opium smokers—questions the fact that opium is addictive, but opium's addictive nature is not a relevant issue here—not unless they are also prepared to condemn and prohibit coffee, alcohol, tobacco, and hundreds of commonly prescribed pharmaceutical drugs as well, all of which are every bit as addictive as opium. Furthermore, the two addictive alkaloids in opium—morphine and codeine—are both legally sanctioned medical drugs, and they rank among the most widely prescribed medications in the world. No hospital could function without morphine and codeine, and both are easily obtained on prescription from doctors. Have we ever paused to wonder why morphine and codeine—the two components in opium that *make* it addictive—are both legal medicines, while whole herbal opium, from which these drugs are extracted, remains strictly prohibited even for legitimate medical use? We shall discuss this paradox later.

Another obvious reason why opium's addictive quality is not relevant to a discussion of its medical value is the fact that the chemically synthesized drugs that the pharmaceutical industry produces today as substitutes for opium are even more addictive than opium itself, and far more difficult addictions to quit. They are also less effective therapeutically and have more dangerous side effects than whole herbal opium. Take, for example, the addictive class of chemical drugs known as benzodiazepines, of which Valium is the most popular and the most frequently abused.

Valium was designed as a muscle relaxant, which is one of the basic therapeutic effects that whole herbal opium provides better and more safely than any of the synthetic substitutes patented by the pharmaceutical industry. Addiction to Valium is swift and causes severe damage to the liver, while withdrawal can be so hazardous that patients run the risk of death from convulsions. Similar risks are associated with addiction to and withdrawal from sleeping pills, painkillers, and antidepressants.

In the year 2003 alone, 213 million prescriptions for pharmaceutical antidepressants were dispensed in America, including 32.7 million for Zoloft and 22.2 million for Prozac, all with the promise of relieving chronic depression. In clinical trials, however, Prozac proved no more effective than placebos in relieving depression, and on March 21, 2004, the FDA issued warnings that high doses of Prozac, Zoloft, and other top-selling antidepressants may in fact cause even deeper depression, as well as mania, violence, and suicide. The growing incidence of suicide and homicidal mania under the influence of widely prescribed drugs such as Prozac and Zoloft is one of the most foreboding trends in modern medicine, but instead of taking steps to curtail their use, the medical profession is expanding the application of some of these dangerous drugs to children as young as six. Several years ago in America, young Kip Kinkel slaughtered both of his parents as well as two of his classmates at Thurston High School in Oregon while under the influence of Prozac. A year later, Eric Harris, dosed up on the antidepressant Luvox, embarked on his infamous rampage of mayhem and murder at Columbine High School. Two years ago in Australia, a seventy-year-old man who had been happily married to his wife for over forty years got up one morning and took his daily dose of Zoloft; half an hour later, while his wife was cooking his breakfast, he walked across the kitchen and stabbed her to death with a butcher knife.

A hundred years ago, before toxic chemical drugs replaced natural medicines, people who suffered from depression took a mild dose of opium, to which they responded in the expected positive manner, and no one was ever known to lurch off on a manic killing spree after smoking a few pipes. Today, however, doctors prescribe expensive chemical drugs for depression, drugs that often fail to relieve depression, sometimes make depression even worse, and occasionally drive users into raging fits of violence that prompt them to slaughter anyone in sight, including themselves. Now, that's depressing!

If opium is judged to be something that is bad and must therefore be prohibited because of its addictive properties, then the same prohibition must logically apply to alcohol and tobacco, and to the even more addictive and far more dangerous drugs—the tranquilizers and sedatives, pain-killers and sleeping pills, antidepressants and antihypertensives—produced by the pharmaceutical industry and routinely prescribed by doctors for conditions for which opium used to be the sovereign remedy.

Having dealt with the issue of good and bad, let's have a look at the question of right or wrong. Is it wrong to use opium, either therapeutically or recreationally? Opium is certainly illegal, so if its prohibition by law is the sole criterion for deciding whether it's right or wrong to use it, then it's definitely wrong. However, if we take a closer look at why opium, after its long and illustrious history as the world's most heroic remedy and most popular relaxant, was suddenly declared illegal both for professional medical use and for personal recreational use, we find some serious doubts about what's right and what's wrong with opium.

We've already mentioned the paradox that morphine and codeine, the two alkaloids that make opium addictive, remain legally available as medicine throughout the world and rank among the most widely prescribed drugs on earth while whole herbal opium, from which these two addictive drugs are derived, has been declared strictly illegal. From a logical medical perspective, this situation is irrational and absurd. But when viewed through the lens of corporate politics, the situation comes into clear focus. Morphine and codeine are still legally tolerated as medicine simply because pharmaceutical chemistry has found no effective synthetic substitutes for either of them. Furthermore, since these natural alkaloids can be extracted from whole herbal opium only by means of a complex chemical process that must be done in properly equipped drug factories, the pharmaceutical industry can control their production and profit from their distribution, even without a patent. By contrast, whole herbal opium—which contains morphine and codeine in much lower dosages and is therefore much safer and less addictive than pharmaceutically extracted morphine and codeine—requires no chemical processing and can easily be purified from raw opium on an ordinary kitchen stove (as discussed elsewhere in this book). This means that if opium was legal for medical use, the pharmaceutical cartels would face stiff competition on the open market from whole herbal opium prescribed by naturopathic doctors because it does not require factory processing to prepare it for medicinal use. That is why pharmaceutical-grade morphine and codeine are legal medicines and whole herbal opium remains illegal: to protect the vested interests and lucrative medical monopolies of the pharmaceutical industry and their powerful political patrons.

This leads us to the core issue regarding the worldwide prohibition of opium for medical use. The American government began to pressure the rest of the world to enforce its strict ban on opium around 1940, at precisely the same time that the chemical pharmaceutical industry began its rise to power in the United States. Opium was then outlawed not because it is dangerous or addictive, but because it's such a consistently effective medicine for so many common ailments that it had become the key ingredient in approximately eighty percent of all medical compounds sold in America. Because opium is a natural herb that works better than chemicals, has fewer harmful side effects, and cannot be patented, the new pharmaceutical corporations knew that they could not monopolize the market for medicine in America and the rest of the world as long as opium remained legally available. Opium was banned to eliminate competition from traditional natural medicine and pave the way for the newly established pharmaceutical industry to take control of the market with patented chemical drugs.

To put the matter another way, if you had a free choice between using natural medicines that contain opium derivatives and provide superior therapeutic results with fewer harmful side effects at much lower cost than the synthetic chemical substitutes produced by the pharmaceutical industry, would you chose the natural medicines or the chemical drugs?

The answer is obvious, and that is why business barons trying to get the chemical-drug industry off the ground in America during the early 1940s had to take steps to get opium banned.

A key player in this scheme was Senator Prescott Bush, grandfather of the current American president. Senator Bush and his political protégés in Washington were among the earliest investors in the pharmaceutical industry, and they orchestrated the passage through Congress of a bill banning opium for medical use. Since the rest of the U.S. government was preoccupied at that time with events leading to America's entry into World War II, the bill banning opium drew little attention, even though it was specifically designed to serve the financial interests of America's most politically influential families, who have been major investors in the pharmaceutical industry from the beginning.

In 1977, for example, Dan Quayle's father—who held a controlling interest in the giant pharmaceutical firm of Eli Lilly—appointed George H. W. Bush as one of Lilly's managing directors, and later Bush picked Quayle as his vice president. Furthermore, since many pharmaceutical drugs are synthesized from toxic wastes produced by the petroleum industry—coal tar, for instance—those who invest in the oil industry, such as the Bushes and other politicians, have found a lucrative market for their toxic petrochemical wastes in the pharmaceutical industry.

While serving as Ronald Reagan's vice president in 1981, George H. W. Bush aggressively lobbied the administration to allow American pharmaceutical companies to dump obsolete and dangerous drugs that had already been banned in America onto the markets of Third World countries. Many of these hazardous and medically useless chemical drugs were recommended for common conditions that had previously been effectively, safely, and inexpensively treated in those countries with natural medicines containing whole herbal opium.

More recently, powerful political friends of the pharmaceutical industry managed to attach a rider to the antiterrorism bill that rushed through Congress in the wake of 9/11 prohibiting families of autistic children from using federal courts to sue pharmaceutical companies whose mercury-preserved vaccines are suspected as a possible cause of autism, thereby protecting the industry from financial liability if such a connection is scientifically proved. By contrast, whenever any sort of natural medicine made from herbs or nutrients causes even the mildest negative reaction, government agencies usually respond by prohibiting the product and sometimes shutting down the producer.

The point here is that opium was not prohibited for medical use because it is dangerous or addictive, nor because it is therapeutically ineffective. It was prohibited in order to cripple competition with the pharmaceutical industry from traditional natural medicine. If whole herbal opium was again a legal medicinal substance, it would soon decimate many profitable medical monopolies held by American pharmaceutical cartels, because not only is whole herbal opium therapeutically superior to the chemical substitutes produced by the pharmaceutical industry, but opium also cannot be legally patented and therefore it cannot be monopolized by private corporations.

Herein lies the crux of the issue: No natural substance extracted from a plant can be patented, and therefore pharmaceutical companies cannot monopolize opium and its derivatives. If opium could be legally patented by private corporations, it would unquestionably remain a legally condoned medicine, and would still be the most widely used medicine on earth, as it was for thousands of years prior to the takeover of the medical industry by private corporate interests.

So where does that lead us on the question of whether the use of opium, particularly for medical purposes, is right or wrong? Suppose, for example, that you know opium is an effective cure for a particular disease that no pharmaceutical drug can cure, and that you or a member of your family suffers from that disease. Assuming you could somehow obtain it, would you feel that you have the right to use opium as a medicine under those circumstances? In light of what you know regarding the reasons that opium is now prohibited for medicinal use, would you let that stop you from using it to save the life or relieve the suffering of a loved one? This is a question that can be answered only by each individual when and if such circumstances arise, but there are in fact some very serious medical conditions for which whole herbal opium is the only safe and reliable remedy, and which the toxic chemical drugs produced by the pharmaceutical industry only make worse. Those conditions for which opium still remains the sovereign remedy will not be mentioned here, however, because such important medical claims must always be supported by concrete clinical evidence, and to do this properly would require another book on the therapeutics of opium.

It may well be time, in fact, to conduct new clinical studies regarding the therapeutic properties of the world's oldest medicine, because recent false claims the pharmaceutical industry has been making about the medicinal benefits of its noxious chemical nostrums have been clearly exposed. Dr. Allan Roses, a senior vice president at Britain's largest pharmaceutical company, GlaxoSmithKline, has revealed publicly what has long been known privately in boardrooms and laboratories of the world's major pharmaceutical cartels. Dr. Roses admitted that most of the prescription medicines produced by drug companies today do not work for most people who take them, and that fewer than half of the patients who use the world's most expensive drugs derive any benefit whatsoever from them. During the same week that Dr. Roses made these incriminating statements about its products, GlaxoSmithKline announced that it would soon release twenty new drugs onto the market, from which the company expects to earn one billion dollars per year.

Dr. Roses pointed out, for example, that the costly drugs that pharmaceutical companies promote as treatments for cancer actually work in only twenty-five percent of patients who take them. "The vast majority of pharmaceutical drugs—over ninety percent of them—only work in thirty to fifty percent of the people," states Dr. Roses. Moreover, not only are most pharmaceutical drugs therapeutically useless, but some of them are also downright dangerous to patients.

By contrast, very few people fail to respond positively to the therapeutic effects of opium. That's because opium, like all other medicinal herbs, is a natural organic substance derived from a plant and unaltered by chemical processing; such natural medicines are always compatible with the organic functions of the human body. Instead of concocting chemical substitutes for opium and other natural medicines to produce synthetic drugs that can be patented, monopolized, and sold at three thousand percent mark-ups, the pharmaceutical industry should be required by law to research and develop ways to improve the utility and potency of natural medicinal plant substances, and to provide them to consumers at reasonable cost. If there is anything wrong in this debate, it's the fact that a private corporation may legally earn one billion dollars per year peddling twenty patented chemical drugs posing as medicine, when eighteen of them will prove to be therapeutically useless and many of them will cause serious harm to most people who use them.

Finally, we arrive at the most basic issue of all: the personal use of opium as a relaxant—that is, to smoke or not to smoke? Like smoking cigarettes, drinking alcohol, using pharmaceutical drugs, racing cars, or skydiving, opium is simply another decision in life to be made by responsible adults, a decision that must be carefully weighed by each individual based on a thorough familiarity with the facts and a clear awareness of the risks. Even if opium was legal, as alcohol and tobacco are, important questions must still be considered before making a decision to smoke opium, and ideally this book will have provided sufficient information to answer most of those questions.

Managing an opium habit without doing harm to one's health requires considerable discipline, but that is equally true of using tobacco and alcohol, racing cars, and skydiving, and it applies even more strictly to the use of pharmaceutical drugs. As with all such decisions, the best advice is to thoroughly study the relevant facts, and if you then decide to proceed, seek a good teacher, find the best-quality product, and try to do it right, as Nick Tosches did when he set out on a global odyssey in search of "the last opium den."

Tosches's travels finally landed him in Thailand, where someone fortuitously introduced him to the author of this book. After reading the nearly finished translation of the manuscript, Tosches refers to it in his *Vanity Fair* article, "Confessions of an Opium Seeker," as "a work of astonishing breadth and depth, and by far the most valuable treatise on opium we are likely ever to have." Guided by a hand-drawn map provided by the author, Tosches flew on from Thailand to Laos, where he finally tracked down his long-sought opium den. Owned and operated by the author's dear friend "Mr. K," this was the den where the old pipe master—last of a dying breed—was interviewed for the final vignette in chapter 7—the same Chinese master fondly recalled by the opium-smoking poet Martin Matz in the last lines of "The Alchemist's Song."

As Tosches ascends the "rickety slat stairs," he immediately recognizes "the most lovely smell on earth" wafting through the window from the room where smokers recline with their pipes in the amber glow of the lamps. Waiting inside is "Papa," who gives him a warm welcome and, knowing exactly why he has come there, "gently kicks one of the supine men, rousing him, summoning him to rise, then gestures that [Tosches] take his place on the mat." After assigning an assistant to prepare his smoke, the old man pours Tosches a cup of hot tea and "tells the pipe man that there is to be no charge . . . It is as if money, even in this poorest of places, no longer has anything to do with any of it . . . It is as if he . . . is here now only to do what he was born to do, and to ward off the end of a dying world of which he alone remains."

Resting his head on the wooden pillow block, the visitor from New York slowly smokes a few pipes of Mr. K's fine highland opium, then gazes around the dilapidated den and sighs, "I am home."

The writer's sentiments echo the feelings of many other Western travelers who, over the course of four decades, found their way to this place by following the telltale aroma up those "rickety slat stairs" and into that smoke-clouded room, where, as a Chinese poet once wrote, "wind and rain, heat and cold, do not occur, and day mingles with night." Regardless of who you were or where you came from, the friendly denizens at Mr. K's always beckoned you to lie down and smoke a few pipes, drink some tea, and commune with them in the rosy aura of the lamps.

The title Tosches chose for the book in which he recounts this experience—*The Last Opium Den*—has proved prophetic, for only two years after the New Yorker found his way home to Papa's place, the congenial Mr. K died of a broken heart when he learned that his beloved eldest son had been shot dead, killed in cold blood by trigger-happy police in neighboring Thailand, where the government calculates the progress of its ruthless campaign to suppress the drug trade by tallying the rising body count of extrajudicial killings.

Mr. K survived fifty years of nonstop opium smoking, thrived happily through a lifetime of poverty, and managed to raise and educate a large brood of children on the meager earnings of his humble den, but the light of his life was extinguished like a lamp in the night by the loss of his favorite son, and with it went the last opium den in Asia where intrepid travelers from the West could find a warm welcome and a friendly invitation to savor "the perfume of unknown flowers" and share what Tosches says "can only be called ambrosia." The demise of this last outpost of the ancient Chinese art and craft of opium is yet another milestone in the rapid degradation of human civilization in these barbaric times.

Part II

THE ART AND CRAFT OF SMOKING OPIUM

10

BLACK GOLD
REFINING AND BLENDING
THE SMOKING MIXTURE

Of all the various and sundry aspects of the opium-smoking habit—the pipes and lamps, the mats and pillows, the cozy room and tasteful decor, the skill of the pipe master and fraternal cheer of the smokers—none is more important than the quality of the opium itself, for the enjoyment of everything else is entirely dependent on it. Regardless of how elaborate the equipment may be and how elegant the setting, if the opium itself is of inferior quality, it is like having a meal of stale sandwiches and flat beer at a table set with sterling silver, crystal goblets, Dresden china, and fine linen.

The quality of the smoking mixture depends primarily on the experience and skill of the person who prepares it, rather than on the quality of the raw opium from which it is refined. Even mediocre opium can be transformed into an excellent smoking blend if the person who prepares it knows what he is doing. Known as yen-gao, or smoking paste, in China, and chandoo in India and Indochina, the refined essence of raw opium smoked by connoisseurs represents the crème de la crème of the opium poppy.

Traditionally, good Chinese opium dens and sophisticated private households always refined their own chandoo from raw opium purchased through a reliable supplier, rather than buying the chandoo ready

182

made. There are two main reasons for this: One is to ensure that the smoking mixture is blended precisely according to the requirements and tastes of the smokers; the other is to ensure absolute purity by discarding not only all of the coarse and inactive plant material from the raw paste, but also whatever contaminants may have been added to the raw opium at the source in order to increase its weight for sale. All manner of noxious impurities are customarily added to raw opium by unscrupulous suppliers to bolster their profits. Among the most common adulterants are powdered silicon, gypsum, thick sesame oil, molasses, gum arabic, egg white, and various vegetable saps and tree mastics. In addition, whenever one purchases chandoo prepared by an unknown supplier, one risks acquiring a product not only contaminated with various vegetable and mineral additives, but also excessively laced with heavy dosages of dross, the highly toxic residue scraped from the inside of pipe heads, which increases the intoxicating properties of the chandoo at the expense of purity and balance. The only way for smokers to avoid such problems is to prepare their chandoo themselves. Let's take a look at how this is done.

The first step in the refinement process is to soak a loaf of raw opium—usually a brick of one to two kilos in weight—in water overnight, using a large cooking pot and enough water to submerge the entire piece in four to five times its own volume of water. Some chefs also add a bottle of brandy or wine at this stage to further emulsify the solution. Jean Cocteau, as noted in his book *Opium,* preferred this method: "I recommend a liter of old red wine in the water in which the raw pill is soaking." However, this is optional and not particularly important to the final result.

The next day, place the pot on the stove and bring the fluid to a rapid boil. While it is boiling, the liquid should be vigorously stirred with a long spoon or a whisk to fully dissolve the raw paste and extract its essence into the water. Today, some opium chefs use an electric eggbeater for this purpose. Since all of the active opium alkaloids are soluble in water, this boiling and whisking process, which should be continued for fifteen to twenty minutes, extracts the active essence of opium from the inert vegetable matter and leaves the alkaloids in solution in the water.

When the cooking is done, turn off the heat and let the pot rest for about half an hour, so that most of the sediment may settle to the bottom. The next step is to carefully filter the fluid, and for this several options are available. In India, they prefer to line a large sieve with a thick layer of cotton wool and pour the fluid slowly through it. In China and Southeast Asia, a bamboo or wicker colander is lined with a piece of finely woven cloth of cotton or silk through which the liquid is slowly strained. Western chefs today often use a large coffee-filtering cone lined with a double layer of paper coffee filters, and this does the job very well. Whichever method is used, the fluid should be poured through the filter very slowly, until the pot is drained of its liquid contents. If the filter becomes overloaded and clogs, use a new piece of cloth or paper, but be sure to reserve all the sediment from the first filters.

Next, return all of the sediment to the pot, add about half as much water as was used for the first cooking, and bring it to a boil again, whisking continuously for another fifteen minutes. Filter this mixture in the same way as the first, then combine the two filtered liquids and discard the sediment. Allow the fluid to rest in a large, covered vessel for about forty-eight hours.

The next step is to filter the fluid again, pouring it very carefully from the vessel into the filter so that any sediment that has collected on the bottom of the vessel is not disturbed and may be discarded. Pour the filtered fluid back into a large cooking pot and bring it to a boil, simmering it long enough to reduce it to about two thirds or one half its original volume but not enough to render it thick and sticky.

Filter this fluid once again and let it cool, then pour it into a tall glass jar, seal the jar, and set it to rest where it will not be disturbed for a week to ten days. If you cannot find a jar large enough to contain it, use two or three smaller ones, preferably of the sort with straight vertical walls and a wide mouth, such as large mayonnaise jars.

This stage of preparation is the most important for obtaining a clean, highly purified grade of chandoo, for it permits the fine micro-sediment that escapes the filters to slowly settle to the bottom of the jar, where it collects in a dense, finely grained layer of sludge. It is truly amazing how much of this subtle particulate matter remains suspended in the fluid

Filtering freshly boiled raw
opium through a coffee filter
to remove impurities.

Boiling raw opium with water
in a copper pot, the first step
in the preparation of
chandoo for smoking.

after so many filterings even when a double layer of the finest filter paper
is used. Allowing the liquid opium to stand so that the residual sediment
may slowly settle to the bottom of the jar makes the difference between
a mediocre and a superior grade of chandoo.

After the sedimentation process is complete, it is time for the final
cooking and reduction of the fluid. If any fungus has formed on the
surface, carefully peel it away and discard it, then slowly pour the
liquid into a cooking pot, taking care not to disturb the layer of sediment that has collected on the bottom of the jar. Bring the fluid to a
boil, then reduce the heat and simmer slowly, stirring it occasionally to
keep it well mixed. At this point, the chef must decide whether or not
he wishes to fortify and balance the chandoo by adding some dross,

and if so, how much to use, so here we must pause in our discussion to have a look at what dross is and how it may be used in preparing opium for smoking.

Known in India as *ilchi,* dross is obtained by using a special tool to scrape the inside walls of clay-pipe heads to loosen the crusty, black residue that collects there during smoking. The gritty dregs are then shaken out into a cup or bowl. The Chinese opium pipe is designed to distill, rather than combust, pellets of opium that are placed into the aperture of the pipe head and held over a lamp for smoking. Thus, instead of producing ash as a by-product of smoking, as a tobacco pipe does, the opium pipe produces a black residue that deposits itself as a sooty crust on the inside of the pipe head as the opium vaporizes over the heat of the lamp. This dry, crusty residue is the dross.

For unknown reasons that probably relate to the volatile properties and relative densities of various alkaloids in opium, much of the morphine from each pellet that is smoked precipitates out of the smoke and is deposited in the residual dross. Consequently, the dross has a morphine content five to six times greater in concentration than pure refined opium. It also contains some additional alkaloids in various proportions, but morphine is the predominant one. This is why the dross is so potent and so highly addictive. In opium dens, most of the dross is reserved and sold in small portions for oral consumption to customers who cannot afford to smoke chandoo. The effects last a long time, but it is highly toxic to the human system, particularly the liver.

The dross may also be used to fortify and balance weak or inadequate opium and bring it up to par. Depending on the quality of the raw opium used, as well as the potency desired by smokers, the chef may add anywhere from a five percent to a twenty-five percent ratio of dross to the simmering chandoo during the final reduction, but it takes a well-practiced hand to get it just right. One should first test the pure chandoo by smoking a few pipes before committing the entire batch to a particular dose of dross, because once it's added it cannot be removed, and even then it's often a matter of luck to strike the perfect balance. Some purists never add so much as a single drop of dross to their chandoo,

Two forms of "gourmet"-grade chandoo, paste and liquid, in enameled ceramic containers.

Silver dross box, pipe bowl, and dross scraper and scraper knife with ivory handles.

regardless of its potency, in the belief that it would spoil the opium's natural character. As Cocteau notes in his diary:

> In preparing raw opium the alkaloids are combined quite haphazardly. It is impossible to foresee the consequences. By adding the dross one increases the chances of success, but risks destroying a masterpiece.

Of course, some jaded smokers deliberately stoke their chandoo with measures of up to fifty percent or more of dross, and there are even some who so relish the stupefaction it imparts that they smoke the dross straight, but this is not a recommended practice, at least not if one wants to stay healthy and in control of one's habit. As Cocteau remarks, "The vice of opium smoking is smoking the dross."

Indeed, this vice can be taken to the point of utter wretched excess by smoking the second dross produced as a residue of smoking the first dross, and even the third or fourth recycled dross, each of which becomes progressively more saturated with morphine and produces a progressively more stupefying sensation. The early-twentieth-century Vietnamese writer and connoisseur of opium Nguyen Te Duc, author of *Le Livre de l'opium,* describes this practice as "repugnant and stupid."

In any case, before the dross can be used to fortify a batch of purified opium, it must be refined and purified itself in precisely the same manner as chandoo. First a jar of coarse dross is placed in a cooking pot and crushed into a fine powder with a pestle or the back of a large spoon. Water is then added, and the dross is left to soak for a few hours or overnight. Next it is boiled and stirred vigorously, filtered into a glass jar, and left to precipitate for a week or two. The clarified fluid is then carefully poured off into a cooking pot, discarding the sediment at the bottom of the jar, and brought to a boil to reduce it to a thick syrup. While cooking, it exudes an extremely strong, unpleasant odor, which a French smoker in Bangkok compares to "cat piss." This syrup, which is extremely potent, is added to the chandoo in the correct dosage during the final cooking and reduction stage. Sometimes addicts also smoke it straight as a temporary emergency measure when they run out of their usual blend of opium.

After adding the dross, the next step in preparing chandoo is to stir in about one cup of brandy, vodka, or other distilled spirits per kilo of raw opium used. This is done for two reasons: First, spirits distilled to a degree of 70 to 90 proof (thirty-five to forty-five percent alcohol) from fermented grain or fruit help to properly blend and balance the active alkaloids and other constituents in opium, rendering a richer magma and a smoother smoke; second, the alcohol sterilizes the mixture, killing any residual fungus spores that may have impregnated the fluid during the final sedimentation period, and this helps preserve the chandoo when it is stored in sealed containers. The spirits perform these two functions as soon as they are added to the simmering mixture, after which the heat evaporates off all the alcohol so that it does not influence the chandoo's volatile properties during smoking.

The last decision to be made is the degree of viscosity desired in the final product. There are basically three grades of thickness that may be obtained in reducing the liquid mixture. The first is a dense fluid about the same consistency as a heavy liqueur. When the mixture has been reduced to this degree, it will begin to form small foamy bubbles on the surface of the boiling liquid. At this point, turn off the heat and let the liquid cool, then pour it through a funnel into presterilized glass or ceramic bottles. Let it cool and breathe in the bottles overnight, without plugging the mouth, then seal them airtight with a cork or cap for storage.

The second degree of viscosity is a very thick, semiliquid syrup, somewhat denser than molasses or honey. When it reaches this stage in the cooking process, it will begin to expand and rise in the pot, requiring careful control of the heat and constant stirring to prevent it from brimming over the edge. As it reaches the desired thickness, turn off the heat and continue stirring for a few minutes, then let it cool in the pot for a while, but pour it out while still soft and warm. The best container for this variety of chandoo is a ceramic or earthenware crock, such as a large mustard jar or tea caddy, with a cork stopper. Sterilize the vessel and pour the thick syrup directly into it, scraping as much as possible off the sides of the pot. Leave it uncorked for at least twenty-four hours to breathe, which permits tiny air bubbles trapped in the syrup to rise to the surface and evaporate. Then plug the container with a cork and seal the edges with paraffin or beeswax for storage.

The last and densest level of thickness in preparing chandoo for smoking is a semisolid gum somewhat like taffy or heavy rubber. To achieve this, the heat must be kept very low while the liquid is continuously reduced in the pot from a sticky syrup to a glutinous gum. Stir constantly and scrape the sides and bottom of the pot with a spatula during heating. When all the water has evaporated, remove the pot from the heat and immediately start scraping the hot gum onto a piece of aluminum foil or wax paper. Let it cool and contract overnight, then leave it to condense into solid form for about a week, after which you may press and cut it into whatever shape and size you want. Wrap each piece well in cellophane or wax paper and seal it with tape for storage.

Such is the process of refining chandoo for smoking from raw opium. Depending on the degree of viscosity to which it's reduced, one kilo (1,000 grams) or 2.2 pounds of raw opium will render 450–550 grams or 18–20 ounces of pure chandoo for smoking, with a volume of 350–450 ml (1.75–2.25 cups). If it is free of impurities and kept well sealed in a cool dry place, chandoo may be stored for many years or even for decades without losing its potency. In fact, when stored as a viscous syrup in ceramic or clay jars sealed with cork and beeswax, chandoo seasons well and improves considerably with age due to gradual fermentation. In Shanghai, the better dens used to season their smoking opium in porcelain jars for at least three years before serving it to their customers.

One should keep out only as much chandoo on a smoking tray as is required for two to three months of use; reserve the rest in sealed containers, replenishing the smoking supply as needed from the reserve batch. This preserves freshness and permits the reserve supply to continue improving with age.

SMOKING GUNS

CHINESE OPIUM CRAFT

The actual origins of the Chinese opium pipe, or Smoking Gun *(yen chiang)*, as it is called in Chinese, have been long lost in the dense blue clouds of vapor it has produced across Asia for the past three centuries. No doubt it was developed soon after tobacco smoking was banned in China in 1641, so that tobacco smokers could smoke opium instead. As with most Chinese inventions, a colorful myth traces the origins of the opium pipe all the way back to the time of the great Yellow Emperor (Huang Ti), the legendary founder of Chinese civilization, who ruled the Celestial Empire around 3000 BCE. The story is told that a red-faced god with six arms appeared before the Yellow Emperor one day and blew a mighty breath across the earth, magically producing a bamboo pipe. With another divine puff he created the poppy, and with a third huff a flame appeared, thereby engendering the three most essential elements for smoking opium: pipe, lamp, and opium.

The exotic assortment of paraphernalia used for smoking opium the Chinese way, the variety of materials employed to make them, and the intricate detail and artistic skill with which they are all designed and crafted testify to the creative talent of the Chinese artisans who produced them as well as the sophisticated tastes of the Chinese smokers who collected and used them. As with everything else in traditional Chinese civilization—food, tea, snuff, furniture, textiles—the utensils and accouterments associated with the opium-smoking habit were designed to please the eye with their beauty and delight the mind with their aesthetic form, as well as to provide practical utility in the hands of those who used them.

The most important implement for smoking opium is, of course, the Smoking Gun, or pipe. This instrument consists of two basic parts: the smoking tube and the distillation bowl, or "head," also known in English as a damper. The most useful material and popular design for the tube is a straight length of plain bamboo 55–65 cm (22–26 in.) long, usually consisting of one natural segment of bamboo plus about a quarter of the next one, with a three-pronged knob left attached at the joint where smaller sprigs branched out from the stem. Near the joint, where the segments meet and in line with the knob, a hole is drilled about three fourths of the way down the length of the tube. The tip of the shorter segment is sealed with a plug made of ivory, jade, bone, or marble; the tip of the longer section is fitted with a mouthpiece of the same material.

Over the hole drilled into the side of the tube near the joint sits a saddle made of metal—usually fashioned from copper, bronze, silver, or gold, or an intricate combination of several metals—with a raised socket designed to receive the stem that protrudes from the base of the bowl. The edges of the saddle must fit snugly against the tube to ensure an airtight seal. Pipe saddles are often ornately engraved or cast in bas-relief with dragons and phoenixes, flowers and trees, and other traditional motifs. Some bamboo pipes are further embellished by plating the surface with tortoiseshell, sharkskin, or snakeskin, adding layers of lacquer, or encrusting it with inlays of cloisonné or mother-of-pearl, but experienced smokers shun such vulgar extravagance, preferring the natural elegance, smooth patina, and earthy tones of a plain bamboo tube.

Over the centuries, other materials have also been crafted to make smoking tubes, including ebony, ivory, porcelain, and jade, and various metals. Some connoisseurs claim that tubes made from the hollowed stems of sugarcane are the best material of all for opium pipes because the natural sweetness of the cane lends a fresh fragrance and mellow flavor to the smoke, but sugarcane tubes have the disadvantage of cracking and shredding, making them impractical for long-term use and negating their value as collector's items. Tubes of wood, metal, porcelain, or jade, regardless of how attractively they are crafted, are spurned by experienced smokers because the interior surface fails to absorb aromatic resins from the smoke. Such pipes cannot be properly seasoned, even with prolonged use, and continue to deliver a harsh, inferior flavor. Ivory is acceptable because it acquires a beautiful patina, and eventually the interior surface develops the degree of seasoning required to render a rich, flavorful smoke, but it takes many years of use to achieve this effect.

In the end, the best smoking pipes have always been made with bamboo tubes; the older they get, the better they smoke and the greater grows their value. The outer surface of a plain bamboo pipe acquires a deep dark patina from frequent handling, while the porous interior seasons quickly from the cumulative absorption of alkaloids and aromatic resins in the smoke. A well-seasoned bamboo pipe greatly enhances the pleasure of smoking not only by improving the flavor of the smoke but also by increasing its potency. Furthermore, owing to the natural width of the interior, bamboo tubes also provide a better draw than materials hollowed out by

Terra-cotta bowl on bamboo pipe stem, with silver frog design.

hand, such as wood and ivory. As Nguyen Te Duc remarks in *Le Livre de l'opium,* "Bamboo is the easiest to obtain (or make), the least expensive, and the most highly recommended material for smoking opium."

In addition to the classic long pipe with the bowl located three quarters of the way down its length, there are several other basic designs. There are both long and short pipes with the bowl located at the extreme end of the tube, usually inserted into a wood or ivory base that is carved in the shape of a clenched fist. For portable smoking kits made for traveling, pipes are often designed with two-piece tubes that fit together and come apart for convenient packing and portability. There are also styles crafted with slightly curving tubes made from bamboo or cane, using the curved sections that grow from the roots.

Collectors usually keep their smoking tubes on a special rack designed for the purpose, a sort of "gun rack," with the sockets plugged to prevent dust from entering and the heads stored separately. This way, each time one wants to have a smoke, a particular tube may be selected and fitted with a favorite bowl.

*   *   *

The key item in the actual transformation of a pellet of opium into pure vapor is the bowl, or damper. Before we take a look at the various designs and materials used in crafting bowls, it is most important to understand the essential technological feature that distinguishes the Chinese opium pipe from all other smoking utensils, such as tobacco pipes, kif and hashish pipes, and water pipes. Unlike all other pipes and paraphernalia used for smoking herbal substances, the Chinese opium pipe is designed to distill rather than burn opium. Indeed, if a pipe loaded with a fresh pellet of opium is held too close to the lamp while smoking, or if the pipe is improperly drawn by the smoker, and the opium catches fire, that pellet is lost and must be scraped away and replaced with a new one. However, when the wick is properly trimmed to produce just the right flame, when the bowl is held at just the right distance and angle from the heat, and when the pipe is properly drawn by the smoker, the opium pellet slowly vaporizes rather than burns, producing a distinctive sizzling sound that echoes in the bowl—the telltale gurgle of opium being smoked the Chinese way.

As the opium slowly vaporizes (but does not burn), it is transformed by the heat into a dense, bluish white cloud that rushes into the bowl through the tiny pinhole to which the pellet is attached. Entering the relatively large chamber of the bowl through such a minute aperture, the hot vapor, which carries solid particulate matter from the pellet, suddenly expands and cools, causing the solid matter to precipitate from the vapor and stick to the inside of the chamber, where it forms a crusty residue, or dross. The remaining vapor, which now contains only the purest volatile and most aromatic elements of the opium in gaseous form, continues traveling through the base of the bowl into the tube and down the pipe to the mouthpiece, where it enters the smoker's lips and descends to the lungs as a smooth, soothing smoke. These fragrant fumes, which constitute the very essence of opium refined by the purifying process of distillation, are therefore free of particulate matter and do not contain the harsh, noxious by-products found in ordinary smoke produced by the process of combustion.

An article in the magazine of the Stanford University Museum of Art, which featured an exhibition of Chinese opium pipes notes, "The configuration and dimensions of the bowl were carefully calculated to maximize the distillation of the opium, rather than permit its incineration during the smoking process." Herein lies the most distinctive feature, as well as the technological genius, of the Chinese opium pipe. By transforming the solid opium into a vapor by the process of distillation rather than combustion, the Chinese opium pipe renders a pure and potent smoke in which all of the active alkaloids contained in the original opium remain intact within the fumes, rather than being damaged or lost by ignition with fire. Furthermore, the fragrant purity of the smoke remains untainted by the acrid, hazardous toxic effluvia produced by incineration. Such an invention certainly belies the common Western notion that ancient China lacked a scientific tradition, although unlike its counterpart in the Western world, traditional Chinese science focused its attention on improving the art of living rather than inventing deadly weapons of war.

Let us now resume our discussion of craftsmanship of the Chinese opium pipe. The most common design in bowls is a smooth, round configuration, somewhat like the shape of a mushroom, with a slightly convex surface on top, in the exact middle of which is a small hole 1–1.5 mm in diameter, designed to receive the prepared opium pellet. The hole itself is usually drilled into a small round insert cast of copper or bronze, or sometimes of ceramic, which in turn fits snugly into a larger hole left for that purpose in the center of the bowl's smooth convex surface. This design provides a recessed indentation around the hole, which helps ensure that the opium pellet adheres to the hole rather than falling off. It also helps to funnel the vaporizing smoke into the chamber rather than allowing it to escape.

The bottom of the bowl is designed with a short stem, around which a metal sleeve of copper or brass is attached. The sleeved stem fits snugly into the socket of the saddle and is held firmly in place with a small length of moistened cloth wrapped tightly around the sleeve, thereby creating an airtight seal between tube and bowl.

Bowls come in many different sizes, ranging from 3 to 7 cm (1–2.5 in.) in diameter across the top surface and 2 to 4 cm (1–1.5 in.) in height

Six excellent old Chinese terra-cotta bowls for smoking opium.

from the hole on top to the base of the stem on the bottom. They also come in an amazing variety of shapes and styles, including octagonal, hexagonal, decagonal, and quadrangular designs, as well as fluted, scalloped, and other multifaceted variations. The rarest designs are those that are molded in high-relief configurations that resemble things like snails and crabs, gourds and shells, turnips and poppy capsules, or the heads of gods, warriors, and other figures.

In Yunnan province in southern China, as well as in the mountainous regions of the Golden Triangle, where the world's best opium is grown today, many hill-tribe people use a simpler type of bowl that seems to have been developed indigenously by these minority tribes and is seldom used by Chinese smokers. This style of bowl is shaped exactly like a miniature flower vase, with a hole drilled into the side and an open mouth at the top serving as a socket into which the end of a short hollow bamboo tube is inserted to make a pipe. A strip of damp cloth is wrapped tightly around the end of the tube to hold it firmly in place and form an airtight seal in the mouth of the bowl. Though simple and unsophisticated compared to the traditional Chinese pipe, these hill-tribe pipes work very well, distilling the opium efficiently and providing a good draw. They are also easy to improvise when a Chinese pipe is unavailable, and they don't require as fine a hand in preparing the pellets for smoking, so they are simpler to use for beginners than is the more demanding Chinese pipe.

Terra-cotta clay, preferably of the same reddish *yi-hsing* variety used for making the best Chinese teapots, is considered by most experienced smokers to be the best material for making pipe bowls. Unglazed clay provides a cooler smoke due to its capacity for rapidly dissipating heat. It is also more efficient at precipitating residue from the vapor during the distillation process, and the exterior surface acquires an attractive patina after prolonged use.

Additional materials commonly used for fashioning pipe bowls are porcelain, celadon, and other ceramics, as well as jade and stone; the latter, however, produce a hotter smoke due to their greater density. Sometimes the entire bowl is glazed with enamel, while in other designs only the top surface is glazed, leaving the sides and bottom bare to preserve the material's cooling properties. The outer rim of fancier bowls is often lined with a border of copper, tin, silver, gold. When the top surface is glazed, it is usually painted first with a traditional motif, such as a dragon or phoenix, fruits or flowers, birds or bats, or perhaps a dreamy landscape, or else inscribed in elegant calligraphy with an appropriate line of verse or a charming quip. Among the inscriptions typically found on Chinese opium pipe bowls are the following:

> *Swallowing Clouds, Spewing Fog*
> *Always the Right Time*
> *Fragrant Fumes of the Immortals*
> *To Celebrate an Auspicious Day*
> *Spring Flowers and Autumn Moon*
> *The Fragrance Wafts for a Thousand Miles*

On the underside of the bowl, around the base of the stem or along the sides below the outer rim, the artisan who designs and produces the piece usually imprints his personal seal-chop, as well as that of the kiln where it was made, and sometimes the year of production. When the piece is specially commissioned by a particular collector, the owner's personal seal is also stamped on the bottom of the bowl. People who collect these bowls as antiques identify them and verify their authenticity according to the various seals imprinted underneath.

Just as the smoking tubes are kept on a special rack when not in use, so the bowls are stored on a stand designed for the purpose. These stands, which are made of wood, metal, or porcelain, have holes cut into the surface so that the stems of the bowls may be inserted into them, leaving the tops exposed for easy identification and ornamental display. Some stands are also fitted with removable trays underneath to catch drippings from residual dross in the bowls, particularly in hot humid climates, where damp heat often causes the dried deposits of dross encrusted inside the bowls to liquefy and drip down in thick, sticky droplets, when the bowls are kept stored for a long time without use. Storage stands are designed to hold from three to ten bowls, either in one straight row or in a double-tier arrangement. There are also smaller models for only two or three bowls that are made to be kept on the tray, so that the smoker may change bowls whenever he wants without having to get up.

The next most important piece of equipment used for smoking opium beside the pipe itself is the lamp, affectionately referred to by some contemporary smokers as the Magic Lamp. This is the item that smokers who quit the habit usually miss the most during withdrawal.

First of all, let's correct one common misnomer: Time and again, Westerners who write about opium but have never smoked it refer erroneously to this piece of paraphernalia as a "spirit lamp," implying that the fuel used to provide the flame is alcohol. Opium lamps are designed to burn oil, not alcohol, for only oil produces the steady flame and relatively low degree of heat required to properly cook the opium pellet without charring it, so it can be smoked without incinerating it. Alcohol burns much too hot for cooking and smoking opium by distillation, and the flame produces an unpleasant chemical odor.

In India and Indochina, pure coconut oil is the preferred fuel for opium lamps. Coconut oil burns at just the right temperature and produces a steady flame without smoke or smell. In China, lard is often the fuel of choice, and it too burns at just the right temperature with a smokeless flame free of odor. However, virtually any common vegetable oil that is sufficiently refined for cooking food may be used to fuel an opium lamp, although some, such as sesame oil and peanut oil, produce a slight odor.

Opium lamps consist of a metal stand on which sits a small chamber that holds the oil. The oil chamber is made of metal, such as copper or brass, or else porcelain or glass. A string wick for conducting the oil upward to the flame hangs into the mouth of the chamber through a metal ring that fits over the lip. A glass chimney is set onto the stand over the oil chamber, so that it funnels and focuses the heat to a point just above the mouth of the chimney for cooking and smoking the opium while preventing air currents from disturbing the flame. The chimney also eliminates any trace of smoke from the flame by serving as an efficient carburetor for mixing the burning oil and air. The best chimneys are made of cut crystal, often engraved with flowers, butterflies, fruit, clouds, and other traditional motifs, but usually ordinary glass is used, and even an old bottle with the bottom and part of the neck cut off will do the job.

The stand must be designed to allow air to enter the chimney from below and be drawn upward toward the flame by the heat inside. Otherwise the chimney will contain insufficient oxygen to sustain the flame. Once the lamp is lit, a new wick must be carefully trimmed with a pair of scissors or tweezers designed for this purpose, so that it produces a flame that is neither too small nor too large and burns efficiently without creating smoke. A properly trimmed wick will usually continue to produce the same steady flame for at least five or six smoking sessions before it needs to be trimmed again.

In China, the best lamps came equipped with a charming additional feature. In order to prevent the flame from irritating the smoker's eyes with its brightness, a small screen that hooks over the lip of the chimney was provided, designed in such a way that it hangs down the outside of the chimney at just the right angle required to block a direct view of the flame from the smoker's eyes. This screen was usually carved in the shape of a cicada or a moth, with its wings spread out, creating the impression that the insect has landed on the lamp at just the right spot to block the smoker's view of the flame through the glass. These pieces were crafted from translucent materials such as colored glass, jade, and rose quartz in order to produce a soft warm glow against the lamp.

Opium is kept on the smoker's tray in a special container called the opium box *(yen he)*. Opium boxes were traditionally crafted from buffalo horn, jade, ivory, ebony, lacquer, silver, gold, copper, bronze, and a variety of other materials, and designed in a wide range of sizes, shapes, and styles. For liquid opium, tall round containers with a narrow mouth and tight lid were preferred, so that the liquid could be carefully decanted drop by drop into a cooking pan without dripping, and could be stored without evaporation. For solid or semisolid opium, flat boxes with a wide opening were used, designed in square, rectangular, round, oval, and other geometric shapes. Opium boxes were often inscribed with auspicious ideograms such as *shou* ("longevity"), *fu* ("good fortune"), and *hsi* ("happiness"), etched with traditional motifs such as dragons, clouds, and flowers or inlaid with precious stones.

The simplest tool on the tray, but one without which opium cannot be properly prepared for smoking in a Chinese pipe, is the spindle, also referred to as a skewer or bodkin. These instruments are generally about 15 cm (6 in.) long, with a diameter of about 1.5 mm (1/16 in.). One end is ground down to a gradually tapering fine point, with a tiny collar fitted about 2 cm (¾ in.) from the sharpened tip. The collar serves to prevent the tip of the spindle from entering the hole too deeply when a pellet of opium is inserted into the bowl. It also leaves a small indentation in the pellet itself when the spindle is withdrawn, facilitating the vaporization of the opium when it's held near the heat, and improving the draw through the hole when smoking. The other tip of the spindle is hammered flat to provide a small spatula that may be used to scrape residue from the aperture after smoking a pellet, to collect opium from the corners of a nearly empty box, or for a variety of other tasks. Since considerable pressure is applied in kneading a pellet of opium against the surface of the bowl when preparing it for smoking, a metal with high-tensile strength such as steel or brass is the best material for making spindles. Softer metals such as copper and silver can easily bend or break or lose their points and are, therefore, not practical. Today, the best material for fashioning one's own spindles at home are bicycle spokes.

Another important tool in Chinese opium-smoking kits is a scraper specially designed to scrape the dross from the inside of pipe bowls, a job that should be done after each use of a bowl. The scraper consists of a metal shaft 5–8 cm (2–3 in.) long and .5 cm (¼ in.) in diameter, with the tip flattened and bent to form a hook. The other end is attached to a handle made of polished hardwood, enameled porcelain, intricately cast metal, or carved horn. The hook is designed in such a way that when it is inserted into the base of a bowl and the shaft is rotated, the tip scrapes loose the crusty deposits of dross that accumulate on the inside surface of the bowl. A simple scraper can be fashioned at home by hammering flat and bending the tip of a long heavy-gauge nail and sticking the head into a large cork to serve as a handle.

After the dross is loosened and crumbled inside the bowl with a scraper, the coarse crumbs are shaken out into a container known as the dross box. Dross boxes are usually made of metal and fitted with a tight lid to prevent the foul odor of this residue from escaping. They are designed in flat shapes with wide mouths so that none of the dross crumbs spills onto the tray when the contents of the bowls are shaken over them.

When liquid opium is used for smoking, a special utensil must be used to precook the liquid over the lamp before it can be skewered onto the spindle for the final cooking and kneading process. This cooking utensil comes in the form of either a spoon or a pan. The spoons are designed with deep round receptacles of about 15 ml (½ oz.) capacity to hold the liquid opium, and are attached to handles fashioned from wood, porcelain, or horn. The pans have a round bowl of about the same volume, with a small handle attached to one side and a round metal rack framed underneath so that the pan may sit stably on top of the chimney without having to be held in place by hand. The best material for these cooking utensils is copper, because when the opium gets thick and gummy during the cooking process and is ready to be gathered onto the tip of the spindle, only copper will release it cleanly and easily without it sticking to the pan.

All of these implements and accessories rest within easy reach of the smoker's hand, gathered together on an opium tray, where the smoker has ready access to them without having to move anything but his arm. Indeed, so basic is this item that among smokers the word *tray* has come to mean the entire kit used for smoking. Trays can be anywhere from 15 to 30 cm (6–12 in.) in width or diameter and up to 60 cm (24 in.) long, and they come in round, oval, square, rectangular, octagonal, and hexagonal designs. The most popular material for opium trays is dark, polished hardwood, such as teak or ebony, but lacquerware and metal are also used. The tray has a lip around the rim to contain everything on it, and often a set of handles is attached. Some trays are ornately inlaid with mother-of-pearl, ivory, jade, silver, and gold, depicting traditional Chinese motifs, or inscribed in elegant calligraphy with charming couplets by famous poets.

Bamboo tray arranged with complete set of opium utensils, ready for a smoking session.

In addition to the tray and the paraphernalia it holds, some other traditional accessories and furnishings are associated with the Chinese opium-smoking habit. Almost all Chinese opium smokers keep a brass spittoon nearby for spitting out phlegm coughed up while smoking. A complete teaset, including pot, cups, caddy, tray, and other utensils required for preparing tea the Chinese way, is usually kept close at hand when smoking, as well as ashtrays for those who like to smoke tobacco between pipes of opium.

Since smokers recline on their sides when preparing and smoking opium, a hard thick pillow about 15 cm (6 in.) high is provided to rest the head. Opium pillows, which have become popular collector's items in recent years, are usually fashioned from hard leather, wood, densely stuffed fabric, or brightly enameled porcelain. The latter, which are the most prized by collectors, come in all sorts of fanciful designs, such as kneeling cherubs, reclining monks, mythical animals, and wine barrels. Porcelain pillows keep the smoker's head firmly aloft and comfortably cool, and although they are hard, after smoking a few pipes of opium, the smoker feels as though his head is resting on a cloud.

Even the surface upon which smokers reclined while smoking became an item of special craftsmanship in China. When smoking on the floor, a mat of polished bamboo slats was used, with the tray placed in the center and a smoker lying on each side. These mats were cleverly designed to allow air to circulate beneath the smoker's body in order to help keep him or her cool and comfortable while smoking, an important feature in the hot humid climates of southern China and Southeast Asia. Mats woven of reed or rattan are also used, but bamboo is by far the best.

In the households of wealthy Chinese opium smokers as well as the better opium dens in China, a specially designed opium bed became an integral part of the furnishings. These consist of broad wooden platforms approximately 2 meters (6 ft.) long and 1.7 meters (5 ft.) wide, elevated about .6 meter (2 ft.) off the floor on four heavy legs. Three sides are enclosed with low panel walls about .5 meter (1.5 ft.) high, leaving one of the long sides open to the center of the room. Two smokers could recline on the platform with their heads facing each other resting on pillows and their backs toward the side panels. A thin mat covered in silk brocade was usually spread on the platform for comfort, and two porcelain footstools were placed beside the edge of the bed to rest the feet of the reclining smokers. Some of these beds are truly beautiful works of furniture craft, with legs and panels intricately carved in high relief, traditional motifs inlaid with ivory, jade, and mother-of-pearl, highly polished hardwood surfaces, and other artistic touches.

THE WAY

THE ART AND PHILOSOPHY OF SMOKING OPIUM

The smell of opium smoked the Chinese way is one of the most unforgettable aromas on earth. Like the smell of gunpowder and the smell of sex, the smell of opium identifies itself boldly with a single whiff, instantly and unmistakably, in the nostrils of anyone who has ever experienced it, even if only once. So distinctive is the smell of opium that it defies description in words or comparison with other aromas. Both bitter and sweet, pungent and musky, sharp yet soft, fragrant but musty, opium has a rich bouquet that turns the head and commands the immediate attention of anyone who smells it. The smell of opium has often been compared to the scent of a woman. Graham Greene, who conducted a passionate lifelong affair with the Dark Muse, noted in his diary that the smell of opium is "like the first sight of a beautiful woman with whom one realizes that a relationship is impossible." It's a smell that has both body and character, and, according to some connoisseurs, intelligence. "The smell of opium," Picasso remarked to his friend and fellow smoker Jean Cocteau (as noted in his book *Opium*), "is the least stupid smell in the world!"

In order to produce that rich, sensuous aroma, opium must be handled as skillfully as an artist handles a brush and palette, as a musician manipulates an instrument, as a soufflé chef wields a whisk. Only when

205

properly prepared for the pipe by a well-practiced hand will opium come to life and release its potent aromatic essence. Next to the quality of the opium itself, the skill of the person handling the equipment and preparing the pellets constitutes the most important factor in the art of smoking opium. Like haute cuisine prepared with the finest ingredients, the final result depends not on the cost of the china and cutlery but on the artistry of the chef who does the cooking.

As with any other art, the first step in the art of smoking opium is to arrange the necessary utensils close at hand and establish the proper setting. A quiet room free of drafts and softly lit provides the best ambience for a smoking session. A firm but comfortable mat or carpet should be spread on the floor, or onto an elevated hardwood platform such as an opium bed, with a couple of hard pillows to rest the smokers' heads. The tray, which is set in the middle of the mat between the smokers, should be replete with all of the tools required for preparing and smoking opium: a pipe properly fitted with a clean, well-seasoned bowl, plus an extra bowl to change when needed; a lamp filled with oil and the wick properly trimmed to produce the right flame; a pair of spindles; a box of opium; a scraper and box for the dross; a spoon or pan for cooking liquid opium. An ashtray, spittoon, and tea tray should also be near at hand for those who want to use them.

Smokers should be comfortably dressed in loose, casual clothing, with ties and shoes removed, collars and cuffs unbuttoned, and belts unbuckled, so that no constrictions are felt at the neck, waist, wrists, or feet. The usual arrangement is for two smokers to lie on their sides facing each other, with the tray between them and their heads elevated on pillows, while other smokers recline comfortably on cushions as they wait their turns by the lamp. The person who prepares the opium for the pipe is usually referred to as the chef or pipe master, and he or she should select the position most convenient for performing the operation. If the chef is right-handed, he or she should lie on the left side, so that the right hand is located above, free to manipulate the utensils over the lamp; if left-handed, the chef lies on the right hip, so that the left hand may conduct the process. The other smoker then takes the opposite place. When smoking in a private home, the host is generally the one who prepares the pipes, but sometimes one of the guests volunteers for the job or is designated as chef by unanimous acclaim due to his superior cooking skills. In an opium den, either the proprietor or a pipe boy makes the pipes for the customers, unless they prefer to cook for themselves.

The first step in preparing opium for smoking is to apply the required amount of chandoo to the pointed tip of a spindle so that it can be cooked in the heat over the lamp. To save some time and trouble, the chef usually cooks a sufficient quantity to make three to six pellets for the pipe, rather than just one at a time. This requires a wad of opium weighing between .5 and 1 gram, or anywhere from the size of a pea to that of a peanut.

If the chandoo used is solid, the required amount is pinched or cut from the block, rolled into a ball between thumb and forefinger, and impaled on the tip of the spindle. When a thick, semisolid syrup is used, the skewer is simply dipped into the opium box and withdrawn with the correct quantity of chandoo clinging to the tip. If liquid opium is used, it must first be precooked in a copper spoon or pan. This is done by dripping the desired amount into the spoon or pan and placing it over the lamp to boil. As it boils and bubbles, the water content slowly evaporates, and the opium becomes thick and gummy. The tip of the spindle is then used to collect the viscous gum by scraping the inside of the spoon or pan and rolling the sticky resin onto the point. Regardless of which form of chandoo smokers use—solid, syrup, or liquid—when a wad of the amount required to prepare three to six pellets has been impaled on the point of the spindle, it is ready for the delicate process of cooking over the heat of the lamp.

Dexterity, timing, and careful attention are required to properly cook a wad of opium and prepare each pellet for smoking. The chef must take care not to hold it too close or too long over the flame to avoid overcooking, for many of the active alkaloids are highly volatile and may be easily lost by evaporation in the heat. Even a moment's lapse of attention can easily ruin the final product, resulting in a smoke that is unbalanced and unrewarding in effect as well as flavor, like a charred soufflé. It therefore behooves the chef to relax and consciously compose himself, focusing full attention on the task at hand as he approaches the lamp with a spindle laden with a wad of opium ready for cooking.

There are two ways to cook a wad of chandoo over the lamp. One is to use the lower hand to hold the pipe near the lamp at an angle that exposes one side of the bowl to the heat, and to use the upper hand to knead the wad of opium against the hot side of the bowl with the spindle, sort of like kneading dough on a board when making bread. This is the method most commonly used by pipe masters in opium dens. The other method is to use two spindles, one held in each hand, to knead and roll the wad between the two points in the heat above the lamp, like weaving knots with a pair of knitting needles. This is how it is usually done by chefs at home, so we'll follow this method in our discussion here.

If the wick is properly trimmed, the flame will produce just the right temperature for cooking opium about one inch above the mouth of the chimney. It is important to keep the wad of opium constantly turning while folding it continuously over and onto itself, so that it does not become charred by overexposure to the heat. This is done by using the tips of the spindles to repeatedly stretch and fold, turn and twist the wad as it cooks in the heat. The kneading must be done quickly and thoroughly to ensure a homogenous blend, so that all of the alkaloids are evenly distributed and none of them are lost to evaporation by over-exposure to heat. Thebaine, a euphoric alkaloid and cerebral stimulant that balances the soporific effects of the morphine and codeine, is par-ticularly vulnerable to evaporation, so if the opium is overcooked, the first alkaloid to be lost is thebaine, resulting in a smoke with excessively heavy sedative effects.

As it cooks, the opium gradually acquires a dense, rubbery texture, and the original jet black color slowly turns to brown, then to tan, and finally, if the chandoo has been expertly refined and purified, it takes on a beautiful hue of burnished gold. The poet Martin Matz, author of *Pipe Dreams*, refers to this purest grade of chandoo as Black Gold. In Viet-nam, opium smokers describe this amber color as "cockroach wings," and its appearance signals that the cooking process is complete and the opium is ready to be formed into pellets for smoking. At this point, with a final flourish of his wrists, the chef swiftly wraps the entire wad around the tip of one spindle, leaving just enough on the other point to form the first pellet for smoking. In her story "The Big Smoke," Emily Hahn describes the first time she observed this cooking process at the home of a Chinese friend in Shanghai:

> As he rotated the needle ends about each other, the stuff behaved like taffy in the act of setting; it changed color, too, slowly evolving from its earlier dark brown to tan. At a certain moment, just as it seemed about to stiffen, he wrapped the whole wad around one needle.

As soon as the cooked wad of opium is removed from the heat, it immediately hardens, like caramelized sugar. The chef then sets the needle with the large wad down on the tray, while keeping the one with the single portion in his upper working hand. With the other hand, he picks up the pipe and brings it near the heat, holding it so that the convex surface of the bowl is fully exposed to view in the lamplight, where it provides a platform on which to roll the pellet into a cone for smoking.

After pulling it out of the heat when the initial cooking process is over, the pellet hardens on the tip of the spindle in an irregular, amorphous shape and must be formed into a tightly rolled, perfectly symmetrical cone before inserting it into the hole of the bowl for smoking. To do this, the pellet is first made soft and malleable by spinning it briefly in the heat, rapidly rotating the shaft of the spindle to evenly expose all of the surfaces. It is then moved to the bowl and quickly folded and rolled against the smooth convex face, gradually forming a small cone. This heating and rolling process is repeated several times, until the pellet has formed a completely homogenous, tightly rolled cone on the tip of the spindle. It is now ready to be inserted into the bowl.

Inserting the pellet into the hole is one of the most delicate and important operations in the entire process of preparing opium for smoking. First the bowl is held inverted over the flame to heat the hole before it receives the pellet; this makes it easier for the pellet to stick to the hole when inserted. Then, while holding the warmed bowl near the heat with one hand, the main working hand is used to rapidly spin the tip of the spindle back and forth over the lamp, so that the hardened cone rotates in and out of the heat, allowing it to slowly soften again without melting or charring. A moment too long in the heat can easily ruin the opium by causing it to incinerate or by vaporizing the most volatile alkaloids.

When the cone is sufficiently soft, the tip of the spindle is plunged swiftly into the hole and pressed down, causing the cone to collapse and compress against the rim of the aperture, where it forms a small compact ring on the hole, like a miniature doughnut. While the opium is still soft and warm, the spindle is given a couple of short, sharp turns in each direction to set it against the hole and separate the opium from the shaft before it hardens. The spindle is then withdrawn, leaving a round hard clump of opium stuck to the rim of the indented aperture, with a hole drilled into the center of the pellet, evenly aligned to the hole in the bowl. The pellet is now ready to be smoked.

Lying with head relaxed on the pillow, the smoker holds the pipe with the upper hand near the mouthpiece and the lower hand by the bowl, inverting the aperture toward the lamp at a 45-degree angle, so that the pellet is exposed to the heat in the sweet spot—about 2.5 cm (1 in.) above the mouth of the chimney. Lips must be pressed firmly against the mouthpiece to form an airtight seal between the pipe and the smoker's mouth; even the slightest leak of air at the mouthpiece will disrupt the draw and cause the pellet to clog the hole. With empty lungs, the smoker then begins to draw slowly and steadily on the pipe, holding the bowl securely in place over the lamp. As heat and air are drawn in through the hole by the force of suction through the pipe, the pellet begins to sizzle and vaporize and the fumes are sucked in a jet stream into the bowl, which instantly cools and distills them. After precipitating the coarser elements onto the inner surface of the bowl, the purified vapors flow onward through the pipe and are drawn down directly into the smoker's lungs, where the alkaloids enter the bloodstream through the walls of the alveoli. The smoke is then immediately exhaled through the mouth or nostrils.

Each pellet should be prepared so that it can be completely smoked with a single breath. Small, tightly rolled pellets vaporize far more efficiently than large ones, which tend to sputter and evaporate unevenly, and to overheat the bowl. Since the smoke is distilled and does not contain the harsh toxic by-products of combustion, it does not irritate the throat, and therefore even those who normally do not smoke

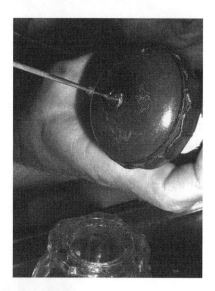

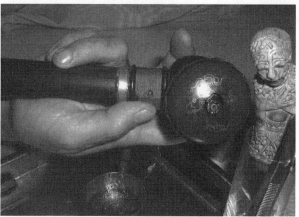

Top Left: Softening a rolled cone of chandoo in the heat over the lamp prior to inserting it into the bowl for smoking.

Top Right: Inserting a softened cone of chandoo into the hole in the bowl in preparation for smoking the distilled vapors.

Center: A perfectly prepared pellet of chandoo ready to smoke, next to a carved Balinese ivory scraper handle.

Bottom: A pellet of chandoo sizzling in the "sweet spot" over the lamp as the smoker inhales from the mouthpiece of the pipe.

tobacco or any other substance can easily inhale a whole pellet of opium in a single breath without gagging. If the smoker runs out of breath before the pellet is completely vaporized, smoke may be released from the lungs through the nostrils while the mouth continues to draw on the pipe, thereby sustaining the suction required to keep the distillation process going and avoid clogging the hole.

When the pipe is finished, the chef clears the hole with the point of the spindle and uses a damp cloth to wipe any residue from the surface of the bowl. He then lays down the pipe and picks up the other spindle with the remaining wad of precooked opium on it. Holding the wad close enough to the heat to let the surface soften, he uses the other spindle to scrape a sufficient amount of opium off the wad to prepare another pellet. Picking up the pipe again, he now repeats the process of alternately heating the pellet and rolling it into a tight cone on the surface of the bowl, then inserts it into the hole for the next smoke. A smoker will usually smoke two or three pipes in a row and then take a break. If one smokes any faster than this, the bloodstream tends to become overloaded with alkaloids too quickly, which for the experienced smoker is simply a waste of opium, whereas for novices, such excessively rapid absorption of alkaloids into the blood—without allowing sufficient time between pipes for the alkaloids to circulate and metabolize—can cause dizziness, fatigue, and nausea.

The biggest mistake that most beginners make when first smoking opium is smoking too many pipes too fast. Opium takes effect slowly, as each alkaloid metabolizes at a different rate and affects different parts of the body. It takes at least one or two hours before the full effects of a few pipes of opium are felt. Therefore, when a novice, whose system is unaccustomed to the effects of opium, smokes five or six pipes in a row, the full impact of the alkaloids suddenly overwhelms him an hour or two later, almost invariably causing a toxic reaction that triggers a prolonged bout of vomiting, clouding the clarity and dulling the subtle sensations that a smaller measure would have provided. With opium, it's usually a matter of smoking less and enjoying it more.

Even for the habitual smoker, the first few pipes of the day, taken with a clear body and mind, always deliver the best effects. Thus the experienced smoker will smoke two or three pipes and then take a rest, savoring the subtle shift of energies as the various alkaloids circulate and take effect throughout the system. Depending on his mood, the weather, the quality of the opium, and other relevant factors, he may then smoke a few more pipes after a while, but when he reaches the point of satiation and realizes that his system is already saturated, he smokes no more. Smoking beyond the point of initial satiation in an attempt to increase one's pleasure is almost always counterproductive. Rather than achieving a further measure of euphoria, one usually gains nothing more than a series of toxic side effects, such as dizziness, fatigue, weakness in the limbs, feelings of heaviness, and indigestion. For experienced smokers, a wider margin for error is possible here, but for a novice, even one or two pipes too many almost always causes adverse reactions, particularly nausea, as the body tries to expel the excess. So for the novice, three to five pipes of opium smoked over a period of two to three hours usually suffices to provide a pleasant experience. For the occasional smoker who is not addicted, six to eight pipes is an adequate measure; the habitual smoker who has already been smoking daily for at least three months may take twelve to fifteen pipes per day, divided into several sessions, without any ill effects. If these three types of smoker were smoking together, each would experience the same pleasant effects from their respective dosages.

After a group of smokers has smoked ten to fifteen pipes from the same bowl during a session, it is time for the chef to change the bowl. First the hot bowl is removed from the tube and the dross is scraped loose from the inside surface. The loosened crumbs are shaken into the dross box, and the bowl is set aside to cool. A second bowl is then fitted into the saddle for the next round of pipes. Before they resume smoking, however, the smokers take a break to drink a few cups of Chinese tea, perhaps smoke some tobacco to supplement the effects of the opium, and relax for a while, chatting or daydreaming as the opium works its subtle alchemy in their system.

The best time of day for smoking opium depends on the habits and lifestyle of the individual smoker. For the habitual smoker who smokes every day and is accustomed to performing his daily duties under the influence of opium, the best time to smoke is early in the morning, before breakfast. Indeed some smokers, particularly writers and artists, like to rise at the crack of dawn to smoke the first few pipes of the day and muse in the pristine stillness and silence of early-morning calm. The next best time for habitual smokers is around noon, prior to lunch. After smoking their first round of pipes either early in the morning or around noon, daily smokers usually have a second round in the late afternoon or early evening, before dinner. Smokers who smoke every day grow so accustomed to the effects of opium that even a few pipes give them a strong burst of energy and gear up their system for activity whenever they smoke. For this reason, they generally avoid smoking late at night, when it would tend to keep them awake.

For novices and those who smoke only on rare occasions, smoking in the morning or early afternoon often precludes further activity for the rest of the day, due to the tranquilizing effects of the soporific alkaloids, particularly morphine and codeine. Since their nervous system has not developed a tolerance to the potent sedative properties of those alkaloids, these smokers tend to prefer smoking in the late afternoon or at night, when they can relax and not worry about having to go out and do something else later. Smokers who are not addicted to opium do not get so highly energized by it, and therefore they usually don't find it difficult to fall asleep when smoking at night, as long as they don't overload their system by smoking beyond the point of satiation.

Regardless of when one chooses to smoke, smoking on an empty stomach is always best. The initial effects of smoking opium always include a temporary suppression in the flow of gastric juices in the stomach, and so smoking on a full stomach tends to cause indigestion. Normal digestive functions are restored about an hour after smoking the last pipe; in fact, when the initial lag in digestive power has waned, the smoker's appetite for food is actually sharpened and his body feels hungry for a good meal. That's why smoking a few pipes of opium before breakfast, lunch, or dinner is a popular custom in countries where opium smoking is socially accepted.

Alcohol, however, is not at all compatible with opium, except in moderate quantities as an accompaniment to a meal or to stimulate circulation after smoking. As Jean Cocteau noted in his journal, "Opium and alcohol are mortal enemies." Those who start drinking liquor after smoking opium, or who start smoking opium after drinking, inevitably end up suffering either nausea or headaches or both, and they enjoy the pleasures of neither the alcohol nor the opium. Habitual opium smokers drink alcohol only for its therapeutic properties, such as to keep warm in the winter or stimulate blood circulation, or to aid digestion with meals, while alcoholics have trouble tolerating even a few pipes after drinking. However, although alcohol and opium do not mix well, an opium addict in withdrawal will often turn to alcohol for solace, and opium can serve as an effective, albeit addictive, cure for severe cases of alcohol abuse.

AFTERWORD
COMING FULL CIRCLE

In the text of this book, we quote the writer Jean Cocteau as saying in his journal *Opium, the Diary of an Addict*, "It's a pity that instead of perfecting curative techniques, medicine does not try to render opium harmless." It seems as if modern medical science has finally made Cocteau's dream come true, for in September 2004, a company in Tasmania, Australia, published details of its genetically engineered opium poppies.* Top-1 (thebaine oripavine poppy 1) mutants do not produce morphine or codeine.

Tasmania is the source of some forty percent of the world's legal opiates; its native crop of poppies is already being reengineered with the mutant strain. Conversely, some investigators expect that the development of genetically engineered plants and microorganisms to manufacture potent psychoactive compounds will become widespread later in the twenty-first century. Research into transgenic psychotropic botanicals and microbes is controversial; genes from mutants have a habit of spreading into the wild population by accident as well as design.

In the top-1 mutant of the opium poppy *(Papaver somniferum)*, the poppy's natural chemistry has a glitch that stops the normal process of making morphine, which is prized as a drug by itself and as a raw

---

*Millgate, A. G., A. J. Fist, and P. J. Larkin. 2004. Morphine-pathway block in top-1 poppies. *Nature* 431 (Sept. 23): 413–14.

material for opiates such as heroin. As a consequence of the synthetic pathway's breakdown, top-1 accumulates two intermediate compounds: thebaine and oripavine.

To make some modern painkillers and addiction treatments, pharmaceutical companies convert morphine back to thebaine and then process it further. Starting with thebaine is more efficient, says Philip Larkin of the plant-industry section of CSIRO, Australia's federally funded research agency. The Tasmanian drug industry has been using top-1 since 1998 for the production of buprenorphine, oxycodone, naloxone, and naltrexone, which are often used for withdrawal from morphine or heroin addiction.

Peter Facchini, of the University of Calgary, Alberta, who studies poppy biochemistry, says that for figuring out details of natural morphine synthesis the new poppy is a very useful tool. To create more desirable varieties, Tony Fist, of the company Tasmanian Alkaloids in Westbury, Australia, treated poppy seeds with a chemical mutagen. He then screened the seedlings and found the top-1 poppy. The company must have set a land speed record for commercialization, says Larkin. As early as 1997, Tasmanian growers turned to the top-1 poppy to sell to pharmaceutical companies.

Larkin and Anthony Millgate, also of CSIRO, compared the activity of some 17,000 individual genes in the mutant and the natural poppy. The mutant's activity fell short for ten of the genes. Low-morphine mutants are common, especially for ornamental gardens, Facchini says, but it's rarer to find a mutant that accumulates something useful.

If ever the restrictions on whole herbal opium are lifted, even if only for medicinal use, then this variety of poppy could provide a completely safe, non-addictive way to use this amazing, multi-faceted medicine to treat a wide range of human ailments, both chronic and acute, without the risk of the severe negative side effects caused by most chemically based pharmaceutical drugs—and at far less expense to the patient. The therapeutic applications of whole herbal opium as a natural medicine and "sovereign remedy" for humanity's most distressful conditions have a history of over 5,000 years, and this new variety of this ancient medicinal herb makes it possible to treat many of these conditions without the risk of addiction.

Appendix
CHRONOLOGY OF
OPIUM MILESTONES

c. 3400 BCE

The opium poppy is cultivated in lower Mesopotamia. The Sumerians refer to it as *Hul Gil,* the "joy plant." The Sumerians would soon pass along the plant and its euphoric effects to the Assyrians. The art of poppy culling would continue from the Assyrians to the Babylonians, who in turn would pass their knowledge on to the Egyptians.

c. 1300 BCE

In the capital city of Thebes, Egyptians begin cultivation of opium thebaicum, grown in their famous poppy fields. The opium trade flourishes during the reigns of Thutmose IV, Akhenaton, and King Tutankhamen. The trade route includes the Phoenicians and Minoans, who move the profitable item across the Mediterranean Sea into Greece, Carthage, and Europe.

c. 1100 BCE

On the island of Cyprus, the "Peoples of the Sea" craft surgical-quality culling knives to harvest opium, which they would cultivate, trade, and smoke before the fall of Troy.

c. 460 BCE

Hippocrates, "the father of medicine," dismisses the magical attributes of opium but acknowledges its usefulness as a narcotic and styptic in treating internal diseases, diseases of women, and epidemics.

330 BCE

Alexander the Great introduces opium to the people of Persia and India.

400 CE

Opium thebaicum, from the Egyptian fields at Thebes, is first introduced to China by Arab traders.

1300s

Opium disappears for two hundred years from European historical record. Opium had become a taboo subject for those in circles of learning during the Holy Inquisition. In the eyes of the Inquisition, anything from the East was linked to the devil.

1500

The Portuguese, while trading along the East China Sea, initiate the smoking of opium. The effects are instantaneous as they discover, but it is a practice the Chinese consider barbaric and subversive.

1527

During the height of the Reformation, opium is reintroduced into European medical literature as "laudanum" by Paracelsus. These black pills or "Stones of Immortality" were made of opium thebaicum, citrus juice, and quintessence of gold, and prescribed as painkillers.

1600s

Residents of Persia and India begin eating and drinking opium mixtures for recreational use.

Portuguese merchants carrying cargoes of Indian opium through Macao direct its trade flow into China.

1606

Ships chartered by Elizabeth I are instructed to purchase the finest Indian opium and transport it back to England.

1680

The English apothecary Thomas Sydenham introduces Sydenham's Laudanum, a compound of opium, sherry wine, and herbs. His pills, along with others of the time, become a popular remedy for numerous ailments.

1700

The Dutch export shipments of Indian opium to China and the islands of Southeast Asia; the Dutch introduce the practice of smoking opium in a tobacco pipe to the Chinese.

1729

The Chinese emperor Yung Cheng issues an edict prohibiting the smoking of opium and its domestic sale, except under license for use as medicine.

1750

The British East India Company assumes control of Bengal and Bihar, two opium-growing districts of India. British shipping dominates the opium trade out of Calcutta to China.

1753

Linnaeus, the father of botany, first classifies the poppy, *Papaver somniferum* ("sleep-inducing"), in his book *Genera Plantarum.*

1767

The British East India Company's import of opium to China reaches a staggering two thousand chests of opium per year.

1793

The British East India Company establishes a monopoly on the opium trade. All poppy growers in India are forbidden to sell opium to competitor trading companies.

1799

China's emperor, Kia King, bans opium, making trade and poppy cultivation illegal.

1800

The British Levant Company purchases nearly half of all of the opium coming out of Smyrna, Turkey, strictly for importation to Europe and the United States.

1803

Friedrich Serturner, of Paderborn, Germany, discovers the active ingredient of opium by dissolving it in acid, then neutralizing it with ammonia. The result: alkaloids of *Principium somniferum*, or morphine.

Physicians believe that opium has finally been perfected and tamed. Morphine is lauded as "God's own medicine" for its reliability, long-lasting effects, and safety.

1805

A smuggler from Boston, Massachusetts, Charles Cabot, attempts to purchase opium from the British, then bring it into China under the auspices of British smugglers.

1812

American John Cushing, under the employ of his uncles' business, James and Thomas H. Perkins Company of Boston, acquires his wealth through smuggling Turkish opium to Canton.

1816

John Jacob Astor, of New York City, joins the opium-smuggling trade. His American Fur Company purchases ten tons of Turkish opium and ships the contraband to Canton on the *Macedonian*. Astor would later leave the China opium trade and sell solely to England.

1819

The writer John Keats and other English literary lights experiment with opium intended for strict recreational use—simply for the high and taken at extended, nonaddictive intervals

1821

Thomas De Quincey publishes his autobiographical account of opium addiction, *Confessions of an English Opium-Eater*.

1827

E. Merck & Company of Darmstadt, Germany, begins commercial manufacturing of morphine.

1830

The British dependence on opium for medicinal and recreational use reaches an all-time high as twenty-two thousand pounds of opium are imported from Turkey and India.

Jardine-Matheson & Company of London inherits the Indian opium trade from the British East India Company once the mandate to rule and dictate the trade policies of British India are no longer in effect.

1837
Elizabeth Barrett Browning falls under the spell of morphine. This, however, does not impede her ability to write "poetical paragraphs."

March 18, 1839
Lin Tse-Hsu, imperial Chinese commissioner in charge of suppressing the opium traffic, orders all foreign traders to surrender their opium. In response, the British send expeditionary warships to the coast of China, beginning the First Opium War.

1840
New Englanders bring twenty-four thousand pounds of opium into the United States. This catches the attention of U.S. Customs, which promptly places a duty on the import.

1841
The Chinese are defeated by the British in the First Opium War. Along with paying a large indemnity, Hong Kong is ceded to the British.

1843
Dr. Alexander Wood, of Edinburgh, discovers a new technique to administer morphine, injection by syringe. He finds the effects of morphine introduced to his patients in this way to be instantaneous and three times more potent.

1852
The British arrive in lower Burma, importing large quantities of opium from India and selling it through a government-controlled opium monopoly.

1856
The British and French renew their hostilities against China in the Second Opium War. In the aftermath of the struggle, China is forced to pay another indemnity. The importation of opium is legalized.

Opium production increases along the highlands of Southeast Asia.

1874

The English researcher C. R. Wright first synthesizes heroin—or diacetylmorphine—by boiling morphine over a stove.

In San Francisco, smoking opium in the city limits is banned. It is confined to neighboring Chinatowns and their opium dens.

1878

Britain passes the Opium Act with hopes of reducing opium consumption. Under the new regulation, the selling of opium is restricted to registered Chinese opium smokers and Indian opium eaters; the Burmese are strictly prohibited from smoking opium.

1886

The British acquire Burma's northeast region, the Shan state. Production and smuggling of opium along the lower region of Burma thrives despite British efforts to maintain a strict monopoly on the opium trade.

1890

U.S. Congress, in its earliest law-enforcement legislation on narcotics, imposes a tax on opium and morphine.

Tabloids owned by William Randolph Hearst publish stories of white women being seduced by Chinese men and their opium to invoke fear of the "Yellow Peril," disguised as an antidrug campaign.

1895

Heinrich Dreser, working for the Bayer Company, Elberfeld, Germany, finds that diluting morphine with acetyls produces a drug without the common morphine side effects. Bayer begins production of diacetylmorphine and coins the name *heroin*. Heroin is not introduced commercially for another three years.

Early 1900s

The philanthropic Saint James Society in the United States mounts a campaign to supply free samples of heroin through the mail to morphine addicts who are trying give up their habit.

Efforts by the British and French to control opium production in Southeast Asia are successful. Nevertheless, this region, referred to as the "Golden Triangle," eventually becomes a major player in the profitable opium trade during the 1940s.

1902
In various medical journals, physicians discuss the side effects of using heroin as a morphine step-down cure. Several physicians argue that their patients suffer from heroin withdrawal symptoms equal to those of morphine addiction.

1903
Heroin addiction rises to alarming rates.

1905
U.S. Congress bans opium.

1906
China and England finally enact a treaty restricting the Sino-Indian opium trade.

Several physicians experiment with treatments for heroin addiction. Dr. Alexander Lambert and Charles B. Towns tout their popular cure as the most advanced, effective, and compassionate cure for heroin addiction. The cure consists of a seven-day regimen that included a five-day purge of heroin from the addict's system with doses of *belladonna delirium*.

U.S. Congress passes the Pure Food and Drug Act, requiring contents labeling on patent medicines by pharmaceutical companies. As a result, the availability of opiates and opiate consumers decline significantly.

1909
The first federal drug prohibition passes in the United States outlawing the importation of opium. It is passed in preparation for the Shanghai Conference, at which the United States presses for legislation aimed at suppressing the sale of opium to China.

February 1, 1909
The International Opium Commission convenes in Shanghai. Heading the U.S. delegation are Dr. Hamilton Wright and Episcopal bishop Henry Brent. Both try to convince the international delegation of the immoral and evil effects of opium.

1910
After 150 years of failed attempts to rid the country of opium, the Chinese are finally successful in convincing the British to dismantle the India-China opium trade.

December 17, 1914

The Harrison Narcotics Act, aimed at curbing drug (especially cocaine but also heroin) abuse and addiction, passes. It requires doctors, pharmacists, and others who prescribe narcotics to register and pay a tax.

1923

The U.S. Treasury Department's Narcotics Division (the first federal drug agency) bans all legal narcotics sales. With the prohibition of legal venues to purchase heroin, addicts are forced to buy from illegal street dealers.

1925

In the wake of the first federal ban on opium, a thriving black market opens up in New York's Chinatown.

1930s

The majority of illegal heroin smuggled into the United States comes from China and is refined in Shanghai and Tientsin.

Early 1940s

During World War II, opium trade routes are blocked and the flow of opium from India and Persia is cut off. Fearful of losing their opium monopoly, the French encourage Hmong farmers to expand their opium production.

1945–1947

Burma gains independence from Britain at the end of World War II. Opium cultivation and trade flourishes in the Shan states.

1948–1972

Corsican gangsters dominate the U.S. heroin market through their connection with Mafia drug distributors. After refining the raw Turkish opium in Marseille laboratories, the heroin is made easily available for purchase by junkies on New York City streets.

1950s

United States efforts to contain the spread of Communism in Asia involves forging alliances with tribes and warlords inhabiting areas of the Golden Triangle (an expanse covering Laos, Thailand, and Burma), thus providing accessibility and protection along the southeast border of China. To maintain their relationship with the warlords while continuing to fund the struggle against Communism, the United States and France supply drug warlords and their armies with ammunition, arms, and air transport for the production and sale of opium. The result: an explosion in the availability and illegal flow of heroin into the United States and into the hands of drug dealers and addicts.

1962
Burma outlaws opium.

1965–1970
U.S. involvement in Vietnam is blamed for the surge in illegal heroin being smuggled into the States. To aid U.S. allies, the Central Intelligence Agency (CIA) sets up a charter airline, Air America, to transport raw opium from Burma and Laos. As well, some of the opium would be transported to Marseille by Corsican gangsters to be refined into heroin and shipped to the United States via the French connection. The number of heroin addicts in the United States reaches an estimated 750,000.

October 1970
The legendary singer Janis Joplin is found dead at Hollywood's Landmark Hotel, a victim of an "accidental heroin overdose."

1972
Heroin exportation from Southeast Asia's Golden Triangle, controlled by Shan warlord Khun Sa, becomes a major source for raw opium in the profitable drug trade.

July 1, 1973
President Nixon creates the DEA (Drug Enforcement Administration) under the Justice Department to consolidate virtually all federal powers of drug enforcement in a single agency.

Mid-1970s
Saigon falls. The heroin epidemic subsides. The search for a new source of raw opium yields Mexico's Sierra Madre region. "Mexican Mud" temporarily replaces "China White" heroin until 1978.

1978
The United States and Mexican governments find a means to eliminate the source of raw opium—by spraying poppy fields with Agent Orange. The eradication plan is termed a success as the amount of Mexican Mud in the

United States drug market declines. In response to the decrease in availability of Mexican Mud, another source of heroin is found in the Golden Crescent area—Iran, Afghanistan, and Pakistan—creating a dramatic upsurge in the production and trade of illegal heroin.

1982

The comedian John Belushi, of *Animal House* fame, dies of a heroin-cocaine—"speedball"—overdose.

September 13, 1984

U.S. State Department officials conclude, after more than a decade of crop-substitution programs for Third World growers of marijuana, coca, or opium poppies, that the tactic cannot work without eradication of the plants and criminal enforcement. Poor results are reported from eradication programs in Burma, Pakistan, Mexico, and Peru.

1988

Opium production in Burma increases under the rule of the State Law and Order Restoration Council (SLORC), the Burmese junta regime.

The single largest heroin seizure is made in Bangkok. The United States suspects that the twenty-four-hundred-pound shipment of heroin, en route to New York City, originates from the Golden Triangle region, controlled by drug warlord Khun Sa.

1990

A U.S. court indicts Khun Sa, leader of the Shan United Army and reputed drug warlord, on heroin trafficking charges. The U.S. Attorney General's office charges Khun Sa with importing thirty-five hundred pounds of heroin into New York City over the course of eighteen months and holds him responsible for the source of the heroin seized in Bangkok.

1992

Colombia's drug lords are said to be introducing a high-grade form of heroin into the United States.

1993

The Thai army, with support from the U.S. Drug Enforcement Agency, launches an operation to destroy thousands of acres of opium poppies from fields in the Golden Triangle.

October 31, 1993
Heroin takes another well-known victim. Twenty-three-year-old actor River Phoenix dies of a heroin-cocaine overdose—the same speedball combination that killed comedian John Belushi.

January 1994
Efforts to eradicate opium at its source remain unsuccessful. The Clinton administration orders a shift in policy away from the antidrug campaigns of previous administrations. Instead, the focus includes "institution building" with the hope that "strengthening democratic governments abroad . . . will foster law-abiding behavior and promote legitimate economic opportunity."

April 1994
Kurt Cobain, lead singer of the Seattle-based alternative rock band Nirvana, dies of heroin-related suicide.

1995
The Golden Triangle region of Southeast Asia is now the leader in opium production, yielding twenty-five hundred tons annually. According to United States drug experts, there are new drug trafficking routes from Burma through Laos to southern China, Cambodia, and Vietnam.

January 1996
Khun Sa, one of the Shan state's most powerful drug warlords, "surrenders" to SLORC. The United States is suspicious and fears that this agreement between the ruling junta regime and Khun Sa includes a deal allowing the opium king to retain control of his opium trade in exchange for an end to his thirty-year revolutionary war against the government.

November 1996
International drug trafficking organizations, including those in China, Nigeria, Colombia, and Mexico, are said to be aggressively marketing heroin in the United States and Europe.

1999
Bumper opium crop of 4,600 tons in Afghanistan. United Nations Drug Control Program estimates around 75% of world's heroin production is of Afghan origin.

2000
Taliban leader Mullah Omar bans poppy cultivation in Afghanistan; United Nations Drug Control Program confirms opium production eradicated.

July 2001
Portugal decriminalizes all drugs for personal consumption.

Autumn 2001
War in Afghanistan; heroin floods the Pakistan market. Taliban regime overthrown.

October 2002
U.N. Drug Control and Crime Prevention Agency announces Afghanistan has regained its position as the world's largest opium producer.

December 2002
UK Government health plan will make heroin available free on National Health Service "to all those with a clinical need for it." Consumers are skeptical.

April 2003
State sponsored heroin trafficking: Korea's attempt to penetrate the Australian heroin market hits rocky waters.

October 2003
U.S. Food and Drug Administration (FDA) and Drug Enforcement Administration (DEA) launch special task force to curb surge in net-based sales of narcotics from online pharmacies.

January 2004
Consumer groups file a lawsuit against Oxycontin-maker Perdue Pharma. The company is alleged to have used fraudulent patents and deceptive trade practices to block the prescription of cheap generic medications for patients in pain.

September 2004
Singapore announces plans to execute a self-medicating heroin user, Chew Seow Leng. Under Singapore law, chronic heroin users with a high physiological tolerance to the drug are deemed to be "traffickers." Consumers face a mandatory death sentence if they take more than 15 grams (0.5 ounces) of heroin a day.

A Tasmanian company publishes details of its genetically engineered opium poppies. Top1 [thebaine oripavine poppy 1] mutants do not produce morphine or codeine. Tasmania is the source of some 40% of the world's legal opiates; its native crop of poppies is already being re-engineered with the mutant strain. Conversely, some investigators expect that the development of genetically engineered plants and microorganisms to manufacture potent psychoactive compounds will become widespread later in the 21st century. Research into transgenic psychotropic botanicals and microbes is controversial; genes from mutants have a habit of spreading into the wild population by accident as well as design.

The FDA grants a product license to Purdue's pain medication Palladone: high dose, extended-release hydromorphone capsules. Palladone is designed to provide "around-the-clock" pain-relief for opioid-tolerant users.

October 2004
Unannounced withdrawal of newly-issued DEA guidelines to pain specialists. The guidelines had pledged that physicians wouldn't be arrested for providing adequate pain-relief to their patients. DEA drug-diversion chief Patricia Good earlier stated that the new rules were meant to eliminate an "aura of fear" that stopped doctors treating pain aggressively.

December 2004
McLean pain-treatment specialist Dr. William E. Hurwitz is sent to prison for alleged "excessive" prescription of opioid painkillers to chronic pain patients. Testifying in court, Dr. Hurwitz describes the abrupt stoppage of prescriptions as tantamount to torture.

May 2005
Researchers at Ernest Gallo Clinic and Research Center in Emeryville, California, inhibit expression of the AGS3 gene in the core of nucleus accumbens. Experimentally blocking the AGS3 gene curbs the desire for heroin in addicted rodents. By contrast, activation of the reward centers of the nucleus accumbens is immensely pleasurable and addictive. The possible effects of over expression and gene amplification of AGS3 remain unexplored.

Chronology courtesy of opioids.com, adapted and expanded from Martin Booth's *Opium: A History* (Simon & Schuster, 1996).

SELECTED READING

Anderson, Edward F. *Plants and People of the Golden Triangle: Ethnobotany of the Hill Tribes of Northern Thailand.* Portland, OR.: Dioscorides Press, 1993.

Berridge, Virginia, and Griffith Edwards. *Opium and the People: Opiate Use in Nineteenth-Century England.* New Haven: Yale University Press, 1987.

Blofeld, John. *The City of Lingering Splendor.* Boston: Shambhala, 1989.

Boyes, Jon, and S. Piraban. *Opium Fields.* Chiang Mai, Thailand: Silkworm Books, 1991.

Cocteau, Jean. *Opium, The Diary of His Cure.* London: Peter Owen, 2000.

Coleridge, Samuel Taylor. *Notebooks.* Edited by Kathleen Coburn. London: Routledge & K. Paul, 1900.

De Quincey, Thomas. *The Confessions of an English Opium-Eater.* London: Oxford University Press, H. Milford, 1934.

Farrère, Claude. *Fumée d'opium* (Black Opium). New York: N. L. Brown, issued privately for subscribers, 1929.

Greene, Graham. *The Quiet American.* New York: Penguin Books, 2002.

Hahn, Emily. "The Big Smoke." In *Times and Places.* New York: Thomas Y. Cromwell Company, 1970.

Hughes, Richard. *Foreign Devil: Thirty Years of Reporting from the Far East.* London: Deutsch, 1972.

Lee, James. *The Underworld of the East.* Somerset, England: Green Magic, 2000.

Linnaeus. *Genera Planarum. See* Linné, Carl von. *Carol a Linné species plantarum.* Berolini, 1797.

Marshall, Chris. *I-Ching.* London: Headline, 1994.

McKenna, Terence. *Food of the Gods: The Search for the Original Tree of Knowledge: A Radical History of Plants, Drugs, and Human Evolution.* New York: Bantam Books, 1992.

Reid, Daniel. *The Shambhala Guide to Traditional Chinese Medicine.* Boston: Shambhala, 1996.

Stuart, G. A. *Chinese Materia Medica: Vegetable Kingdom.* New York: Gordon Press, 1977 (extensively revised by G. A. Stuart from F. Porter Smith's work).

Symons, Arthur. "The Opium Smoker." In *Poems.* London: W. Heinemann, 1902.

Te Duc, Nguyen. *Le Livre de l'opium.* Paris: Guy Tresdaniel, 1957.

Tosches, Nick. *The Last Opium Den* (first appeared as an article in *Vanity Fair,* September 2000, "Confessions of an Opium Seeker"). London: Bloomsbury, 2002.

Von Bibra, Baron Ernst. *Plant Intoxicants: A Classic Text on the Use of Mind-Altering Plants.* Translated by Helvig-Schleiffer. Rochester, VT: Healing Arts Press, 1995.

Wakeman, Jr., Frederic. *Policing Shanghai: 1927–1937.* Berkeley: University of California Press, 1995.

Westermeyer, Joseph. *Poppies, Pipes, and People: Opium and Its Use in Laos.* Berkeley: University of California Press, 1982.